NEVER GUILTY, NEVER FREE

NEVER GUILTY, NEVER FREE

GINNY FOAT
with LAURA FOREMAN

 RANDOM HOUSE, NEW YORK

Library of Congress Cataloging in Publication Data

Foat, Ginny.
  Never guilty, never free.
  Includes index.
  1. Foat, Ginny   2. Feminists—United States—
Biography.   3. National Organization for Women.
I. Foreman, Laura.   II. Title.
HQ1413.F63A34   1985   305.4′2′0924 [B]   85-6261
ISBN 0-394-54141-3

Manufactured in the United States of America
Designed by Oksana Kushnir
98765432
First Edition

To KTQT
for keeping the magic and the dream alive

I thought how unpleasant it is to be locked out;
and then I thought how it is worse, perhaps, to be locked in.

—Virginia Woolf, *A Room of One's Own*

Acknowledgments

I hope that my Kafkaesque experience of 1983 will finally be put to rest with the publication of this book. Writing it was a very difficult task that was mixed with cathartic, enlightening, and anger-provoking experiences that helped me grow. I began by not wanting to write this book and ended being proud of what we had produced. I give the book as a tribute to those people who helped me to endure, overcome, and go on. I owe all of you an enormous debt of gratitude. Listing everyone who helped would be an impossibility, but some of you must be named:

Ivy Bottini, Jeane Cordova, Jean O'Leary, and Robin Tyler, who within hours of my arrest formed the Ginny Foat Defense Fund; Dani Adams, Jolin Astin, Patty Duke Astin, Lia Belli, Gail Campbell, Dorothy Huebel, Gloria Kapp, Midge Costanza, Sheila Kuehl, Michael Linfield, Ramona Ripston, who contributed their time and energy to the board of GFDF. A special thank-you to Jean Conger, whose administrative skills, warm heart, friendship, and love kept the GFDF together on a daily basis. To Jan Holden, whose love, caring, and personal commitment gave me the courage to go on and the strength to see it through. To the northern California contingent of the GFDF—Ilene Brettholz, Claudia Cappio, Katherine Cogswell, Brenda Roth, and Andrea Wachter, who licked hundreds of stamps, stuffed and "bulked out," and never let me go a day without feeling loved. To my "roomie" who coordinated the northern GFDF, Sandy Morris, for keeping the home fires burning, the other "roomie" together, and the dogs alive. To Brighton, Dog Face, and Koshka, for their cold noses, bright eyes, and silly smiles. To Crickett, for holding down the fort in San Francisco. To Judy Haddad, Peggy Mitchell, Chris Wagaman, and all the volunteers who handled the endless but necessary office work created by the fund-raising efforts. To WAVAW and NCJW, who opened their offices on my behalf, and to NOW members and chapters around the country who had the courage to stick by their feminist principles and do battle for their sister. To Norma Hair and Carol Schmidt, whose dedication to righting the wrongs of this world and capacity to care allowed them to give me so much of themselves. To Pat Kuta of Marin Abused Women's Services, for sharing her resources on battering. To

Debbie Jones and Pat Berlly, who opened their home and their hearts, and who are and always will be family. To Judy Davis, Julie Gertler, and Susan Wolford, Myra Rydel, Trish Manning, Cheryl, Torrie Osborne, Barbara Lampert, Peggy Kemeny, Jack Meyer, Lisa Meyer, Raymond Foat, Danny Angelillo, Marie and Al Greco, Tisa Blackburn, Megan Costello, Keith Weitzman, Dan Marcheano, Ellie Schneir, who helped and cared and gave of themselves. To my friend Clara Sparks, who through all these years has kept me in her prayers and her heart. To Savina Teubal, whose brilliance, dignity, and courage will never be forgotten. To John Boyd, for his help and caring. To Bob White, whose faith helped free me and who is, I hope, himself free now. To Kim Gandy, Betty Spencer, Adriane, Susan, Nancy, Bob, Clay, and the women and men of the New Orleans area who formed the strong support network that made some sanity out of insanity. To Bridget Bane, for introducing me to New Orleans, its fine people, and the Feelings Café D'Aunoy. To the Marianites of Holy Cross, for their prayers and support. To the twelve people of the jury, who saw through the whole thing. To Nikki Kearby, whose courage and incredible sense of sisterhood and caring enabled her to post a bond for a woman she did not know. My thoughts of freedom will always start with Nikki Kearby and Betty Caldwell. To Anne Teachworth, who through her caring and sharing and talent helped me to meet Ginny Galluzzo and, most important, to forgive her. To my friend and attorney Kay Tsenin, who coordinated all our efforts and put together my legal defense team in California. To that team, Richard Hirsch and Michael Nasatir, for their untiring efforts and brilliant briefs. To Bob Tuller, for his support and caring. In Nevada, to Annabelle Whiting Hall for her insight, perseverance, dedication, legal theories, tears, and laughter. In Louisiana, to Robert Glass and John Reed, to whom I can never adequately express my love, gratitude, and respect for their brilliance, their legal powers, and their feminist hearts; and to their wives, for their support of them and me. To Gary Eldridge, the supersleuth, and Jan Tucker, the California connection. To Terry Waller and the National Jury Project.

To those who were most important in coproducing this book and leading me through the foreign world of publishing: my dear friend and agent, Peter Skolnick, our editor, Charlotte Mayerson, Buddy Cianfrani, who read and encouraged each step of the way. And, most of all, my coauthor, Laura Foreman, for her patience, understanding, tenaciousness, love, and ability to make sense out of it all.

To my family, especially my mother and sister, who never lost faith in me or doubted that truth would prevail, and my beloved father, who did not live to see that truth prevailed. And finally, my most special thank-you, love, and eternal gratitude to my beloved friend Kay, who put all the holidays I missed in a box, who never let me lose sight of the happy ending, whose courage, love, commitment, and stubborn will never let a day be bad until it absolutely had to be. I could not have written this without her, nor could I have survived.

—Ginny Foat

I especially thank: journalists Rinker Buck and Richard Boyd, who generously shared with me some of their own research into the facts surrounding Ginny's trial; Jean Conger, whose phenomenal memory and insight helped me toward a better understanding of feminism; Dona Munker, whose faith in me literally made my work on this book possible; and Kay Tsenin, whose humor, kindness, keen eye, and unfailing wit helped me over many a rough spot.

I am most grateful to our brilliant editor, Charlotte Mayerson. She kept us on track.

And most of all, I thank my husband, Buddy Cianfrani, for his love, support, and astounding patience.

—Laura Foreman

NEVER GUILTY, NEVER FREE

My world is a cage, six feet by ten feet.

My possessions are a schoolroom desk bolted to a wall, a cot, a metal closet, a sink, and a toilet.

My companions are my jailors and my past.

Convicted of no crime, I'm living at Sybil Brand, the Los Angeles County Prison facility for women. It's February of 1983, the second month of my second stay here. I'm privileged this time around. I have a cell of my own in a special prison unit reserved partly for high-publicity cases. I'm special, all right, and I get special treatment.

On days when I have to go from jail to court, I follow a set routine for high-profile prisoners at Sybil Brand. A guard wakes me at 5:30 in the morning and a trusty brings me breakfast in my cell. Breakfast is cold powdered eggs, lumpy oatmeal, two pieces of un-toasted stale bread, a greasy piece of fried bologna.

Breakfast done, I take off my prison nightgown, a white cotton sack, and dress in my own clothes. Somewhere in the cell block, women deputies have already checked each item carefully before giving the clothes to a trusty to hand through the bars to me. The deputies have to make sure the clothes haven't somehow accumulated contraband while in the care of the prison.

I have fifteen minutes to dress. At 6:00 A.M. the bars that make up my cell door open automatically. I step outside the cell, and the bars slam shut behind me. I walk down a corridor lined with bars. At the end stand male deputies, men from the county sheriff's department. I hold out my wrists to them. They snap on a pair of handcuffs. (Still, in my dreams, I hear the click of locking manacles.)

The deputies lead me out of my underground cell and up to the prison's main level to line up with other women to board a bus. I stand in line behind bars. The bars open to let me into another cage. When all the women are in the cage its doors open, and we file out into a courtyard enclosed by the prison's high walls. The bus waits there.

It, too, is a cage, an old converted school bus with bars on the windows. Since I'm special, I have a special place in the front of the bus, an area sealed off by bars from the regular seating area in the rear. I have a cage within a cage.

I'm loaded onto the bus first. I sit and wait while the other women, some in leg shackles as well as handcuffs, climb in and find seats. The bus sputters into motion. The walls open to allow it into the street.

It's about 6:15 now. The bus labors up a hill and onto the freeway. Early commuter traffic whizzes by—free people on the freeway, headed for their jobs. (I used to play a game on the bus. I would look at the people in their cars and try to imagine what jobs they were going to, what kind of lives they led. I would project myself into their cars, setting out for a busy day with work and friends. I would be crying by the time I got to court.)

After about ten minutes the bus leaves the freeway for a stop at Men's County Jail. Women going to courts other than the Los Angeles Court are unloaded here for transfer. They exchange pleasantries with the men boarding their own buses. ("Hey, blondie, ah bin fuckin' sumbody luk jes' lak yew." "Yeah, boy, I bet she ain't as good. Gimme your booking number so I can write you a letter.") It's like pulling into a foreign country, hearing a foreign language.

The thirty-minute stopover ends. The bus chugs off on the short last leg of its journey, through downtown Los Angeles to the court building. On this particular day I'm going to court to hear a decision on one of the innumerable writs my lawyers have filed in my case. The low gray sky begins to drizzle. We pass City Hall, and I look out through the bars. It's still too early for downtown traffic.

The streets are silent. City Hall is deserted. It looks eerie, as unreal as a movie set.

Suddenly, I'm no longer on the bus. My mind, uncaged, travels back to a day filled with sunlight. Throngs of people crowd the City Hall steps. It's Mayor Tom Bradley's inauguration day, a day of celebration for all of us who worked for his election. People are happy and laughing. Bands blare. As a Bradley backer and the leader of some forty thousand feminists, I've been invited here as a special guest. Dressed in a stylish suit, I trade welcomes with the smiling people who come up to greet me. Members of the mayor's staff usher me to a special seating area. . . .

Special then. Special now. My head moves and my focus changes from far vision to near. City Hall fades. I can see only the bars on the windows.

The bus has reached the courthouse. It pulls into a driveway running underneath the building and rolls inside a cage of its own, which locks around it. (A cage within a cage within a cage, now.) I'm unloaded from the bus first and taken inside the building to a holding tank. The other women are put into other holding tanks, ten or twelve to a room. I'm alone. Deputies come in, take off my handcuffs, and leave.

My new cage is about twice the size of my cell at Sybil Brand. I've been here often, and by now I know it well. It's a windowless room. The front wall is dominated by a steel door. On either side of it is metal grating. There are concrete benches along two of the remaining walls. There's a dirty toilet in one corner and a drain in the middle of the floor.

There's not an inch of bare space on the side and rear walls. They are covered with graffiti, the scrawls in all sizes, in pencil, ink, lipstick, eyeliner. Along with the usual obscenities are comments on the criminal justice system: *Angela is a snitch. Pled gilty but Im inocent.* I try not to stare whole-focus at any wall for too long. I know that if I do, the writing will begin to close in on me. Instead, I view each wall a piece at a time, memorizing the graffiti bit by bit. I know maybe half of them by now. In time, I'll know them all. I feel desperately tired, but I dare not lie down. The benches are too narrow to stretch out on, the floor too filthy to fall off on. I read the walls for two and a half hours.

The door of the holding tank slides open by remote control. It's time for me to go to court. I walk out into a glass-enclosed basement room filled with deputies. A voice from a loudspeaker says, "Walk and stand in front of elevator number three." I obey. The elevator doors open. I step in. They close. The elevator glides automatically to the right floor. The doors open. The mechanical voice says, "Step out of the elevator." I walk down a long corridor studded with uniformed police officers. At the end of the corridor, a deputy locks me into another holding tank, this one directly behind the court-room.

Some thirty minutes later I enter the courtroom for a ceremony that lasts about two minutes. (Writ read. Writ denied.) I walk back into the holding tank to begin the morning's trip in reverse.

Back in the basement about 12:15 P.M. I'm told I've missed the noon bus to Sybil Brand. The next bus will leave at 5:00 P.M. Lunch is served: an apple, a sandwich of salami and cheese on a dry hard roll. I munch on the apple and go back to memorizing the messages left on the walls by my sisters. Finally, the bus comes to take me home.

In my own cage again, I wait for the worst part of all. The women deputies come for the strip search.

One deputy stands outside the bars of my cell, the other at the end of the cell-block hall. I take off my clothes, handing them out a piece at a time. The deputy examines each piece for drugs or other contraband. I hand her my shoes. She scrutinizes them.

When I'm stripped down to nothing, she tells me to stand facing away from her, to bend over and spread the cheeks of my buttocks. Watching from between my legs, I see her peer at my anus, my vagina. Satisfied, she hands me my prison uniform and leaves.

I put on my little-girl clothes: prison-issue tennis shoes, white knee socks, and a pink pinafore. Demurely dressed for my forced regression to childhood, I go to my cot and sit. I hear somebody crying. I can't comfort her. It's not allowed.

The only things abundant in prison are anguish and time, and there's not much to do with the time but think. The future is too frightening to contemplate and the present too bleak to acknowl-edge, so there's only the past to think about.

My mind begins to gnaw at it, chewing painfully, obsessively, at the gristle of old mistakes and failings, of stale, recurring ques-tions: How did I get here? How did the wide expanse of my life narrow to this cage? What happened to that good little Catholic girl named Virginia Galluzzo, growing up in upstate New York and dreaming her sugary Disney dream that someday her prince would come?

He did come. That's what happened. That's why I'm here.

chapter 1

My grandparents, Charlie and Ida Liuni, were the first members of my family to leave New York City. They had reared their five children in Brooklyn, where my grandfather owned a little fruit and vegetable stand that catered to the neighborhood's Italian tastes. By the early 1940s the children were all grown, the old neighborhood had changed, and my grandparents resettled some eighty miles north in a pretty town called New Paltz in the foothills of the Catskills. All their children, with their own families, would follow them there in time. In New Paltz, Charlie and Ida bought a rambling old farmhouse and two acres of land on top of a hill and set about raising chickens and tending their apple trees and vegetable garden.

I remember how big and roomy it seemed, so different from my parent's apartment back in Brooklyn. I loved the smells—the sweet warmth of my grandmother's baking, the tang of my grandfather's homemade wine fermenting in the basement. And I loved my grandparents.

I spent the summer with them the year I was five. It was 1946, and my mother had given birth to my sister, Emilia, in March. My rambunctious nature must have been even more of a trial for Mother than usual, with a new infant on her hands, so she sent me off to New Paltz. I welcomed the exile.

Grandma never seemed impatient with me. I would follow her around all day, watching her clean and cook and wash and iron, trailing along while she fed the chickens or brought in the sun-fresh clothes from the clothesline. At night I would watch as her plump little fingers crocheted the lacy collars and cuffs and afghans and bedspreads she still occasionally sold to the New York department stores to bring in extra money.

I was a fanciful little kid, and Grandma never discouraged my babbling about how special I was going to be when I grew up. She enjoyed my fantasies, in fact, and she liked to help me embroider them. I was going to be rich and famous. That meant, of course, that I was going to marry somebody rich and famous. I would probably marry the king of England, we decided. When I was queen, Grandma would have beautiful gowns and jewels. That would be nice, she said, and maybe I could also get her somebody to help pick the beans and tomatoes and do some of the ironing for Charlie.

As befitted the man in an Italian family, Grandpa Charlie was absolute master of the household—at least to all appearances. He made the major decisions and handled all financial matters, as my father did in my parents' house. (Before my father's death my mother never wrote a check or owned a credit card with her name on it.) Grandpa expected, and got, a well-kept house, a constant supply of clean, starched shirts, and meals that were served on time and to his liking. After all, he was the provider. He ran things.

I wonder if he ever suspected to what extent Grandma ran him. She criticized him constantly in a pattern of marital guerrilla sniping that she probably inherited from her mother and certainly passed on to mine. This was usually done out of earshot, though Grandma wasn't shy about face-to-face confrontation when she thought it necessary. *"Fatti i fatti tuoi!"* she would yell at him. "Go mind your own business!" Grandpa would usually shrug, or smile contemptuously, to show that such female ranting was beneath his notice. Yet he often went along with her wishes, at least on matters involving the home and family, and he seemed to try to please her in small ways. I assumed that their behavior had to do with what it meant to love each other and be married, and that her feistiness and his disdain were all part of it somehow.

I don't know whether Grandma ever imagined a life different from her own. She seemed to enjoy the mammoth labor that went into holiday dinners, when the whole family would come to visit—

her five children, their spouses, and the grandchildren, my seven cousins and I. She would make miles of pasta, laying it out to dry on floured sheets on every bed in the house, upstairs and down. She would pick apples for pies and send Grandpa out to select and kill four or five of the fattest chickens for the main course. Then she would assemble ingredients for her sauces and salads and desserts and begin to cook. The preparations sometimes lasted for days.

Then the big day would come, and twenty of us or more would wedge ourselves around the dining-room table. Grandma would serve everything herself, bringing each dish to Grandpa at his place at the head of the table. He would fill the individual plates, serving himself first, then the sons and sons-in-law, and finally the women and children.

The feast would start with loaves of hot Italian bread and a huge platter of antipasto, rich with oily olives and peppers and salami. Then came big bowls of spaghetti, with a separate platter of meatballs, veal, pork, beef, and sausages, which had cooked in the spaghetti sauce. When these modest appetizers were cleared away, the main course arrived, the chicken, with mashed potatoes and home-grown vegetables. Next came a heaping green salad to help clear the palate for dessert. All of it was washed down with the red wine from Grandpa's operation in the basement. Even the children were allowed a small glass on really festive occasions.

We all needed a break after the salad, so the men would go into the living room and talk while the women cleared the table and reset it for dessert. When we reassembled, Grandma would bring out her pies, along with cream puffs, pizzelles, cannolis, and fried dough balls dipped in honey. The meal would end about two hours after it began, with black coffee and anisette for the grown-ups.

I liked the holiday dinners not so much for the food but because they brought together at one time, under one roof, all my cousins —my younger cousins. I was the oldest of the grandchildren. In fact, I was the firstborn of the firstborn of the firstborn, going back four or five generations. This gave me a certain status even among the adults in the family, and it made me the undisputed leader among my cousins.

I was the one who invented most of the games and planned most of the activities—and caused most of the mischief. Grandma hardly ever told on me unless it was for major naughtiness. One summer an incident did push her to it. I was going into town to get some ice cream with my cousins Joseph and Joan. As we walked along the country road below my grandparents' house, an older boy on a bicycle rode up and began to tease us. "Guinea, guinea, wop, wop," he yelled, circling us on his bike. Joseph started to cry. I was furious, but decided it wasn't the time to stand and fight. As we walked home, I planned revenge. Something I remembered from a television cartoon gave me the idea.

We found some rope and took it down the hill. Joan and Joseph crouched in the roadside ditch, holding one end of the rope. I hid on the other side and held the other end. Before long the big kid came pedaling toward us at a good clip. He didn't see us until it was too late. We executed the plan perfectly and it worked just like in the cartoon. He went flying over the handlebars headfirst onto the asphalt.

But then I saw that he was bleeding and screaming and crying. Something was wrong! Nobody bled in the cartoon. My cousins fled and hid and I ran up the hill to get Grandma. Much confusion followed, but I remember watching her clean the blood from the boy's face and calm him down. I was sweaty with guilt and dread. "He's not going to die, is he?" I wailed. Grandma just looked up at me and glared.

As it turned out, all the blood came from a rather small cut on the boy's head, and he was able to get back on his bike and ride away. Grandma led me into the house, and I waited while she telephoned his parents and told them what had happened. Then she sat me down in the kitchen. There was a long silence.

"This time, I've really got to tell your mama," she said at last. "You could have killed that boy."

We sat in silence for what seemed like hours. She shelled beans. I fidgeted. Then I heard a car coming up the driveway, and I knew it was my parents. Grandma went to let them in, and when they finally found me hiding under a bed, Daddy dragged me out and administered a thorough whipping. I had no doubt I deserved it.

My father was manager of one of the Gristede Brothers food stores when we lived in New York. He often worked from eight in the morning until ten at night during the week, plus a half day on Saturday. By the time I was about six years old, he had saved enough money to move the family into a house of our own in the suburbs. We moved from Brooklyn to Queens Village in the eastern section of Queens.

Our new home, part of a tract development, was a brand-new one-story brick house, exactly like every other house on the block. Our neighbors were solid, working-class people, all of them strongly ethnic, many of them Jewish. We lived there for six years or so, and all I recall as extraordinary about that part of my childhood was how perfectly ordinary it was.

I was jealous of my baby sister, but not especially so. I went to public school and made good grades without having to work very hard. I liked to roller skate and to play games that got my clothes dirty and I had little interest in the pretty dresses that Mother would starch and iron for me, standing them stiffly around the living room until she was finished. In fact, I irritated my mother constantly, mostly by resisting her efforts to prepare me for a life as a good Italian housewife.

Mother encouraged me to make friends with the other little girls in the neighborhood. "Girls play with girls, and boys play with boys," she said. I preferred the boys. The girls seemed prim and dull. Boys had more freedom and more fun and I spent most of my time with them.

We would write our names in the wet cement of new sidewalks being installed in the expanding neighborhood, or, as we got older, experiment with cigarettes in the woods that bordered a field at the end of our block. Once we accidentally set the field on fire.

I took piano lessons for a while from a woman down the street, but she quit in despair after only a few months with me. I never learned to read a note of music and could barely locate middle C on the piano. Nevertheless, I decided to display my skill at a school talent show one year. The other little girls twirled batons with some expertise, or played proper, formal little piano pieces. When my turn came, I settled my starched ruffles on the piano bench and pounded with a flourish through a random series of notes I made up as I went along. Mother was embarrassed, I think. Daddy said I did fine.

Like most families, I guess, mine fell into a pattern of alliances. Mother seemed to prefer my sister, Emilia, who was more pliant than I, and who seemed able to express her emotions to Mother in ways that I couldn't, or wouldn't. Only in the past few years have my mother and I become close, loving friends. As a child I was much closer to my father.

Though Daddy was home very little, the time we did spend together was almost always happy. He seemed proud of me, maybe finding some worthwhile spirit in what Mother considered my way-ward and stubborn nature. It was Daddy I ran to for a hug when I needed one.

He had many ways of showing how much I mattered to him. If I needed a new dress or had my heart set on some special toy, he would see that I got it, even if the family had to do without something else.

Despite our closeness, Daddy was my disciplinarian for misbehavior that Mother considered serious. Her "Wait 'til your father gets home" was a dire threat, and I was as frightened by it as she meant me to be. When he came home from work Mother would tell him what I'd done wrong and why I deserved to be punished. Then my father would come for me and lead me downstairs to the basement. There was a post in the basement, and hanging on it was a leather strap he would whip me with.

The whippings were not a common occurrence; I remember only four or five of them throughout my whole childhood. If they were painful to me, they seemed to hurt my father even more. I never blamed him for them. Still, I've wondered whether it might have been there, in that basement, that I first began to believe in the rightness, the acceptability, of being beaten by a man I loved.

Though my parents did quarrel about how to handle me, a bigger problem in their marriage had to do with religion.

Mother has always been a devout Catholic, and she tried to instill in Emilia and me her passion for religion. When I was a child, that passion was easy for me to share. I understood little about Catholic doctrine then, but the mysticism and pageantry of the Church appealed powerfully to my imagination and love of fantasy. I made my first Holy Communion when I was seven, and I suspect my reaction to the event was a common one among little girls. Kneeling at the altar, bathed in incense and candlelight, staring at the statues of saints and at the priests in their white-and-gold robes, I was momentarily certain that God meant me to be a nun. (Happy as that would have made my mother and grandmother, it was a notion that quickly faded.)

We went to mass every Sunday—at least Mother and Emilia and I did. My father, though born and reared a Catholic, had no interest in the Church at all. I think he believed in God, but Gus Galluzzo was not, in any traditional sense, a religious man. As if to underscore his indifference to Catholicism, he joined the Masons a few years before we left New York City. Membership in that secret society was grounds for excommunication in those days, and Daddy was officially severed from the Church.

His rejection of religion was a source of enormous grief and anger for my mother. She didn't talk to me about it much, but my impression was that she was sure he would go to hell. I was learning in Sunday school what sin was, and what Catholic hell was all about, and I was terribly frightened for him. For several years after my first Holy Communion I would go to mass not once every Sunday, but twice. I would receive the Host once for my own soul and then once more for the soul of my father.

Another source of conflict in my parent's normally placid marriage involved where to live. Mother had objected to the move from Brooklyn to Queens, and she was horrified at the prospect of leaving the city entirely and moving to New Paltz. Though it was her parents we would be joining, Mother cried off and on for weeks after Daddy announced the decision to move. Unfortunately, she didn't have much choice but to go along.

The years of long hours at work were beginning to tell on my father's health and he was told that he would have to slow down. I'm not sure why he chose to look for a new job in New Paltz, but I suspect it had to do with his closeness to my grandparents. Daddy had always been Ida and Charlie's favorite son-in-law. Mother loved her parents, too, but she also loved the city. Since my father had no job when we sold the house and moved to New Paltz, Mother prayed for weeks to her favorite saint, Anthony, that my father wouldn't be able to find work and we would have to move back to New York.

Saint Anthony is sometimes called the Bread Saint, because he fed the poor. When Daddy finally got a job driving a truck for Wonder Bread, Mother must have felt doubly betrayed.

I sometimes think about how different my life would have been had we stayed in New York. New Paltz was a town where social accept-ability meant belonging to one of two groups. The first was made up of families descended from the French, English, and Dutch founders of the town. The second consisted of the administrators and faculty of the SUNY college at New Paltz.

I was twelve years old and just entering junior high school when we moved there. I was in that awful limbo between childhood and true adolescence and probably would have felt a little awkward no matter where I lived. But in New Paltz I felt like a Martian. I didn't fit in at all.

I had come from a big school where there was a niche for almost everybody. Now I found myself in a class of only sixty or so children, who belonged to a rigid caste system. Those in the "in" group were overwhelmingly Protestant. I was Catholic. They could trace their American ancestry back two centuries. I was the granddaughter of Neapolitan and Calabrese immigrants. Many of them had parents who were deans or professors—professional people who earned high salaries by my family's standards. Neither of my parents had gone to college. We were working-class.

To make matters worse, I was a city kid. Though New York was only an hour and a half away, few of the New Paltz youngsters had ever been there. They thought the city was a wild place, a kind of Sodom to the south, where all preteens smoked, drank, and generally worked at becoming juvenile delinquents. The popular girls at school looked on me with suspicion as too citified. And I, wanting desperately to be one of them, told myself that they were snobs and hicks.

Worst of all my handicaps, I looked different. I had reached puberty when I was nine, and unlike other girls of my age, I had what I thought of as "growths" on my chest, which seemed to attract a lot of interest. Boys would stare at me, then go off into corners and whisper together and giggle. Even grown men looked at me in a new way, a way I didn't like.

I was mortified. My early-blooming breasts were just one more sign that I was different, odd; and the way males reacted to them made me feel dirty in some way that I couldn't understand or name. I wore baggy, oversized blouses in a vain attempt to hide my hated curves. Because I was afraid it would make them more pronounced, I put off wearing a bra until Mother absolutely insisted on it.

Then, very slowly, I began to realize that, different or not, my looks could be a tool. I was getting attention because of the way I looked, and attention might lead to acceptance. Some of the boys told me I was pretty and I began taking special pains to see that my long black hair was always clean and glossy and styled the same way as the other girls'. I started wearing a little makeup to emphasize my large, dark eyes. If the girls were still standoffish, the boys were not.

I set out to conquer New Paltz with a calculation born of the desperation known only to teenagers who are outsiders and see a slight crack in the door that leads in. The first target of my campaign was a handsome boy whose father was a dean at the college. I flirted with him as well as I knew how, and it worked. He began to walk with me between classes and escort me to school dances, and some of his popularity spilled my way. Even the girls began to thaw. My phone rang more often, with invitations to pajama parties or Saturday afternoon movies with the erstwhile snobs and hicks, now my wonderful new friends. But I was living in a time when girls considered themselves competitors for a limited and precious commodity —boys. We measured one another's worth by how popular we were with boys, and we formed alliances accordingly. But we tended to be wary of one another.

The dean's son was my steady beau when I was thirteen, and he was the first boy I brought home to meet my parents. They weren't entirely pleased. He was a nice boy, but he wasn't Italian or Catholic and wasn't, therefore, "suitable." Mother and Daddy figured that I would marry right after I finished high school, as good girls from my world always did, and it was never too soon to weed out unacceptable prospects.

I brought the next boy home when I was fourteen. His name was Fred Schindler. He wasn't suitable either—of German descent and a member of the Dutch Reformed Church. I didn't care. I was in love.

My parents eventually grew to like Fred, though they never completely approved of him as a prospective son-in-law. Mother's worst fears were realized when I was a junior in high school. I left the Catholic faith and joined the Dutch Reformed Church.

Fred wasn't my only reason for making the change. Living among people who belonged to other faiths, I no longer believed that only Catholics went to heaven. Once I questioned that, I began to doubt the other lessons I'd learned in catechism class.

Mother was hurt literally beyond words. After I told her I was leaving the Church she didn't speak to me for days. I think she was finally able to do so again only by blaming Fred for my error, and by praying constantly to God and Saint Anthony that I would one day realize my mistake and return to the fold. My parents' objections slowly waned as Fred and I stayed inseparable and our marriage began to seem inevitable. Two years ahead of me in school, he was attractive, polite, and very bright. He was planning to go to college and become a chemist. We assumed almost from our first date that we'd get married one day, and we saw each other virtually every day or night until he graduated. Just before my own graduation we became engaged.

Being with Fred encouraged the venturesome side of my nature. He taught me to scuba dive and ride motorcycles and work on car engines. Once we even built a boat together. And my status as his steady girl friend ended any lingering question about my social acceptability. More secure now, I became a leader in the school's social and athletic life. I played on the girls' varsity basketball, softball, and tumbling teams. I gained a reputation as a good organizer and was always asked to serve on committees that planned school dances and proms. I sang in the school chorus and joined the yearbook staff. Like Grandma, I thrived on activity.

Fred left for college when I was a junior but he would come home for big occasions like proms, and I would visit him on weekends at Wagner College on Staten Island.

With more time on my hands, I got an evening job waitressing and helping with the management of a drive-in restaurant. I liked the work, and I liked the feeling of independence I got from earning my own money for the first time. Not that I planned to make a habit of it. It wasn't uncommon for women in my family, where the work ethic ran deep, to have jobs before marriage. Mother, for instance, had been a saleswoman in a New York department store. But after marriage the breadwinning was traditionally left to the men, and I anticipated that Fred would take care of me.

I finished my last year of high school and earned an honors diploma. Graduation ended a part of my life that had most of the elements of what was supposed to be the American girl's ideal life: the stable family, the nice boyfriend, the proper circle of friends, the healthy activities, the seemingly assured future. I suppose I should have been perfectly content, and yet I was restless and felt a nagging discontent whose source I couldn't pinpoint.

All I knew of marriage was what I saw in my extended family —safe and secure and respectable people. Part of me wanted that, wanted to marry Fred and have his babies and take care of his home, to be protected and cared for in return, to have the approval of my family and the community. But another part of me—a larger part, it seemed sometimes—wanted a lot more. I wanted romance and adventure. I wanted to travel, to see new places and meet different kinds of people. I wanted to accomplish things on my own. What things? I had no idea. Just something . . . different.

One day when I was in junior high there was a Career Day at school—professional people came to talk to us about their careers. I went home afterward and announced enthusiastically to Mother that I wanted to be a lawyer.

She laughed at me. "Where would we get the money to send you through all that school?" she said. "You know you're just going to get married anyway. It would be a waste. Be realistic."

I knew my parents were already saving for my wedding. They would gladly spend thousands of hard-earned dollars to make that event special for me. If I had been a boy instead of a girl, they would just as gladly have used the money to send me to school. They would have been proud that I wanted to be a lawyer. Somehow it didn't seem fair. It would be many years before I would understand why, but I felt instinctively that there was an injustice here.

On the other hand, I thought, Mother was probably right. Girls from my background did get married—unless there was something wrong with them. A rare woman here and there pursued a profession and became successful at it. But even then, people assumed that she was just making the best of the fact that no man wanted her. Besides, law schools generally accepted few if any women.

I was being unrealistic, just as Mother said. I was aiming over my head. I'd always dreamed too much. Maybe there was something wrong with me. Maybe the things I wanted were unnatural. I should remember who I was.

More and more, I came to feel guilty about my vague longings and doubts. I couldn't make them go away completely, but I tried to suppress them as much as I could. I wanted to do the right thing, to be a good girl.

The world of mid-century America in which I lived was more stable than the present, but the stability was built on constraint. The word "feminism" was barely part of the language. The program for "good" girls of the 1950s was closely prescribed, and "good" girls went along with the program. Suited for it or not, they got married, had babies, tried to keep their men happy, and hoped for the best.

It was the stagnant calm before the storm of the sixties, when many Americans would question the foundations of their complacent dream and begin to shake those foundations.

chapter 3

For me, the time had come to settle down and get married. My parents expected it. Fred expected it. And the closer I got to it, the more frightened and restless I became. I was engaged, but I hedged again and again at setting a wedding date. When our friends began to give us engagement parties I got really panicky. For years Fred and I had agreed on everything; now I picked silly fights and found trivialities to argue over. Finally, I gave him back his engagement ring. We still saw each other, and everybody assumed we'd get back together sooner or later. I guess I assumed so too, but I knew I wasn't ready yet for anything so permanent, so final, as marriage.

My parents were confused and upset by all this flightiness, and I still wanted to please them, to conform to their traditions. But their ways and mine weren't altogether the same anymore. Mother and Daddy had grown up with a set of customs and expectations that fit them comfortably. I couldn't seem to settle into their kind of life, but I couldn't find a new one of my own either.

I had come to New Paltz a scared little outsider, afraid I would never fit in. By the time I was a senior I did fit in, or at least I seemed to. Now I was about to be different all over again. My friends were going on to college. I wasn't. Some of them were going to stay at

New Paltz State, while others were going off to Ivy League schools. Some planned to get married and continue their schooling; others were still unattached. But all of them were going on to a new and wider world, and I was being left behind.

I had several discussions with my father about the possibility of my going to New Paltz State.

"Why would you want to do that?" he said. "You're going to get married soon. Maybe what you should do is go to secretarial school."

He wasn't being cruel, any more than Mother had been when she laughed at the idea of my becoming a lawyer. Both of them were simply dealing from the only frame of reference they knew. Besides, I thought, maybe the family couldn't afford to send me to college. Maybe it was time I learned to type and looked for some secretarial job to mark time until I got married.

Again, I felt that I'd been venturing out of reality. What was I doing hanging around with people who were going to Harvard and Yale? I was an Italian Catholic young woman from a working-class family, and college wasn't part of my sphere.

Twelve o'clock, Cinderella. Time to go home.

I enrolled in a secretarial school in Poughkeepsie, across the Hudson River from New Paltz. I lived at home and commuted— though not necessarily to school. School was a disaster or, more like it, I was a disaster. I took to the typewriter about as well as I had to the piano. As for shorthand, those squiggly little lines the instructors tried to teach me were a complete mystery. I couldn't draw them and I couldn't read them and I didn't want to.

Before long I found myself leaving home in the morning only to spend the day at the movies, or at the library reading books and magazines. I felt guilty about not being in school, but the guilt was no worse than the inadequacy and dissatisfaction I felt when I did go.

The problem got solved easily when I flunked out after the first semester. Daddy was very disappointed. What would I have to fall back on now if it turned out that nobody wanted to marry me? I was sorry for the whole debacle, but I was also immensely relieved. Besides, I had a new plan.

On one of those endless days at the public library, I had come across an advertisement for Grace Downs Academy, a school in New York that trained young women to become airline attendants. It sounded perfect to me. I'd be living away from home, out on my own at last. I'd be learning a job that paid well and that used what I considered my strength, dealing with other people. No typing! No shorthand! I'd make new friends. I'd get to travel. The prospect seemed incredibly glamorous.

My father objected at first but eventually agreed to look at the school. He and Mother and I drove down to New York to look the place over. It was in Manhattan on First Avenue, across the street from Bellevue Hospital. At least medical help would be close at hand. The staff seemed friendly and the program sound, and there appeared to be enough supervision to satisfy my father's requirements. I arranged to get a job as a part-time receptionist to help with the tuition and Daddy decided I could go. I liked Grace Downs almost as much as I'd loathed secretarial school. We learned some things about airplanes and airports, but most of the program had a finishing-school flavor. We learned to walk with books on our heads to improve our posture and acquire grace. We had courses in how to apply makeup and groom our hair. We learned the niceties of tray-serving and passenger-greeting.

I enjoyed living in a dormitory, much like college would have been, I imagined. I made some close friends and I developed a very active social life. For the first time, I didn't have a steady boyfriend. Playing the field was part of my new freedom, and I savored it.

Not unexpectedly, Fred and I were growing further apart. We couldn't see each other as often as we once had, and when we were together things weren't the same between us. I wasn't so emotionally dependent on him as I had been, and possibly he was threatened by the changes I was making in my life. For my part, I was getting a taste of the less restrictive life I'd dreamed about and I wasn't ready to give it up. Finally, we stopped seeing each other altogether. The ultimate break was painful for me. Fred had been part of my growing up, a mainstay of my life for five years. But again, a large measure of relief went along with the pain. I had severed one more tie with the past.

And, too, there was somebody else who was now special in my life, someone I had met when I was still in high school. He was a brawny, dark-haired, good-looking boy, whom I'll call Tony, the star of the football team in nearby Highland, New York. During my senior year Tony was at a college on a football scholarship, but we spent a lot of time together whenever he was home. After he injured his knee during his freshman year, he had to give up his scholarship. The loss of his football-hero status gave him a new and appealing vulnerability, and our relationship intensified as Fred faded from the picture. After I went off to Grace Downs, Tony was a frequent visitor.

I was very attracted to him and flattered by his interest in me. He was a catch. Along with his other assets, he had unqualified approval from my parents. Unlike Fred, he was an Italian Catholic from a family much like mine—solid, working-class people. His parents owned an apple orchard, which gave the family a modest but adequate income. They doted on their son, the only male of three children. Tony was respectful and attentive to my parents. More, he seemed completely at home with them, and they with him. By the same token, I got along well with his sisters and with his parents, who were as enthusiastic as mine about a potential match.

Still, I wasn't ready for a commitment. Besides, there didn't seem to be any need to hurry. Tony and I had talked about marriage, but he wasn't really pressuring me. For the time being, he seemed as content as I was just to date and see how the relationship would evolve.

I graduated from Grace Downs in the summer of 1960 and was hired by Allegheny Airlines. I went through a short training course in Washington, D.C., ending with a ceremony in which I was awarded my wings. I felt so proud as one of the airline executives pinned the metal badge on my brand-new stewardess uniform. It was a momentous event for me, almost a rite of passage. At the age of nineteen I was flying off on a real career. My past travels outside the state of New York consisted of a couple of trips to visit cousins in Rhode Island. Now I was going to see the world.

The first part of the world I got to see was Cleveland. I was based there, assigned to Allegheny's commuter run between Cleveland and Newark. I wasn't exactly jet-setting between Rome and Paris, but by and large I liked my job. It gave me a sense not just of independence, but of identity. An airline attendant was not only what I was, it was who I was. I was something more now than a confused adolescent. Some of the work was tedious and grubby, but I liked getting to know the passengers. Several of the regular commuters became acquaintances and I even dated a few from time to time. Maybe I wasn't fulfilling my ordained role as wife and mother, but I was serving men, in a way, as I had surely been born and bred to do. That part of the job seemed wholly natural.

My mother joined me on one of my early flights, and she seemed proud of the way things were working out for me—at least at first. As the months went by, my parents' visits to Cleveland became marked by pointed questions: How long did I plan to fly? Was this all I wanted to do with my life? When was I going to come home and settle down? As if to emphasize the point, they sometimes brought Tony with them. His interest in marriage seemed to be increasing with every visit. He, too, now wanted to know when I was going to come home and settle down.

Obviously, the tug-of-war between worlds still wasn't over. Too many of their doubts echoed my own. There was no promise of permanence in my job. I knew I'd have to stop flying when I got married or arrived at my thirty-fifth birthday. (Apparently, either event was supposed to cause the brain to atrophy—or, more likely, the body. Unbelievably, it never occurred to me in those days to question the discriminatory retirement rules. Fortunately, it did occur to others. Under pressure from feminists, the rules have long since been changed by all the major airlines.)

I knew it would take years, in any case, to advance to one of the better flight runs. Was my job a dead end? Was I letting everybody down? Maybe they were right. . . . But couldn't I put all the debate and doubt aside and just enjoy my life for a little while? That didn't seem too much to ask.

One of the fairly frequent passengers on my run was a pleasant, bright young man who was a student at Bucknell. There was no great romance between us, but we were friends and sometimes had dinner together when our schedules coincided. I liked him, and I was thrilled when he invited me to his college for a homecoming weekend.

A homecoming weekend! It was a chance to enter, however briefly, into the collegiate world that my old high-school friends now belonged to. I prepared for the weekend extremely carefully, picking out a nice blazer and skirt to wear to the football game, choosing just the right shoes. I spent half a month's salary on a new dress for the formal dance that would follow the game. The price was outrageous, but I didn't care. It was so important to look my best, and the dress I'd found was beautiful.

It was a stiff taffeta in various shades of light blue and turquoise. The bodice featured a darker blue foldover and tiny spaghetti straps. The skirt, worn over crinolines, was enormously full, a bell-shaped cascade that ended in a scalloped hemline at the ankles. Ballerina length, it was called back then.

The night of the dance my date came for me, carrying a corsage that was perfect for the dress. But the minute he saw me, the wide smile on his face faded. He stood speechless for a minute, just staring at me in an odd way. I hadn't had enough experience to judge what the expression on his face meant.

The minute we got to the dance, I knew. From the door I could see that the other girls were all dressed in soft, straight dresses, sleek silks and floating chiffons. I stood out among them like the awful hick I was. My dress was horribly wrong. I looked ridiculous. I *was* ridiculous. I was a fraud, a silly, stupid, pretentious intruder, and everybody in the room knew it. I didn't belong there. I could never belong there.

My cheeks burned with embarrassment. I saw contempt and laughter in every pair of eyes that met mine. I wanted only to run away somewhere and hide and cry. I'd done it again. I'd ventured out of my depth, out of my world, out of my role, out of my class. How could I be such a fool?

A month later, less than a year after I became a stewardess, I went home to New Paltz and got engaged to Tony.

chapter 4

Tony and I were married on August 20, 1961, in an Italian extravaganza of a wedding. I had just turned twenty.

Neither the wedding nor the marriage got off to a very auspicious start. The first problem had to do with my return to the Church. I wasn't a Catholic anymore, but I was marrying one. I'd never developed into an especially ardent Protestant anyway, and it was unthinkable to deprive my parents and Tony's of a traditional Catholic wedding. Consequently, I went to see my family's parish priest to talk about my rejoining the faith.

The priest was a stern, elderly man whose Bible studies apparently had skipped any mention of returning prodigals. He lectured me about the seriousness of my defection and wanted to know why he should allow a sinner like me the sacrament of marriage. After a long harangue he finally dispensed penance—an endless string of Our Fathers and Hail Marys—and agreed, with great reluctance, to perform the ceremony.

Mother and I got busy assembling my trousseau and planning the wedding. The engraved invitations were sent out. More than two hundred guests were invited to both the wedding and the reception, which was to be a seated dinner, complete with champagne, at a local nightclub. For several weeks before the event there was an exhausting round of engagement parties and bridal showers.

I asked Emilia to be my maid of honor. Several high-school friends and older cousins were enlisted as bridesmaids, and I also chose two flower girls. My attendants would wear long dresses of pink and blue satin and chiffon. My own gown would be white, of course, with tiers of ruffles down the skirt and a long veil.

The ceremony went off without a hitch and I was very aware of its gravity. This was, after all, the most solemn of a woman's rites of passage, the one I was born for. I was stepping into a new life that was to last forever. As I made my vows to Tony, I also made a promise to myself. I would be a good wife, faithful, loving, and supportive. I would make my husband happy in every way, and he would love me and take care of me.

Thinking back on it, I believe my marriage really ended about the same time it began. We were both so young. We accepted completely the traditional romanticism that surrounded the idea of marriage in those days. When the reality turned out to be something else entirely, both of us were disillusioned and unable to adapt.

Tony's disillusionment would come later. Mine began right at the start of our honeymoon. My airline gave free honeymoon plane tickets to stewardesses who were quitting to get married. Tony and I decided to use our passes to go to Miami, then on to Mexico City. Exhausted, both of us read and dozed on the long flight from New York to Florida. Then, as we got close to the Miami airport, I heard a grinding noise that I'd learned to recognize during my days as a stewardess. I put down my book and turned to my new husband.

"It sounds like they're having a little problem with the hydraulic system," I told him. "They may have trouble getting the wheels down."

I went back to my book, confident that the pilot would find a way to land the plane safely, with wheels or without. But a few minutes later I looked over at Tony and saw that he was terrified. He was clutching the armrests so hard his knuckles were white.

I took his arm reassuringly and said nothing. But at that moment I felt all my comfortable preconceptions about marriage and sex roles begin to crumble. This was my hero, my brave protector who was supposed to defend me from all the dangers of the world? We'd been married only a few hours and already I was having to protect and comfort him. Something was definitely wrong here. Either something was wrong with Tony, who was not what he was supposed to be, or else everything I'd learned about marriage from my mother and father, from my whole culture, had been a big lie. Either possibility seemed too awful to think about. Now, that kind of measure of human strength and weakness seems ridiculous to me, but at the time it was the only measure I knew.

The plane landed safely after all and I shelved my doubts as best I could; this was no time to be having second thoughts. I tried to act the part of the ecstatic honeymooner, and I succeeded fairly well during our stay in Miami. We spent a pleasant week sightseeing and enjoying the beaches. Then we were off for our week in Mexico City.

Our first night we went to an elegant restaurant that somebody back home had recommended. The food was superb, but I was too sick to enjoy it. The altitude and thin air were getting to me, and I was dizzy and very nauseated. I finally stood up and tried to run out of the restaurant, but somehow I got lost and ended up in the kitchen, where I threw up in the nearest sink. Too late I realized that the sink was full of dishwater and dirty dishes, dishes that somebody was going to have to fish out.

I remember making some kind of mortified apology to the kitchen help, who, all things considered, couldn't have been nicer. They led us to the back door and hailed a cab for us. We went back to the hotel, and I spent the next two days sick in bed.

Tony, who was fundamentally a sweet and caring guy, was very understanding about the whole thing, but I suspect the sight of his new wife retching into a dirty sink might have been as much of a shock to him as the sight of his fear on the plane was to me. By the end of the week we were both ready to go home.

I guess, after the honeymoon, I expected the proverbial rose-covered cottage to materialize in some magical way. I would become the perfect homemaker, even if I also had to work for a while to help Tony finish his education. He would go back to school and maybe work part-time, and we'd get on with the business of living happily ever after.

That's not what happened.

We got an apartment right down the road from Tony's parents' house. His mother contributed most of the money for the furniture. Tony did go back to school, enrolling at New Paltz to study art and physical education, and I got a job. Almost immediately, we started growing in different directions.

Tony thrived in the carefree student world. He became totally absorbed in campus activities and campus social life. He had a wide circle of friends he felt comfortable with. I did not. I was about as at home with them as I'd been at that homecoming dance at Bucknell. I felt excluded, and I felt my husband and his friends were childish, insulated from the real world in a cozy little collegiate cocoon.

Because we lived mostly on what I made, the marriage was nothing like what I'd been conditioned to expect. Tony was supposed to be the provider, the responsible male who shouldered most of the load. It wasn't that I minded working. In fact, I liked it very much. What bothered me was the confusion of roles, and the contempt I couldn't help feeling for what I then saw as Tony's failure to hold up his end of things.

I thought that by getting married I'd finally done the right thing. Now, the right thing was turning out to be more complicated than I ever could have imagined. I resolved the conflict simply by putting it on hold, by giving less and less attention and energy to the marriage. When Tony got out of college and went to work things would be different, I told myself. Then he'd be the husband he was supposed to be, and I'd get back to trying to be the perfect wife. In the meantime, I had my own survival to worry about and my own life to live.

I had taken a job as a receptionist at the Wiltwyck School for Boys, whose main facility was just outside New Paltz in a complex of old frame and fieldstone buildings that had once been part of an estate. Wiltwyck was a school for emotionally disturbed boys from inner cities. There were perhaps a hundred children, most of them between the ages of five and ten, who had been sent to the school by court order. Some of them had adjustment problems in New York's public schools. Others had been in trouble with the police. Others were wards of the court, sent to us because their home situations were intolerable. Almost all were black, as were most of the school's counselors, though most of the higher-paid personnel, the therapists and school administrators, were white.

I started out at Wiltwyck answering phones and typing an occasional letter for the executive director, but he needed a troubleshooter more than a receptionist, and within a few months I was promoted to assistant to the executive director and given an office of my own.

My boss was a compassionate and talented man, good with the staff and good with the children, but he didn't have much patience or a knack for handling details. In a crisis he would simply to tell you to fix it. How you fixed it was your problem.

On one occasion, for instance, he was worried about a drought in the area, which threatened to dry up the well that supplied the school's water. All he said to me was, "If this drought doesn't end pretty soon we're going to be without water, and it's going to be a disaster. Handle it."

Running out of water was an emergency, I reasoned, and in an emergency you call either the police or the military. I settled on the military. I called a nearby Air Force base and eventually got a promise that help would be forthcoming if and when we needed it. I was very pleased with myself for working it all out.

Unfortunately, some fine point of timing got lost somewhere along the Air Force chain of command. A school counselor called me at home the night after I'd made the contingency arrangements. The Air Force had just delivered two huge tanker trucks full of water, he said. Where did I want to put it?

I told him to thank the Air Force, store as much water as possible, and do whatever had to be done to get rid of the rest of it. Put it in the toilets and keep flushing, if he had to. The military had to be convinced that we were in desperate need, just in case we turned out to be later on.

Luckily, most of my troubleshooting worked better than that, but the great impact Wiltwyck had on my life came not from the work itself but from the people I worked with. My political awareness and my anger at injustice were born at that school.

I'm ashamed to say it, but before I went there the subject of race prejudice seldom entered my mind. There weren't many black people in New Paltz and I'd had very little contact with those who were there. I hardly noticed the existence of the few blacks at my high school. It never occurred to any of the white kids, including me, to try to befriend them. I never would have thought of inviting one of them to my home, nor did I doubt what my parents' reaction would have been if I had. My mother and father didn't think of themselves as bigots, but their attitude toward blacks was the standard one of their class and culture at the time. Blacks belonged with blacks and whites with whites, Jews with Jews, Catholics with Catholics. That was the way things were and were meant to be. People should stick to their own. It was an attitude as ingrained and basic as it was unfair and irrational, and it was so much a fact of life that it was never even discussed. Racism was a state of mind I never

— 29 —

noticed and never questioned. And so, I guess, it was a state of mind I shared.

Now, at Wiltwyck, I was confronted with the results of racism every day. I saw children not yet ten years old who were drug addicts. I saw children whose developing minds had been stunted by malnutrition. I saw little boys who had been sexually molested by their mothers or fathers. I saw forty-year-old eyes in the five-year-old faces of children who'd had to survive on their own on the streets because the adults around them were too poor and degraded and beaten down to help. Some of these kids were so brutalized, so scarred psychologically, that their lives were beyond hope almost before they began.

I couldn't ignore racism anymore, or fail to question it. It was impossible not to feel compassion for these children. It was impossible not to be outraged by a system that caused such misery or allowed it to exist. And it was impossible not to be outraged at myself for my own past indifference and ignorance.

My anger began to take political shape. The civil rights movement had begun to stir in the South, sending out the first shock waves to other parts of the country. Many of my black colleagues were part of the movement. Their political philosophies were well formed and their passion for their cause was total.

There's no way to overstate the influence they had on me. I spent hours with them, listening to their ideas, asking questions, trying to absorb the strength of their commitment. The experience was like waking up to a new world after years of sleep.

The employees' union at Wiltwyck was the United Mine Workers, which was a focal point for civil rights activism at the school. The Student Nonviolent Coordinating Committee (SNCC) and the Congress of Racial Equality (CORE) were influential as well. By 1962 I was in all three organizations.

The work I did with them was a revelation because, for the first time, I was able to channel all my energy into a cause I believed in completely. It was also an escape because it diverted my attention from a marriage that I knew was a mistake. If I kept busy enough, I didn't have to confront the mistake or deal with its implications.

Gradually, more and more of my time was taken up with meetings. I didn't arrange my weekends to suit Tony's plans anymore, or rush home to him right after work every day. Along with my local activities there were occasional regional meetings in New York. I wouldn't get home from those until two or three o'clock in the morning. If Tony was awake when I got in, we argued. If he was asleep, the fight would be delayed until the next morning. But there was always a fight.

If I'd been disillusioned earlier, now it was his turn. Maybe he wasn't a very conventional husband, but he'd thought he was marrying a conventional wife. He had little patience with my time-consuming devotion to the civil rights movement. His happiness and welfare had always been the number-one priority for his mother and his sisters and he'd expected them to be the number-one priority for his wife. Why was I letting him down? What was wrong with me anyway?

My parents were asking the same questions, and others. What was I doing running around with all these colored people? Where did I get all these strange ideas and learn to behave this way? If I didn't watch out I was going to lose Tony, and that was unthinkable. There had never been a divorce in my family. "Let the colored take care of the colored," my father told me. "You should be home taking care of your husband, instead of trying to save the world."

At first I tried to make all of them understand how I felt and what I was trying to do. When that failed, I just tried to sidestep discussions and avoid confrontations. With Tony that proved to be impossible. The arguments got more frequent and more bitter. Finally, they began to lead to separations—short ones, at first. A vicious shouting match would end with my spending a few days at my parents' house, or his stalking off to spend the night with his parents. I was usually the one who weakened in these situations. When things calmed down I would go to Tony and ask him to come home. He'd relent. We'd get back together, try to patch over the widening split between us, and go on for a while longer.

I could never bring myself to think of a permanent separation. That idea was too frightening, too foreign to everything I'd ever believed. No. Tony would grow up a little more someday, and I'd settle down a little more, and we'd make things work. We'd get the marriage back on an even footing, if not an altogether happy one.

With that, I'd put the problem out of my mind again and throw myself even deeper into my work, into the life I had apart from my husband.

In the spring of 1963, I was one of millions of Americans watching television while a sad and sorry show unfolded in Birmingham, Alabama. That April, young blacks holding sit-ins at white lunch counters in that torn city, or sit-ins at the public library, or even kneel-ins in churches, were arrested and jailed. Dr. Martin Luther King, Jr., was thrown into jail for marching in defiance of a court order forbidding demonstrations. On May 2, hundreds of schoolchildren, some as young as eight years old, were jailed during a protest march. The next day, Birmingham Police Commissioner Eugene "Bull" Connor unleashed fire hoses and attack dogs on a crowd of peaceful blacks, mostly teenagers, who were leaving a meeting at a black church.

The horrors of Birmingham made my friends and me more determined than ever to add our voices to a national protest. Now all our efforts were centered on one goal: to help make Dr. King's forthcoming March on Washington a statement that couldn't be ignored.

I was one of the organizers in charge of sending a delegation from upstate New York. Throughout the summer I worked as I never had before, rounding up volunteers and chartering buses.

At last the bright, hot day came when we melted into a flood of people, more than a quarter of a million strong, blacks and whites, young people and old, marching arm in arm in ragged ranks, singing, laughing, crying. On August 28, in the one hundredth year after the Emancipation Proclamation, we surged into the quadrangle in front of the Lincoln Memorial. Both sides and both ends of the memorial's long reflecting pool were packed with shouting, joyous people.

I remember how we wept and cheered as Dr. King stood in front of the statue of Abraham Lincoln and told us, in words that are legend now, what he dreamed for America.

His words expressed exactly what I felt. Free. "Free at last!" I had never known such certainty, such complete and undivided joy. No inner fears or nagging doubts. I stood in the hot sun with tears streaming down my face and listened to this black preacher from the South talk not of sin and punishment but of love and forgiveness. I'd never heard words like these before, but I felt the rightness of them. I felt that the people around me were my thousands of brothers and sisters, who believed as I did and as he did. We couldn't all be wrong. Nobody could ever tell me again that we were wrong! At last I knew who I was and where I belonged. I was sure, on that day, that my life had changed forever. Yet it wasn't long before the door that opened so wide for me that August afternoon slammed shut.

· · ·

I'd been living at home with my parents when I went off to march on Washington. Tony and I had separated again, but again, I didn't consider that the break might be final. After the march we'd talk, I thought. We'd put things back together the way we always had before. This time, I was wrong.

I don't remember how I found out. Maybe he told me himself, maybe somebody else did. But I learned that my husband had been having an affair with a student at the college. It had been going on for some time, and it was serious.

I do remember the shock I felt. I think I may even have gone a little crazy. I went to Tony and begged him to come back to me. I pleaded with him to go away with me somewhere and try to work things out. I begged his family to intercede for me and persuade him to give me another chance.

It wasn't that I suddenly fell back in love with my husband, but I couldn't bear the disgrace I felt, or the sense of being alone and a failure. Whatever new directions my life may have been taking, I'd never really abandoned the traditional dream. When I saw it slipping away, I knew nothing else to do but clutch at it.

Finally, I got Tony to agree to go away with me for a week, but we came home after only three or four days. The only thing we'd agreed on was to start annulment proceedings. The marriage was beyond retrieval.

I told my parents about the forthcoming annulment, and watched them both cry, and wished that I'd never been born. I hated myself for hurting them. Why hadn't I listened to them when they warned me this would happen? They'd been right, after all, and I'd been so wrong.

Tony's affair was the explanation I gave them for the end of the marriage, but in my own mind it was only a smoke screen, a convenient excuse to help ease the crisis for them and deflect blame from me. I couldn't stand any more blame.

Despite what I told my mother and father, it never really occurred to me to blame Tony for having an affair. If only I'd been more of a woman, I thought, it wouldn't have happened. If I'd been a better lover, or a better housekeeper, or a better cook, he wouldn't be leaving me. If only I'd paid more attention to him, had made him the center of my life the way he expected, the way a good wife was supposed to do.

If only I hadn't gotten so involved in my job. If only I hadn't gotten so caught up in all that civil rights business. Once again I'd been a fool, doing something I shouldn't have done and going somewhere I didn't belong. And this time, it was going to cost me everything.

It was just a month or so after the hope and certainty of Washington, and now I was completely lost. I was only twenty-two years old and already I'd ruined my life. Nothing could be worse than this.

Then I found out I was pregnant.

chapter 5

During my trial in 1983 one of the prosecutors asked me where I went to have my baby. I refused to answer the question. When he pressed the point I refused again.

"I don't want to say anything here that will tell anyone who this child is or who the father of the child is," I told him. "I am not going to hurt anybody else."

I feel that some of the details of my child's conception and birth must remain secret. He's not a child anymore, of course. He's a young man in his early twenties, living his own life somewhere. Maybe he's even married by now, with children of his own. I don't know anything about his life, although I've wondered and worried about him for years and will for the rest of my life.

About the father: I knew when I found out I was pregnant that the baby was not Tony's. The pregnancy was the consequence of an incident that happened during one of the rocky times when Tony and I were separated. I don't think the father ever knew I was pregnant.

I didn't know myself until I was almost four months along. Strange as it may sound, I knew so little about my own body that I wasn't really sure what the early signs of pregnancy were. Then too, it happened at a time when my life was in such a tailspin that I wasn't alert to my body's signals—or to much of anything else, for that matter.

The failure of my marriage had left me in such a deep, guilt-ridden depression that my whole personality changed for a while. I began sleeping more than usual, sometimes as much as ten or twelve hours a night. During the day I dragged around the house, aimless and listless, trying to avoid the looks of concern and puzzlement on my parents' faces. For the first time in my life I began to drink, regularly and heavily. And for the first time, I started seeing a lot of different men, looking for appreciation, for some validation of my womanhood, or just some escape from my misery. Certainly, there was no pleasure in that kind of life—not in getting drunk and not in the frantic dating. But if a man or a drink could numb my thoughts and feelings temporarily, that was enough.

I had no morning sickness, and I failed to notice the missed periods, or perhaps their significance failed to register. But I began to feel changed physically, and vaguely ill. Every time the thought of what it might be tried to edge its way into my mind, I pushed it away. It just wasn't possible. It just couldn't happen.

But I must have known that it was possible. When I finally decided to see a doctor, I didn't tell my parents about it, and I didn't go to our family physician in New Paltz. I found somebody in Poughkeepsie instead. He confirmed that I was between three and four months pregnant.

For several days I was too dazed and frightened to face the situation. I was still married to Tony and I did not want to trick him into thinking the child was his. The father was not someone I could marry.

I thought about abortion, but only briefly. It wasn't legal anywhere in the country, and I had no idea how to go about getting an illegal one. Even if I'd known where to look and wanted to try, I was probably too far along. But the factor that made me rule out abortion completely was that the very idea scared me to death. In those days you were gambling with your life.

While I was at Grace Downs I got to be casual friends with a fellow student who came to me one day and told me she was pregnant. She was terribly frightened. She wanted me to go with her to a certain street corner, where some people she didn't know were going to pick her up and take her to have an illegal abortion. She asked me to memorize the license tag of the car that came for her. That way, she said, there would be some way to begin to trace her in case she didn't come back. I did what she asked and I agreed to meet her the next day at a specified time on the same street corner. That's where she was going to be dropped off after the operation was over.

I was on time the next day, but she was already there. She was leaning against a building and appeared to be about to collapse. Her normally fair complexion was milk-white. She told me she was bleeding badly. Something had gone wrong. I half-led, half-carried her to the emergency room at Bellevue, and she was admitted to the hospital immediately. She was hemorrhaging. She almost died. She would never have children.

There was only one choice left. I would go away and have my baby and give it up for adoption. I spent the next few weeks with only two thoughts in mind: hiding my condition until I could get away, and finding a home for unwed mothers where I could have the baby safely and in secret.

I was well into my fourth month now, and the changes in my body were obvious—at least to me. Somehow, no one else seemed to notice. My parents never commented on my looking any different. I'd always been slender. Maybe it just appeared that I was putting on weight, as women in my family tended to do.

I began dieting to keep my weight down as much as possible. Still, my clothes didn't fit anymore. I started pinning my slacks and skirts closed at the waist with safety pins. When the pins wouldn't reach any longer, I just left the clothes unbuttoned and covered over the gaps with oversized sweaters and blouses. It was winter, and the coats and bulky clothes helped with the camouflage.

Once in New York I'd seen an advertisement for a home for unwed mothers that was run by a religious organization. But New York was too close to home. I still had relatives there. I called the place and asked for information about homes run by the same organization in other cities. I settled on one in a large city in the Midwest. I didn't call ahead to make any arrangements. That would have made the prospect of going there too real, too immediate, and I still wasn't strong enough to face it.

The next worry was money. I'd left Wiltwyck when I was trying to reconcile with Tony, and I hadn't worked since. I was nearly broke. The only thing of any material value I'd salvaged from the marriage was a little red MG convertible that I loved and worked on myself to keep it in top condition. I sold it and bought a cheaper car, telling my parents I needed something more practical because I was planning a trip.

I told them I needed to get away. I wanted to travel around for a while and visit old friends, roommates I'd had when I was with the airline. Mother and Daddy seemed happy about the plan, even relieved. I hadn't been myself since the breakup of my marriage. Maybe a change of scene would do me good.

By January I couldn't delay leaving any longer. I was between six and seven months pregnant. I got a road map, put one suitcase into the trunk of the second-hand Studebaker I'd bought, and started driving west. I'd been on the road only a few hours when it started to snow—just a dusting at first, then heavier and heavier. I couldn't see enough to drive anymore, so I pulled over to the side of the road to wait out what had become a blizzard.

Hours went by. I don't remember how many. I sat and watched the snow pile up around the car. It climbed up to the door handles, then to the bottom of the windows, then midway to the window tops. Nothing was moving on the highway and the car was freezing. I was shivering, partly from cold and partly from fear.

Maybe I'll die here, I thought. The idea was almost welcome, almost comforting. There would be no more problems, no more trouble for anybody. But if I died, so would my baby. I curled my icy feet under me and huddled deeper into my coat, trying to keep warm.

At last I heard a heavy, grinding noise. Snow plows were clearing the road and one of them was able to push my car out of the snowdrift.

It took me three days to reach my destination. It was a huge, anonymous city and I didn't know a soul there. I felt completely alone.

I was afraid to go to the home, afraid to commit myself to giving up my baby. I checked into a YWCA and spent the night.

The next morning I wandered through the unfamiliar streets, trying to come to terms with the decision I'd made. Finally, in the afternoon, I called the place. The woman on the other end of the linc sounded very pleasant. The home was a nice place, she said, a haven to help girls through troubled times. With its help and the help of Jesus Christ, I could put my life back together again. There were certain ground rules for admittance, she said. You couldn't be married. You couldn't plan to keep your baby. If you had any money, a percentage of it would go to the home for your care.

I was wearing my diamond engagement ring, the only valuable piece of jewelry I owned. I took it off and wrapped it in a sock and stuffed the sock into a corner of the trunk of the Studebaker. Then, following the directions the woman had given me, I drove to the home.

It was a large gray stone building with a forbidding institutional look. But there was no turning back now. I parked the car and went inside.

It was like checking into jail. I went to the admittance office and met with the woman in charge. I gave her a false name, as, I learned later, many of the "patients" did. At first the administrator seemed kind and sympathetic. We had a short, friendly talk about my problem, and what I'd decided to do about it. Then she got down to business.

I was handed a list of several pages of rules. Among other things, it outlined what the daily routine would be—what time we "girls" were to get up in the morning, what time we were to make our beds and dress, what time we were to appear for breakfast, what time we were to attend prayer services, what time was allotted for our cleaning duties, what time we were to go to lunch and dinner, what time we were to go to bed. It spelled out some of the niceties of behavior to be observed. First names only. None of us was supposed to know anyone else's last name.

I was taken to a closet filled with used maternity clothes and allowed to pick what I needed. Then I was taken to a dormitory room with six cots and a chest of drawers. I was told to put my own clothes, and any other personal articles I'd brought, into my suitcase. Most especially, I was to put away any cosmetics. Cosmetics were not allowed at the home. The suitcase would be locked up. I'd get it back when I was ready to leave.

From that day on, every moment I spent in that place was an exercise in guilt. We were constantly told in subtle, tacit ways that we were worthless, and we were also told it outright. Like untrustworthy children, we were strictly regimented. It was as though leaving us to our own thoughts, even for a moment, would encourage us to commit some new and terrible sin. Our beds were checked every morning to see if we'd made them properly, if we'd drawn the covers tightly enough to bounce a dime. We filed into the dining room together for every meal. We were required to eat exactly what was on our plates, no more and no less. The sin of gluttony was not to be tolerated, and neither was the sin of waste.

Every morning after breakfast, and every night before going to bed, we were required to attend religious services. There was always a sermon with the same theme: We were sinners, filthy with the sin of carnal lust. We had done the devil's work, tempting men with our bodies. Pregnancy was God's judgment on us. We must repent and atone. We must subdue the flesh.

To help us, we all had housekeeping chores that kept us busy for most of the day. It was my job to clean part of the chapel. I scrubbed its marble floors, cleaned the windows, polished the elaborate mahogany woodwork. In a way, I enjoyed it. The hard physical work was soothing, and the chapel itself was beautiful and peaceful.

Just as they checked our beds, the home's supervisors inspected the quality of our housecleaning every day. One day while I was washing the floor, one of the supervisors came into the chapel. She ran her finger over a wooden railing I'd just polished, looked at her finger, then looked down at me. "It's as dirty as you are," she said.

There was never any rhetoric of the sort heard from the so-called right-to-lifers today about the blessings of adoption or providing the joy of a child to a childless couple. There was only a mixed message that was drummed into us every morning and every night: We were awful because we got pregnant. We were even more awful because we were going to abandon our children. Yet we were most awful of all if we showed any sign of wanting to keep our babies. Giving them up was part of our "atonement."

Any woman who indicated in any way that she might be thinking of keeping her baby was confronted immediately with a social worker or a member of the home's staff. How would she support the baby? she was asked. How could she think of bringing such shame on her family? How could she consider bringing a child into the world with no one to care for it but a sinful mother? It would have taken an incredibly strong woman to fight successfully to keep her baby under that kind of pressure. No one I met while I was there seriously tried.

What comfort we women had, we found in each other. We were all in the same situation. Among ourselves we didn't have to feel ashamed. We made little jokes about painful things—about our own swollen bodies, for instance, or about no-good boyfriends, or about life at the home.

I made some friends though we all knew the friendships would be temporary. It was considered a great sign of intimacy and trust to give your last name to another patient, yet the last names given were seldom the true ones and nobody ever exchanged addresses or telephone numbers. None of us wanted any reminders of the home once we'd left it.

We weren't allowed out on weekdays, but every other weekend we could sign ourselves out for a day, provided the staff had no complaints about our work or behavior. I remember signing out twice. The first time, I went to a movie. When I realized I wasn't concentrating on it and had no idea what I was watching, I left. I got in my car and drove around, thinking of nothing in particular, until it was time to go back.

The second time, I spent the day pretending. I pretended I was happily married. My husband and I wanted the baby. We couldn't wait for it to be born. We were trying to decide what to name it. We were fencing in our back yard so the baby would have a place to play. We were decorating a nursery, all in yellow and white. Our child was going to have a beautiful home and loving parents. Everything was going to be wonderful.

I walked through one department store after another, looking at cribs and bassinets and strollers, sorting through baby clothes. I had only the weakest hold on reality by then. I was very near the edge.

One night, not long after that, I was lying on my cot, trying to get to sleep. I couldn't find a comfortable position. There was a terrible heaviness deep in my belly and pain in my lower back. We had regular medical checkups at the home, and the doctor had told me at my last examination that the baby could come any day. I felt a hard cramp, and suddenly I was wet all over. The water had broken. I was in labor.

We weren't given any instruction in natural childbirth at the home, but natural childbirth was the standard method of delivery. My baby was born that way. I don't remember how long I was in labor. Time seemed to stand still, then to race. I drifted in and out of consciousness. The pain came in waves, surging and ebbing. I remember thinking it might go on forever, like the ocean. I remember screaming. Then people were telling me to push, and I did. And again, harder. And again.

Then it was over. I felt an overwhelming relief, and at the same time a sense of utter loss. I was empty. A part of my body was gone, a part of my womanhood.

I asked if I could see my baby. Nobody answered. I slept.

The next thing I remember is waking up in what must have been a recovery room. A social worker was there. She was carrying papers.

I asked her about my baby. Was it a boy or a girl?

It was a boy, she said. He was healthy.

Could I see him?

No, she said. It wasn't allowed.

I knew it wasn't allowed. I only wanted to hold him once and see for myself that he was all right. She handed me the papers, a standard form relinquishing the baby for adoption. I signed them.

I wonder sometimes if it would have made a difference—if I still could have signed—had I known I was giving up the only baby I would ever have.

Five days later I put on my own clothes, repacked, and got ready to leave. On the way out I stopped at one of the offices and paid the home one hundred dollars for my care.

Driving back to New Paltz, all I could think of was three people I loved and had hurt. My baby. What would happen to him? Would he find a good home? My parents. They had been so upset over my annulment, and now, though they didn't know it, I had given away their first grandchild. They mustn't ever know. It would break their hearts.

In fact, I think my father never did know and my mother only found out twenty years later, just before I had to tell the story to a packed courtroom and the whole world.

I thought I'd had my last contact with the home the day I left it, but that didn't turn out to be exactly the case. For the next fifteen years or so, I'd call there from time to time. When I was tired or depressed or when I'd had just enough drinks to work up the right combination of desperation and courage, I'd call to ask what had happened to my baby.

I'd always call at night, and I'd always get the same recording: "We are closed. Call back during business hours." Of course, I never did. I don't know precisely what I would have said or what I could have learned. They didn't give out information about their adoptions. I knew that when I signed the papers.

In one of the hundreds of newspaper articles about me years later, a writer described me in my stewardess days and just after as being "young, but no ingenue." No doubt that writer would be amazed to know just how much of an "ingenue" I really was.

I predated the sexual revolution by some twenty years, and I was very much a child of my times. Throughout all my adolescence and much of my young womanhood, the birth control pill didn't exist. Married people on television slept in separate beds. *Peyton Place* was the scandalous ultimate in dirty books. Nudity and four-letter obscenities were unheard of in mainstream movies.

A woman who had an illegitimate child was a worthless tramp.

A woman who had premarital sex, or any sex outside of marriage, was a slut—at least if she got caught at it. One slip might be marginally forgivable if the girl planned to marry the boy in question, but by and large, sex was something nice girls didn't do, or talk about, or even think about, if they could help it.

I was a nice girl. Yes, I developed young and started dating early. And yes, I did my share of necking, and even had my share of heavy petting in back seats. Still, I was so ignorant about my own body that I didn't know the physical technicalities of what a virgin was until after I stopped being one in my late teens. By today's standards my premarital sexual experience was pretty limited.

On the other hand, I'll have to concede that the writer's mistake was mostly a matter of timing. After a failed marriage, after getting pregnant out of wedlock, after going back to New Paltz to start an ever-steeper downhill slide, I was no ingenue anymore.

Guilt and loss, loss and guilt. Back in New Paltz in mid-April 1964, I rebounded dully from one emotion to the other. There was the old guilt of the failed marriage, and the newer, sharper guilt of my abandoned baby. But there was also another loss that was harder to name. It was the loss—I don't know how else to say it—the loss of my *shine.* I was tarnished now. I was dirty and used and old. Nothing in the world was pretty or clean or hopeful anymore. There was no promise to life.

My parents were happy to welcome me home, but I could barely manage the smiles and hugs that the reunion called for. The secret of the baby isolated me from my family. Sometimes I felt oddly invisible to them, as though I were crying and they couldn't see me, screaming and they couldn't hear.

I'd been depressed after the breakup of my marriage, but that seemed hardly more than a mild case of the blues compared to what I felt now—or what I didn't feel. I started sleeping too much again, but this time the pattern was different. Sleep was no escape anymore. It was too likely to be full of dreams, nightmares about my baby, usually about his being dead or lost somewhere beyond help. I came to be afraid of sleep, and the periods of sleeping too much alternated with bouts of insomnia. I started to drink again, to deaden me for sleep and to deaden the sleep itself. During the days I spent most of the time just sitting and staring, my mind as empty as I could make it. I saw almost no one outside the family. I felt nothing, wanted nothing, and responded to no one.

My parents had no idea what to make of the fact that their daughter had come home a virtual vegetable. I'd been gone for more than two months, supposedly to get myself straightened out after my annulment, and now I was worse than ever. Sometimes I thought I could see questions in their eyes that they were afraid to ask out loud, and I was grateful that they didn't ask, because I couldn't have answered. But the unspoken questions lay between us, another barrier. As the days stretched into weeks with no sign of renewed vitality in me, their pleasure at having me home gave way to frustration, then to anger and even disgust. The word "depression" wasn't part of their vocabulary—or mine, at the time. If it had been, maybe we would have recognized the symptoms and looked for help before things got worse. As it was, though, they could only see that their grown daughter, almost twenty-three years old now, was sitting around her parent's house doing nothing, instead of getting on with her life.

Mother tried hard for a while to be sympathetic. She thought I was still mourning the loss of my marriage, and she still blamed Tony, not me, for that debacle. But my father, my biggest supporter and staunchest defender for all my earlier years, was losing patience. I should cut out all this moping around and get a job, he said. Better yet, I should be thinking about getting married again, and really settling down this time. I didn't have any problems that the right man couldn't fix.

Eventually I did rouse myself enough to go out and look for work. The Wiltwyck School had moved, so there was no chance to go back to the fulfilling job I'd been good at and enjoyed. Instead, in the summer I got a job at a car rental agency in Poughkeepsie. I lived at home and made the short commute.

The job wasn't much, but then neither was I. Certainly, I was less than the ideal employee. Many mornings I came in late, or hung over, or both. I made a habit of long, wet lunches. After some six or eight months the rental agency started cutting back on its staff and I was among the first to go. Nobody told me it was because of the drinking, but nobody had to. I knew it. Now I was unemployed again, a grown woman still living with her parents, a nothing, a zero.

In the spring of 1965 I found work again, this time as a waitress at one of the many resorts in the Catskills that attracted different ethnic groups. This particular resort catered to affluent Puerto Ricans from New York City. The people were nice, and the air was always full of spirited Spanish music and the delicious smells of spicy rice dishes or sizzling pork. I neither liked the job nor disliked it. It was a living, marking time, treading water. In any case, I wasn't there long.

About the time I'd started working at the car rental agency I'd also started seeing men again. My father, still screening the field for prospective husbands, didn't care much for my new dates. These weren't the nice boys who made polite conversation with the parents while the sweet young daughter readied herself for an innocent evening at the movies. These were men, older and much tougher, who took the daughter God knew where and didn't bring her home until all hours of the night, if not the next morning. My father would have been far unhappier if he'd allowed himself to see those dates for what they really were. I'd gone out a lot after my breakup with Tony. But, again, the pattern was slightly different this time. Then I was only dating. Now I was sleeping around.

I wasn't particular and I wasn't discreet. Some of the men I saw were the adult versions of boys I had known in high school. Others were men I met through them. All were pretty much interchangeable as far as I was concerned, and all were dispensable. It wasn't a cast of thousands. There were, perhaps, six or seven of them in all. But that was more than enough in a small town like New Paltz, where word got around fast. So I wasn't just a divorced woman anymore (annulment or divorce—just a technicality, after all). Now I was, if not the town tramp, at least very close to it.

I didn't care. Why should I? I wasn't looking for a husband. Marriage? That was a laugh. What kind of man would want me for a wife? I didn't deserve to be a wife. I was nothing but a worthless slut. All right, then, I'd act like a worthless slut. A woman with my track record might as well. I'd live it up and look neither forward nor back. Nothing was going to hurt me anymore. What the hell, nothing mattered anyway, and besides, I was getting to be—or trying to be—a very tough broad.

And I was so scared, and so alone.

I'll never forget the night I met Jack Sidote.

It was the spring of 1965. I'd been home from having the baby for a year, an awful, directionless year of too much booze and too many men and too many fights at home, a year when my sense of self-worth bottomed out at zero.

One Friday night I'd made plans to spend the evening with a woman friend named Marie, who came from a well-to-do Italian family in the restaurant and nightclub business. Though she was a local girl, she had moved away and was working in New York. I admired her savvy and independence, and when we were together, when she came home for weekends, I tried my best to match her sophisticated air. She picked me up that night, and I agreed to her suggestion that we drop by for a drink at a nightspot whose owner she was friendly with.

The Villa Lipani was a successful resort near New Paltz that drew a wealthy clientele of Italo-Americans from both New York City and upstate. There was a bar and dining room in the main building and a scattering of rustic guest cabins dotted over its well-kept grounds, as well as a stable, a swimming pool, tennis courts, and the bocci court customary at resorts for the Italian trade. The conservative townspeople of New Paltz considered it something of a fast-track place, with Cadillacs cramming the parking lot and minks and silk suits in the dining room. It was the kind of place where Italian men might take their families for a weekend—or might just as likely take their girl friends. I'd never been there before.

When we arrived I met the owner, John Lipani, a middle-aged Italian. While he and Marie were talking, I looked past them across the long nightclub, toward the bar.

Standing behind the bar was an aggressively good-looking man who appeared to be in his middle to late twenties. He wasn't very tall, but he had a lean, broad-shouldered, compact strength. His hair and eyes were black, and his face seemed very dark above his ruffled bartender's shirt. He was laughing with one of the patrons at the bar when I first saw him. There was a compelling vitality about him, a sort of magnetism that I could feel even at a distance.

Marie and I made our way across the floor of the club and sat down at the bar, and she introduced the bartender. "This is John J. Sidote," she said, "known to his many friends as Jack."

I couldn't take my eyes off him. At close range I could see the deep scar that ran the width of his forehead, but instead of detracting from his looks it added somehow to the impression he gave of total, overpowering masculinity.

"Glad to have you here," he said. "What can I get you?"

Marie gave her order. I asked for a Cutty on the rocks with a twist (I thought it was much classier to order by brand than to drink the bar Scotch) and watched his hands while he made the drinks.

Jack Sidote didn't just tend bar; he performed. His movements were graceful, quick, and absolutely sure. He would throw ice into the air, then catch it in a glass behind his back, all the while keeping up his banter with people at the bar. You couldn't imagine his missing, and he never did. You couldn't imagine his charm failing, either. He seemed to know and like everyone there, and everyone seemed to know and like him.

For an hour or so he did his job while Marie and I chatted and finished our drinks and ordered a second round. Jack came over once in a while to exchange a few pleasantries, the way a good bartender does, but he paid me no special attention. Then, all of a sudden, he jumped from behind the bar onto the stage that adjoined it and picked up a microphone.

"Here goes Jack into his Sammy Davis number," Marie remarked. "Everybody calls him the white Sammy Davis, Jr., around here."

Sammy Davis, Jr., was one of my favorite entertainers, and I recognized that Jack was, in fact, doing a very creditable imitation of him. Singing "Mack the Knife," he would toss the microphone casually from hand to hand, then hunch over it and croon, his eyes closed. He punctuated the song's phrases with the body's sways and jerks and dips characteristic of Davis's delivery. He had a good voice, but his style was what carried the act. Jack on stage was like Jack behind the bar—completely in control of the song, his body, his audience, certainly in control of me.

"Mack the Knife," given a warm reception, was followed by "Bojangles" and "Candy Man." Then he started to sing "There Will Never Be Another You," and this time, for the first time, he was looking directly at me. I couldn't believe what I thought I saw in his eyes.

I guess it would be too melodramatic to say that I fell in love with him that first night we met, but I do know that I'd never in my life felt so drawn to a man or so excited by one. I loved the way he looked and the way he moved, and I loved what I saw as his confidence, his aura of strength and power. That, I thought, was exactly what I needed in a man.

My obvious interest in him wasn't lost on Marie, and driving home, she tried to warn me away. "It's your business," she said, "but if I were you I'd back off."

"Why?"

"He's married, for one thing," she said. "At least, his wife is. He's got this wife and a kid over in Wappingers Falls, but he must have half a dozen girls on the side around here. Right now he's got this big thing going with the singer at the Villa."

"Why tell me?" I asked, and I meant it. Yes, I was tremendously attracted to him, but I had no real reason to believe he felt the same way. I was a nobody, after all, and from my vantage point he was a star. It seemed likely enough that he might be interested in a casual lay, but not in a serious relationship, not with me.

"I'm telling you because I saw the way you were looking at him," Marie went on, "and I'm also telling you that he's nothing but an arrogant little punk. He tries to act like a big shot. He hints around about how he's connected—you know, how he's got an in with big guys in the Mafia. It's all crap."

"But he *is* a big shot," I countered. "He's not just a bartender, he's got a following. It looked to me like a lot of people go to that place just to see him."

"They do," she said. "All the same, he's bad news. Just remember I told you."

The subject was dropped, and Marie and I went on to discuss how we were both going to be free again the next night. We decided to get together and make another night of it. She asked if there was anywhere special I wanted to go.

"Yes," I said. "The Villa Lipani."

By the time we walked from the dining room to the bar the next night our drinks were set up and waiting. Mine was a Cutty on the rocks with a twist. I was flattered beyond words that he remembered. We talked more that night, and the talk was less casual. He told me that he was married but that he and his wife were separated. She was a strong Catholic and would never give him a divorce, he said. They had a little girl, five years old, and he was crazy about the kid. He lived at the Villa, but sometimes he went home on his days off, only to see his daughter. The marriage itself was really over, as far as he was concerned.

I wanted to believe him, so I did. I told him about my own marriage and about the annulment, tossing the whole thing off as though it had only been a minor annoyance. I could never have told him—not then—how shattered I'd been over the failure of the marriage or what a disaster my life had become in the last year. I was trying so hard to impress him with what a worldly sophisticate I was, and I wasn't about to undermine the image with some soppy confession of grief and pain. I must have succeeded pretty well because again, that night, he sang "There Will Never Be Another You," and this time I was sure he was singing it for me only. And again, that night, I went home with nothing but him on my mind.

The next day was a Sunday, and Marie went back to New York. That night I went to the Villa Lipani alone. Jack coaxed me—it wasn't hard to do—into staying around until four in the morning, when he closed the bar. Then he asked me to go to his room.

"No, Jack," I said. "I'm not going to be just another one of your numbers."

If sex was all he wanted I was more than willing to give it to him, and I knew it, but I wasn't going to make it all that easy. I wanted so badly for him to take me seriously. As it turned out, though, the resistance I offered was pathetically small. We went to a diner and had coffee. We talked for a while. He joked about what an unlikely seduction scene it was—his getting me bombed on coffee at a diner. Then we went to his room.

For me, before that night, sex had been a tool, something I could use to please men or make them like me, something I could barter for attention, affection, and companionship. I never especially liked the act itself. It wasn't that way with Jack. Mutual passion was a strong bond between us, at least at first.

Ours was a very romantic courtship. It was typical of Jack to call me when he got off work and have me join him at the Villa. Sometimes we'd go for long, wild horseback rides with the sun just reddening the sky above the mountains. We'd swim or play bocci in the afternoons before he went to work. On his days off he'd take me to expensive restaurants, often in New York. Sometimes we'd go to the racetrack at Yonkers. We never sat in the stands. There were always tickets to the clubhouse, where we'd have dinner and hobnob with people Jack knew. The track officials and horse owners and other track regulars seemed impressive and important to me, and Jack seemed to fit in with them perfectly. Here, as at the Villa, he seemed to know everybody.

On nights when I went to the Villa and stayed at the bar while Jack worked, I had my own special seat. If the bar was crowded, people would be moved so I could sit in my regular place. Jack saw to it that there were always people around to keep me company and amuse me until he was free. As a small-town girl, I was awed by this VIP treatment.

There was nothing secretive or back-street about our affair. Jack seemed proud to have me on his arm, proud to introduce me to his friends. There appeared to be no question that he and his wife really were a dead issue, and I was the woman in his life. Being the woman in his life made me proud beyond words.

It took hardly any time to establish the pattern of our early relationship. I quit my job at the Puerto Rican resort soon after we met so I could more easily arrange my life around Jack's schedule. We saw each other nearly every day or night. Sometimes I'd meet him in the afternoon, then go home, sleep for a few hours, and wait for the phone call telling me to join him at three or four in the morning at the Villa. Other times I'd stay with him throughout his shift and we'd go to his room afterward. Almost from the first I felt I had no real existence apart from him. I ate, I slept, I waited to be with him, I was with him. That was my life.

Virtually before I knew it was happening I found that my commitment to him was total. My veneer of self-assured sophistication cracked wide open. I held nothing back from him. I told him again and again how much I loved and needed him. I told him everything about my life. In tears, I even told him about my baby. When he seemed to think no less of me for that, when he actually tried to comfort me, I loved him even more.

Jack wasn't particularly verbal about his softer feelings. It wasn't in his nature, for instance, to tell me that he loved me. But I could see it in the way he looked at me, and the way he presented me to other people, and I could feel it when he touched me. And he did tell me often how beautiful he thought I was, and how very special. Always that—how special I was, how unlike any woman he'd known before.

Even more than the passion, it was that specialness he made me feel that bound me to him in those early days. I felt that he was giving me a whole new chance at life. He was giving me back my self-esteem. I couldn't be a nobody if this vibrant, handsome, popular, talented man wanted me. He was a star, and I was his woman. Only with him did I feel good about myself, important and worthwhile—and alive. I'd been dead inside before I met him. I needed him the way an addict needs a fix.

Writing this, I'm amazed at myself, amazed that I can get past all the ugliness and horror of what came later and remember how we were then, and what I felt for him. It isn't easy. But remembering is the only way to answer the question that I'm asked so often now: "How did you ever get involved with a man like that in the first place?"

People who ask that question forget how easy it is for women to fall into the trap of measuring their worth by the man they're with. As to my own situation, it was almost twenty years ago that I first met Jack, and in twenty years people change a lot. Jack and I have both changed almost beyond recognition. The answer to the question of how I got involved then is really very simple. I loved him.

chapter 7

If we'd been able to live alone in a vacuum, I think I might have been completely happy with Jack during those first few months I knew him. But we lived in the real world, and our affair came under heavy outside pressure from the very beginning.

My problems were mostly at home. My parents had been upset with me almost constantly since my return from the Midwest a year before—first about my moodiness, and then about the increasing drinking and the running around and the on-again, off-again jobs. When Jack entered the picture the tension between them and me took a decided turn for the worse. What began as little arguments soon became all-out war that raged throughout the late spring and summer, especially between my father and me.

Mother had heard bad things about Jack from some friend of the family whose daughter had dated him a few times. He'd mistreated the girl, Mother said. She was vague about the details, but she thought Jack had "been rough" with the girl in some way, maybe even hit her.

I told her the story was ridiculous. Jack was gentle. He'd never do anything like that. Probably he just got tired of the girl, and she was telling all these stories to get back at him. But my assurances on that score did nothing to ease Mother's mind, maybe because they had nothing to do with the real issue. Mother was a good Catholic. Even if Jack was the best person in the world—which she doubted—he was a married man and ought to be home with his wife. There was nothing else she needed to know about him and nothing else she had to say. She seemed to hate and almost fear the conflict between my father and me, but she left most of the domestic combat over Jack to him.

Daddy had plenty to say. He began with occasional comments that were comparatively bland: Why had I quit my job? When was I going to get another one? Why was I arranging my whole life around a married man who couldn't give me a future? Jack had a bad reputation. Look where he worked, the kind of people he was around. Why couldn't I find a respectable man who was prepared to marry me?

At first I tried to reason with both my parents and argue them out of their objections. They didn't know Jack, I said. If they did, they'd like him. He came from a family just like ours, I told them. His mother and father were good Italian working people in Wappingers Falls, a nearby town much like New Paltz. He'd graduated from high school and been in the Marines and gotten an honorable discharge; then he'd gotten married and settled down. What was so bad about any of that? He had a steady job and seemed to make good money. And maybe it wasn't his fault that his marriage had gone bad. After all, so had mine. Jack didn't live with his wife. It wasn't as if I was breaking up his home. Anyway, the important thing was that Jack and I loved each other and made each other happy. Maybe it was a second chance for both of us.

The arguments cut no ice at all, and after a while I stopped trying to bring Mother and Daddy around. I could see that as Jack and I went on seeing each other they liked him less, not more. He very seldom came by our house, since our usual arrangement was for me to drive somewhere and meet him for dates. When he did come for me, he almost never came to the door. Instead, he sat in his car in the driveway and honked his horn, a practice my father found intolerable.

Daddy hated the telephone calls that woke the whole family in the middle of the night. He hated the way I stayed out until all hours and then came home, smelling of liquor, to sleep through the day. Once Jack and I had an argument while sitting in the driveway, and my father overheard it through an open window. Jack used some bad language, and my father hated that. He hated Jack and sometimes

I felt he even hated me. I began trying to avoid him whenever I could. As he got angrier and harsher I got more belligerent and rebellious. When we did confront each other, there were terrible, hurtful shouting matches that left both of us drained and shaking.

"As long as you're under my roof you'll follow my rules," Daddy would scream at me. "You'll come home at reasonable hours and act decent."

"I'm twenty-three years old, and you're going to set me a curfew?" I'd lash back. "If you don't like the way I'm living, then you can kick me out and I'll live in the streets. You can't stop me from seeing Jack, and I don't give a damn what you think."

"Maybe you belong in the streets," he'd rage. "I won't have any daughter of mine acting like a . . ."

He could never quite bring himself to finish that sentence. I prayed he never would.

Complicating everything, it was during this time that my sister got married. On the one hand, my parents' preoccupation with Emilia's wedding took some of the pressure off me. But on the other, the contrast between Emilia's status and mine seemed to focus and solidify all my parents' discontent with me. While my life had turned into such chaos, in their view, Emilia was doing exactly the right thing. She was marrying an Italian Catholic boy who had my parents' wholehearted approval.

I'd thought that my own dream of marriage, that old, elusive dream of a strong man to take care of me for a lifetime, was dead. But now that I was in love with Jack I found myself dreaming again. Maybe I *could* make it work. My parents didn't like him now, but if I settled down with him, if we made a home, they'd come around. They'd be happy for me and proud. Hard as I tried to act contemptuous of the stability and respectability my parents wanted for me, I knew I wanted it too. If Jack didn't quite fit the mold of the ideal prospective husband, I'd find some way to make him fit. He'd made a home once, with another woman. Why not with me?

My parents weren't the only ones who wanted to put an end to my affair with Jack. While I was under siege at home, he was under siege at work. John Lipani and Jack were more than just boss and employee. Lipani was almost like a father to Jack, an older man whom Jack respected and looked to for approval and advice. Lipani's advice regarding me was that Jack ditch me as soon as possible. Jack was, Lipani thought, getting in way over his head.

Lipani had an Old World attitude about women that I'd seen

often among Italian men of his age. It was okay for a married man to have a little something going on the side, but never at the expense of the wife and family. The marriage might not be much of a going concern, as Jack's was not, but the family must be kept together at all costs. John had been tolerant of Jack's casual carousing, probably even amused by it. But he could see that there was nothing casual about Jack and me, and he let Jack know that he wanted the relationship ended.

Jack pretended not to care what his boss thought, but the pretense was pretty thin. He'd be noticeably less attentive to me when I was at the bar and Lipani was around, and he'd often have me leave his room at the Villa in the mornings before the sun came up so John wouldn't know I'd spent the night.

Not all of Lipani's objections to the affair were on moral grounds. Now that Jack and I were spending so much time together, Jack was no longer available to John at all times and for all services that John wanted rendered. I was never sure what those services entailed, but I knew that Jack was more than a bartender. Some of his functions didn't seem to be connected with the bar at all. For instance, Jack made round trips to New York for John on a more or less regular basis. He told me he was running errands for John. It never occurred to me to ask for information beyond that. It wasn't a woman's place to ask a man about his business. That's what I'd been taught growing up. And, more significant, that's what Jack had been taught.

Along with complaints from Lipani, I suppose Jack was also getting complaints from his wife during this time. Perhaps he wasn't spending as much time with his daughter as he used to. Perhaps his wife had other expectations of him that he wasn't meeting anymore. I didn't know for sure because I tried hard not to know. Jack talked sometimes about how much he loved his daughter, and he griped sometimes about having to give money to his wife. Other than that he seldom mentioned his home. I was always sympathetic when the subject came up, but I never asked questions. I was jealous. Maybe he loved me, but there was the undeniable fact that some other woman had his name, his child, and his home. I didn't want to think about it, and I couldn't stand his thinking about it, about her, when he was with me.

Whatever the pressures on Jack, I saw that he was under increasing stress. I also saw the first inklings that Jack under stress could be very different from Jack when everything was going his way.

One night around the middle of June we were supposed to have a date, and Jack didn't show up or call. I didn't see him for two days, in fact, and the next time we did meet there was a very bizarre scene in his room at the Villa Lipani.

He told me he had been arrested for possession of a gun. The police had stopped him during one of his trips to New York for Lipani and found a gun in a bag he was carrying. He told me he needed the gun for protection when he was driving through rough neighborhoods in New York. Anyway, he said, he'd convinced the police that he didn't even know the gun was in the car, and the charges had been dropped.

Then he took a gun out of a drawer and showed it to me. He started waving it around the room. "I've killed a lot of people with this gun," he said.

He said it as though it were a joke, and it never occurred to me that it could possibly be anything but a joke. I laughed.

"Oh, Jack," I said, "you could never kill anybody."

Suddenly, he rushed across the room and grabbed my shoulders. He started shaking me, hard, saying something like, "You don't believe I could do it? You don't believe I could do it?"

Jack, who had never touched me violently, was hurting me, scaring me. But what was really frightening was the look in his eyes. It was a maniacal look, a scary, crazed look that I never could have imagined on his face.

"You better believe I could do it," he said. "You better believe it!" Then suddenly he started to laugh. It was wild laughter that went on and on.

Couldn't I see, right then, that there might be something very wrong with this man?

Of course I could see it, but I refused to let it register. Loving Jack was my rock, the one solid truth of my life, and nothing was going to shake it. If cracks appeared in the rock I wouldn't look at them, and if doubts whispered in my mind I wouldn't hear. And so, for the first of many, many times, I rationalized. Jack was upset. He was just making a bad joke. Jack could never hurt anybody. Certainly, Jack could never hurt me. I pushed the whole scene out of my mind.

On we went together that summer, with Jack taking more and more control of my time, my thoughts, my will, and my life. He came to insist on knowing how I spent every minute away from him. If I had to be with my family for some special occasion, he wanted to know every detail of the event. And though family obligations were marginally tolerable, spending time with women friends was not. "What do you need with those bitches?" Jack would say.

It was then that I noticed how Puritanical he was about women. In one category he put mothers, wives, and a few other acceptable types—mostly unattached women who seemed straitlaced, and who were friendly to him. All other women were "whores." Most especially, attractive women who didn't like him were whores.

To please him I began cutting myself off from my friends, just as I was cutting myself off from my family. Jack was no longer merely the most important thing in my life; he was getting to be the only thing. I didn't worry about my growing isolation and I didn't resent his possessiveness. On the contrary, I was delighted by it. It showed that he wanted me all to himself, I thought. It showed how much he loved me.

However, it wasn't proof enough. When I first started seeing Jack it was enough just to be with him, to have him as long as I could, on whatever basis he dictated. But he himself had raised my sights from that, had made me feel worthy of something more. The longer I was with him and the more I loved him, the more I became desperate for some kind of commitment. I wanted a future.

I never pressed him for marriage; I was afraid that might be going too far. Instead, I talked about finding a way we could "be together." If he really loved me, I told him, he'd figure out some way to get a divorce. Jack didn't like being pinned down, and he didn't like confronting unpleasant situations. He tried to avoid discussing the future altogether. When I pressed him he'd either tell me to shut up—which I'd do instantly—or he'd try to pacify me with anything short of specific promises or definite plans. He also liked to keep me in line by keeping me off balance, swearing one day that he'd never leave me, then going the next day or two without even calling. Now and then he talked about our running away together, to Florida maybe, but I wasn't sure he meant it.

Sometimes the frustration would get to be more than I could stand. Once I tried to force his hand by leaving. He obviously didn't love me enough to make a life with me, I told him, so I was walking out. I left his room at the Villa, hoping frantically that he'd try to stop me. He didn't.

My little insurrection lasted only a matter of hours. Once away from him I was desolate at the thought that I might really have lost him. I sat in my room at home crying, thinking about what my life had been before Jack and how utterly impossible it would be to go back to that kind of emptiness. He called that night and I rushed back to him, content just to be in his arms again, in his bed, momentarily safe.

Then fall came, and with it a new ultimatum from me. The season was over at the Villa, and Jack's vacation was coming up. He told me he was going away for a week with his wife and daughter.

This, at last, was more than I could bear. I was crushed, outraged, and terrified, all at once. How could he treat me this way? Did this mean he was going back to his wife? I told him that if he went, I wouldn't be around when he got back. Again, I walked out. This time, I told myself, I'd never crawl back.

He called a day later and said he'd changed his mind about his vacation. "Pack your bags," he said. "We're going to Montreal."

We had three glorious days in Montreal, though we spent too much time in bed to see much of the city, and when we returned to New Paltz we were inseparable again. But still there was no real commitment. Jack was as elusive as ever, and I was no less frustrated than I'd been before the trip. He had a way of giving with one hand and taking away with the other. In Montreal he reminded me more than once that he was supposed to be with his wife and daughter.

I began to tell myself that everything would surely work out if only we could get out from under some of the outside pressure. I had to get away from home. Jack had to have some distance from John Lipani and from his family. I came up with a number of schemes, none of them very rational. Most involved my finding a job in New York. I'd get an apartment there, where Jack and I could be together with nobody snooping around, and somehow one or the other of us would make the commute between New York and New Paltz.

One day I drove down to New York alone and applied for a job as a bunny in the Playboy Club. Inconceivable as such an idea would be now, in those days being a bunny was my fantasy of an ideal job, with lots of glamour and good pay. I was a little afraid to tell Jack what I'd done, thinking he might not like the idea of other men watching me walk around in a scanty costume, trying to look sexy. To my surprise, he loved the idea. For years afterward, he would often tell people in introducing me that I'd almost been a Playboy bunny. It seemed that, for Jack, Playboy bunnies, like the Mafia, represented some ultimate in class.

I never got to test his assessment firsthand. I guess I must have looked like Frieda Frump from the sticks to the Playboy personnel people because they decided I wasn't what they had in mind. I was afraid to tell Jack that, too. My being a bunny appealed to him so, I didn't want him to know I'd been rejected. Maybe he'd think I was less of a woman, less desirable. I told him I was going to have to go back for another interview.

I did go back to the city again, this time to an employment agency, where I applied for various receptionist jobs. I never found out what happened with those applications, though, because soon after that Jack and I left New Paltz.

He called one day in October and said he'd decided to go to Florida. Somebody had offered him a partnership in a bar and restaurant down there, and it was a big chance. I could come along if I wanted, he said, but only if I got some money together to help with expenses. He was going to leave the next day.

It was anything but a romantic invitation to elope. It was far less romantic, in fact, that those dreams he'd occasionally spun about our running off together. There was no "together" about this. He was going. I could come along if I wanted, provided I got some money. There were no promises about divorce or marriage or where I would stand once we got to Florida. Take it or leave it. Either way, he was going.

I didn't know what to make of his coldness, so I simply ignored it. I rationalized: Jack sounded distant because, understandably, he was nervous about leaving. It was a big step. He didn't say he was leaving so we could be together, but that's what he meant. The money was just a detail, probably a loan that he'd pay back as soon as we got to Florida and his deal came through. Maybe he'd had to give his wife all his money so she wouldn't make trouble about a divorce. We were going to start a new life together. (The rose-covered cottage again.) He'd be successful in business. We'd get married and have children. My parents would come down and spend the winters with us in our beautiful house on the beach.

All this I got from "You can come too if you get some money."

But what was the alternative? I couldn't lose him. He was my life. I couldn't go back to being nothing again.

There was nothing to decide, really, and I lost no time debating with myself. I was going. That same day I pawned the engagement and wedding rings Tony had given me. The wedding ring had several small diamonds in it, and the engagement diamond was more than a carat. I accepted some absurdly small sum for them, something under two hundred dollars. (I found out later that my father redeemed them for me after I left town.) I borrowed another two hundred dollars from a friend and put the money together with what savings I still had from my jobs. It all came to a little under five hundred dollars. I hoped Jack would think it was enough.

Though I packed my bags, I waited 'til the last minute to tell my parents. That way, I reasoned, I wouldn't have to listen to all their garbage about what a mistake I was making. They'd be hurt, I knew, but it would be all right later, when Jack and I were married and everything was settled.

I was dressed and ready the next morning when I heard his car horn honking in the driveway. I got my bags and went into the living room. Mother and Daddy were there, and I told them I was leaving.

I don't remember everything that was said, only that all the words, theirs and mine, were bitter. I do remember how it ended. My father stood very close to me and looked directly into my eyes.

"You whore," he said softly.

Then he slapped me. My father, who had not raised a hand to me since I was a child, hit me hard across the face. Then he cried. With tears streaming down his face he watched me pick up my bags and leave.

chapter **8**

All I could think of as I hurried to the car was that I was about to be with Jack and he would make everything all right. I'd tell him about the horrible thing that just happened with my father, and he'd put his arms around me and comfort me, and I'd feel better. Then we'd start out on our new life together.

But as I got near the car and looked inside, I saw that Jack wasn't alone. Sitting on the passenger side in the front seat of Jack's new Pontiac Bonneville was a kid from the Villa Lipani named Wasyl Bozydaj. I knew Wasyl only as a boy in his late teens who'd worked at the Villa several summers as a bar boy, running errands for Jack, dancing attendance on him in much the same way Jack did for John Lipani. Wasyl had sandy brown hair and an open, likeable face. I don't think we'd exchanged ten words.

Seeing him in the car stunned me. Something was all wrong here. Jack and I were supposed to be making this romantic new start, alone. What possible reason could there be for anyone else's intruding on the dream?

"Why is he here, Jack?" I whispered as we walked around to the trunk of the car to load my luggage.

"He's my bar boy," Jack laughed. "By the way, did you get the money?"

I handed over my wad of money, and Jack flipped through it before stuffing it into his pocket. "Fine," he said. Then he walked back to the driver's side and got in, and I climbed into the back seat. There'd been no time to talk, to tell him what had happened or to ask any more questions. We pulled out of the driveway and set off, driving south. I didn't look back.

Jack and Wasyl took turns driving, chatting and joking with each other in the front seat. They seldom spoke to me, and I didn't pay much attention to their conversation. I sat in the back seat, alone with my thoughts, trying to sort things out. I was still too upset over the fight with my father to think very clearly about anything, but I tried to reason out what Jack might have had in mind in bringing Wasyl along.

"He's my bar boy" told me nothing, obviously. Wasyl was a local kid who'd probably never been anywhere. Maybe he heard about the trip and thought it sounded like a big adventure and asked if he could go along, and Jack was good-hearted enough to say yes. It must have been like that, a spur-of-the-moment thing. Surely Wasyl wouldn't be staying with us very long. Probably we'd drop him off somewhere. Wasyl had always idolized Jack. Maybe it was reassuring for Jack, heading off toward an uncertain future, to have someone along who appreciated what a star he was. I could understand that.

Slowly I brought myself to terms with this latest rift in the dream, and the hours passed. Night was falling now, and I looked out the window to see how far we'd come from New York State. We passed a sign saying we were a few miles outside Washington, D.C. Wasyl was driving.

It occurred to me that I'd been unusually quiet all day. Maybe I ought to try to join in the conversation. I leaned forward and asked Jack some question about what we were going to do when we got to Florida. I don't remember exactly what it was, but I think it had to do with money—had he already invested in the restaurant, or had he decided whether we'd look for a house right away? He stared at me strangely for a second, then turned to Wasyl.

"Stop the car!" he barked.

Wasyl instantly swerved the car to the shoulder of the highway and screeched it to a halt. Jack flung himself out and jerked open the back door. He grabbed my arm and dragged me out, pulling me along behind him toward the rear of the car. I was stumbling and starting to cry.

"What did I do, Jack? Please tell me what I did," I begged.

He grabbed my shoulders and pulled me to him, then slammed me down backward across the trunk of the car. I felt a sharp pain in my back. He was standing over me, yelling. Through a haze of shock and fear, I tried to focus on what he was saying.

"What do you mean, asking me about my business?" he screamed. "Who do you think you are? You're not my mother. You're not my wife. You're just some whore I brought along for the ride. Anytime you don't like the way I'm handling things you can leave! You want to leave now?"

He grabbed one of my hands and slapped the car keys into it.

"You want to leave now?" he said again. "Open the trunk and get your stuff out. We'll leave you right here!"

He stood there, his hands on his hips, watching me and waiting. I was still lying against the trunk, sobbing. On one level my mind was struggling to right itself, to assimilate what was going on. On another level it was racing: I was on the side of a road at night in the middle of nowhere with this crazy stranger, who happened to look like the man I loved, standing over me and screaming. I didn't even have change for a phone call. There was no one to call, anyway. Leave? Where could I go? Every bridge was burned. I couldn't go back home. I couldn't crawl back to my parents, a failure again. I couldn't face another failure myself. Not this time, not when I'd been so sure of what I was doing.

Slowly I pushed myself upright and faced Jack. I held out my hand, offering him the keys. That was my answer. I was staying. He snatched the keys away and turned on his heel, and we both got back into the car. Wasyl started the engine, and we kept driving into the night.

Jack didn't seem angry anymore. In fact, he seemed almost gleeful, treating the whole incident as though it had been a good joke. He made a hateful game out of it.

"Pull over, Wasyl," Jack would say. "Let's let her out here." A few miles later Jack would do it again. "This looks like a good place. Want to let her out here?"

I huddled down in the back seat, crying as quietly as I could, wishing only that both of them would ignore my existence. My thoughts were tumbling over each other. Why was he torturing me like this? What did I do? Jack had never treated me like this, never talked to me in that horrible way. What made him do it? Was it the stress of breaking with his past? Maybe it was partly that and partly the drinking he'd been doing all day. But maybe it was something more. Maybe there was something really wrong with him, wrong with his mind. (No, don't think that.) Maybe I'd made a horrible mistake. (No, don't think that. Can't think that.)

Finally I willed myself not to think at all.

I remember nothing else about the trip to Florida, and I don't remember the name of the town where we finally stopped.

Perhaps I should say something here about not remembering. There's a lot I don't remember about the five years I knew Jack Sidote. Some memories are all too vivid. But there are also many blanks in my recollections of those days, blanks that I couldn't fill in, even with a therapist's help, years later when, literally, my life depended on it.

One reason I can't remember everything is, of course, that it all happened so long ago. Another reason is that I spent years afterward trying as hard as I could to forget. I understand "repression" to mean a mental mechanism of self-protection in which a person takes incidents that are too painful to deal with and locks them deep in some sealed compartment of the mind. After Jack, I got to be an expert at repression.

When he accused me of murder, first in 1977 and again in 1983, I had to break the seal on that mental compartment in order to defend myself. It was a difficult, agonizing, sickening thing to do. It involved examining the weakest part of myself at the lowest ebb of my life. But the seal is broken now, and memories that were dredged up get clearer all the time. Even in writing this book I find that more details come back to me, a bit here and a bit there.

But remembering is still hard, and it still hurts, and I suspect a lot of the blanks may never be filled in. Maybe that's just as well.

So. I don't remember the name of the town where we finally stopped. I didn't see much of it anyway. My impression is that it was a small place on the beach on Florida's Atlantic coast. We checked into a motel that had a kitchenette, a living room with a sofa bed for Wasyl, and a bedroom for Jack and me. The first night we were there Wasyl went out for a pizza and brought it back, and after we ate we went to bed. All of us were tired. I was completely drained.

The next morning Jack told me he and Wasyl were going to see the man who was offering the restaurant partnership, and they left. I spent a long day just waiting, watching some television, trying not to think about how hungry I was. I had no money for food. Jack and Wasyl got back fairly late in the evening, and we all went out to dinner. It was a pleasant enough night. Nothing was said about the business deal, and I didn't ask about it.

I did ask for grocery money the next morning before the two men went out again, and Jack gave me a few dollars. In the afternoon I walked a mile or so to the nearest grocery store and bought all the fixings for a nice dinner. I'd never cooked dinner for Jack before, and I was excited about it. Maybe we were staying in a second-rate motel, but to me it felt like a place of our own, our first place, and I felt almost like a wife. I spent the rest of the day carefully preparing the food and cooking it, but it all went to waste. Jack and Wasyl didn't come home until late that night. The dinner was ruined, and Jack was angry and disgusted with me.

"How could you do something so stupid," he said. "You should have just bought stuff for sandwiches, not this whole meal thing."

If someone said that to me now, I'd be furious and would fight back. Then, I just felt stupid. I felt Jack was right.

The third morning in Florida started off pretty much like the other two, with Jack leaving early, but this time Wasyl stayed at the motel with me. We made a little small talk during the day, but mostly we kept to ourselves. He would watch television, and I would read a magazine or go for a walk. We still didn't know each other very well, and we had little to say to each other. He was Jack's friend, not mine.

Besides, I felt more like thinking than talking. I was worried and nervous. Jack still hadn't said anything about his business deal or what his plans for us were. I wondered how long it would be before Wasyl would leave and I could begin making a real home for Jack and me. We couldn't stay in a motel forever. We couldn't live like gypsies.

When Jack came back that night, I knew the instant he walked through the door that something was terribly wrong. He'd been drinking. His face was flushed and his eyes looked wild. He was in a rage. He didn't speak to me. He didn't even seem to notice I was there. He started pacing up and down the length of the living room, yelling and cursing, talking to Wasyl. He said the deal had fallen through. There wasn't going to be any partnership, or any job, or any money.

I edged my way into the bedroom and closed the door. I didn't want to hear any more for the moment. No money. No job. What were we going to do now? Everything seemed to be falling apart.

I was getting undressed for bed when Jack came into the bedroom. He had that look in his eyes that I was then beginning to recognize and fear, a look I can only describe as crazy. I was afraid to ask him anything, but I was too upset and worried not to. I went on undressing, turning away from him so I wouldn't have to look at his face.

"What's going to happen now?" I said. "Maybe we should go back to New York . . ."

He strode over and grabbed me from the back by the shoulders and whirled me around to face him. Then—and I couldn't believe it was happening—he balled his right hand into a fist and hit me full-force in the stomach. I doubled over, the breath knocked out of me. He wound his fingers into my hair and jerked me upright, snapping my head back. He hit me in the stomach again, then in the ribs, then in the breasts.

"Stop nagging me," he said, hissing the words. "I told you before that it wasn't your place to ask questions. I make the decisions."

He hit me in the chest again, then he threw me onto the bed and got on top of me, sitting astride my stomach. The blows kept coming, not fast or in flurries, but slowly, deliberately, and as hard as he could throw them. It was like a nightmare in slow motion, and I couldn't make myself wake up.

Then he stopped. He was talking now, whispering something.

"You're a whore," he said, "just like the whore I just killed . . ."

"What are you saying, Jack?" I choked out. I was crying almost too hard to talk. "What are you talking about?"

"I cut her tits off and watched her bleed to death," he said. "She didn't give me the money . . ."

He reached down and with his finger drew a line around one of my breasts, then the other. He kept doing it, over and over.

"Her tits weren't as big as yours," he said softly. "It would take a lot longer to cut your tits off."

"Please don't say that," I begged. "Stop staying that. You didn't kill anybody. It's not true."

"Yes it is," he said. "Yes I did."

"No," I whimpered. "You wouldn't do that. Please stop, please stop, please, please . . ."

He hit me again.

"Now I'm going to fuck you," he said. "It's going to be the best you ever had."

He dropped on top of me. Jack had always been forceful and dominating in sex, but never brutal. He was brutal now, punching my body again and again, even while he made love to me.

Sex seemed to drain away the last of his rage and craziness. Suddenly he was holding me gently, kissing me and stroking my hair. I saw to my utter amazement that he was crying. He was saying he was sorry, he didn't mean to hurt me, he'd never hit me again. He didn't mean all those things he said about killing somebody. Of course that wasn't true. He was only trying to scare me. He wouldn't say those things again, not ever. I wasn't a whore, he said. He didn't mean that. I was beautiful. He loved me. He was just upset, he said. I had to forgive him.

When he fell asleep, I slipped out of bed and went into the bathroom. I showered for a long time, feeling filthy in a way soap and water couldn't touch. I was still terrified and I was hurting. But even as I looked down at the patchwork of purple bruises on my body, I started making excuses for Jack. Years later I'd finally understand that what had been going through my head was the standard list of excuses made by battered women. My "case," incomprehensible though it may seem, turns out to be fairly typical of the pattern of abuse and compliance that occurs every day, in every layer of society.

I told myself I shouldn't have asked him any questions. I should have trusted him to take care of everything. He was the man. He was upset and I nagged him. I should have comforted him instead. That's what a real woman would have done. He'd never said so, but I knew he'd left everything just to be with me. He'd left a place where he was an important man and a star, and now he didn't even have a job. Of course he lost his temper. He was under so much stress. I'd have to figure out some way to help him. I'd try not to nag him anymore, for one thing. It was my fault that he hit me. I'd have to do better.

chapter 9

The morning after the beating neither Jack nor I mentioned what had happened the night before. I wanted to talk about it. I thought if we discussed it I might be able to understand better why it happened and what I should do so it wouldn't happen again. But I was afraid to bring it up, and maybe there wasn't really much more to say. Jack had already apologized, and said that it had only happened because he was upset, and that it wouldn't happen again. I'd forgiven him, and besides, now he was on his very best behavior. I wanted to keep it that way.

For the next few days he was sweet and attentive to me, almost courtly. He spent more time with me, the days as well as the nights, and he was unusually solicitous about my feelings and preferences. How did I want to spend the day, he'd ask, or where did I feel like having dinner. Wasyl was still around, but now more as a silent accompaniment than as Jack's main companion. If he'd overheard the beating, he never mentioned it.

We stayed at the motel another couple of days. Jack and I went to the beach. I'd worried about people seeing the bruises. I didn't want anyone to know, or guess what had happened. But my one-piece bathing suit covered everything. Jack had hit me in places where it wouldn't show. We swam, and ran in the surf, and lay in the sun holding hands. He talked about things he wanted to buy for me—jewelry, clothes, a fancy car, and a big house. It was fantasy, of course. We had very little money, as far as I knew, and no immediate prospect of getting more. Still, it made me feel warm and good to hear it. Money and possessions meant a lot to Jack, and talking about them was one of his few ways of verbalizing affection.

Things were still going well between us when he decided we should see more of Florida. The three of us set out on a random tour of the coast, driving from town to town, spending a few hours here, a night there. I remember seeing Cape Canaveral and Daytona, but beyond that I can't recall the itinerary. The palm trees and beaches began to get redundant after a while, and all the driving seemed pretty aimless. But Jack was in a good mood, and he was being nice to me, and that was enough to keep me content. Somehow, everything was going to work out after all.

We'd been in Florida about a week when he decided it was time to move on. We'd head west, he said, and maybe look up some Marine buddies of his in Baton Rouge.

Driving or riding for long stretches seemed to make Jack edgy, and he passed the time by drinking. The car was always full of bottles, and it got to be impossible for me to ignore how quickly those bottles emptied.

Back in New Paltz Jack had been a big drinker, but then so had I. Drinking was a part of the environment we lived in. After all, Jack did work in a bar. But now he was using alcohol constantly, depending on it for his emotional survival. The liquor heightened whatever mood he was in. When he was up, drinking made him manic. When he was down, it made him mean.

One night en route to Baton Rouge he swung his arm over the back of his seat and hit me in the face. He said immediately that it was an accident, that he didn't mean to do it, but I couldn't stop my nose from bleeding. I was afraid it might be broken. We stopped at a hospital, and an emergency room doctor determined that there was no break. He asked me what had happened. I told him I'd bumped into something.

It must have been a Friday or Saturday night when we got to Baton Rouge, because we had a hard time finding a place to stay. It was football season, and all the motels were overflowing with fans in town for a Louisiana State University home game. We finally checked into a place several miles out of town, and the next morning

Jack drove me into the city to go job-hunting. Money was running low, he said. I'd have to go to work.

He ferried me from one restaurant to another until I found one that hired me as a waitress. It was a little Italian place that served lunch and dinner. I don't know what Jack did during the day while I worked, or whether he looked for work himself. I only know that he drove me to work every morning and picked me up at night, usually with Wasyl. Every night I gave him the tips I'd collected during the day, and at the end of the week I handed over my paycheck. It never occurred to me to keep any money for myself. I didn't need it. Jack paid the motel bills. Jack bought the meals. Jack took care of everything.

I must have worked at the restaurant about two weeks, because my second paycheck was due, when Jack told me to pick it up and then pack. We were leaving. I packed and we left, the three of us. By now the whole trip was taking on the quirky pace of a bad dream. I never knew where we were going next or why, or how long we'd stay when we got there, or how we could afford it. And I never asked questions. I'd learned back in Florida not to ask questions.

Our next stop turned out to be New Orleans, and Jack was in good spirits during the short drive down from Baton Rouge. New Orleans was his kind of town, he said. Wide open. Lots of action. And he'd heard from somebody in Baton Rouge, I guess from one of the Marine buddies, about a guy in New Orleans who would give us both jobs.

When we got to town we looked for a hotel that would satisfy our need for a fairly cheap two-room suite. We settled on the John Mitchell, a hotel that was well located, only a couple of blocks from Canal Street, the city's main thoroughfare, and from the French Quarter on the other side of Canal.

Our first two or three days in New Orleans we didn't worry about getting work. We played. We went sightseeing during the day, and at night we barhopped in the Quarter. The city was endlessly exotic and exciting, especially to two people as small-town as we were. Jack loved it, and I began to hope he'd decide to stay.

Sometime during that first week Wasyl got a job as a soda jerk at a drive-in restaurant. Jack and I, following up the lead he'd gotten in Baton Rouge, went to see the owner of the Ponderosa Bar. We were hired at once, I as a bartender and Jack as a bouncer.

The Ponderosa was in a commercial area on Canal Street within walking distance of our hotel. It wasn't an exclusive lounge by any means, but neither was it a dive. It was just a bar, one of hundreds in the city that got by mostly on tourist trade overflowing from the French Quarter. There was one big room, done in a sort of faded Wild West decor, with a bar running almost the entire length of one wall. Behind the bar was a stage, where go-go girls danced to music from a record player.

I thought it was a dreary sort of place, especially on the nights when business was too slow to require Jack's services and I was working alone. Sometimes during those long nights my mind would flash back to my life long before Jack, to my days as a stewardess or as an administrator at the Wiltwyck School. And I'd catch myself thinking, just for a minute, What am I doing here? What went wrong?

One night not long after I started working there, two men in business suits came into the bar and sat down at a table. I started to go over to take their order when one of the other bartenders stopped me and pulled me aside.

"You can't serve those guys," she said.

"Why not?" I asked.

"Are you blind?" she sneered. "It's a white guy with a nigger."

Suddenly, so clearly, I saw in my mind the March on Washington. I stood there watching another barmaid go over and ask the two men to leave, and I wanted to cry, or scream, or both. There was a time when I never would have permitted anybody to say such a thing in my presence, or let it pass without protest. For a minute I didn't recognize myself. Who was I? What was I turning into?

We were in New Orleans at a time when the city government was having one of its periodic crackdowns on something called B-drinking, a practice in which barmaids, dancers—any women working in bars—drank with the customers, either to sell more drinks or as a prelude to prostitution and, sometimes, robbery. The customers were charged inflated prices for the women's drinks, which were either watered down or entirely free of alcohol. The practice was fairly widespread and was bad for the city's tourist business. To stop it, guidelines were issued about what female bar employees could and could not do. For one thing, we were supposed to limit our conversation with customers to asking what drink they wanted and telling them how much it cost. The rule was being strictly enforced at the time and I was careful to observe it.

One night when Jack and I were both working I served a drink to a man who appeared to be pretty drunk already. He tried to start a conversation with me, and when I cut him short he started to get obnoxious. He grabbed my arm and tried to make me sit down with him, and I couldn't break away. I got scared, afraid it would look like I was breaking the rule, and I called Jack over to handle the situation.

Clearly furious, Jack pulled the man out of his chair, shoved him toward the door, and dragged him outside. When several minutes passed and Jack didn't come back I got worried, though whether for him or for the drunken customer I couldn't have said. I ran outside to the alley that ran alongside the bar and found them there. The drunk was dazed and bleeding. Jack was holding him by his coat and slamming his head against a concrete wall, again and again. I started screaming. Jack looked over at me and dropped the man, just as other people started coming out of the bar to see what was wrong. Somebody called the police, and they came and took the drunk away. They did nothing to Jack.

Back in the bar, he raged at me. I was stupid, he said. I should have seen that the guy was drunk and refused to serve him. I should have pointed him out to Jack right away, and Jack could have gotten him out of the bar before there was any trouble. Things were going wrong because these crumbs we worked for didn't know how to run a bar, he said. He ought to be running things. If he were in charge, shit like this wouldn't happen.

"From now on," he concluded, "if anybody comes in who's drunk, you point him out to me as soon as he comes in."

I apologized for what happened and promised to do as he said. From then on, I notified Jack when I had even the slightest suspicion that a customer might be drunk. Some of the men I pointed out were probably as sober as saints, but I wasn't taking any chances. I'd been warned. If there was any more trouble, I'd get blamed. It would be my fault and Jack would be mad at me. I'd do anything to keep that from happening.

A couple of nights later I pointed out a customer who seemed a little tipsy. Jack left with the man. It was a busy night, but I kept glancing nervously at the clock as I worked. He'd been gone ten minutes, twenty now, half an hour. More than an hour passed before he came back, and by that time I was frantic. I couldn't stop myself from asking where he'd been. Instead of answering me he just laughed. I was relieved. The laugh must mean that nothing bad had happened, nothing was wrong.

When we got off work late that night, Jack didn't feel like going back to the hotel. He said he wanted to party. We got something to eat and then went to an after-hours club in the Quarter. Jack was spending money freely—where he got it I didn't know—and he was in a wonderful mood. It was one of our good nights, one of the times I felt very close to him. We danced and drank and laughed together, and then we strolled back to the hotel arm in arm.

Wasyl was out, I was happy to see. I didn't want anything to violate our privacy or fracture the mood. We walked into our bedroom and closed the door.

"Get undressed," he said.

Something in his tone of voice made me freeze. Then I looked at his eyes, and I knew what was coming.

It was just like what happened in Florida, except now he had a new horror story to recite while he beat me.

"Don't you ever ask me again where I've been," he said. "I don't have to answer to you, you whore. You want to know where I was? Remember all those drunks you pointed out? Remember all those drunks? You want to know what happened to 'em? Well, I took 'em outside and stuck a knife in their kidneys to drain out the alcohol. I took their money. They didn't need it. They aren't really men. Then I took their bodies and threw 'em in the dump in back of the bar."

Then there was the awful, angry sex, and afterward his tears, his apologies, his promises, his assurances that none of those bad things he'd said was true.

I didn't know what to make of it. I'd tried to believe that the beating in Florida was a freak incident. Now I had to recognize that it might have been something else. It might have been the start of some pattern I had to learn to understand. I had to figure out how this wonderful man, who loved me, could turn into a raving animal.

I told myself that his spells of craziness might have something to do with the scar on his forehead. He'd once been in a bad car accident. Maybe there had been some kind of brain damage that left him with a condition like epilepsy. I'd have to make sure he saw a doctor as soon as we could afford it. Maybe he couldn't help himself. I'd have to try to see to it that the rages didn't get triggered. I'd have to find a way to make our financial situation better. Jack never had to worry about money back in New Paltz. He made a good salary and got lavish tips. Now, because he had left all that to be with me, he was reduced to being a bouncer in a cheap bar. He should be a bar owner, or maybe a singer in a good nightclub. If only I could get a better job, making more than the few dollars I earned now, then Jack would be free to look for work that was worthy of him. Then we'd be happy, and he wouldn't hurt me anymore.

Most of all, I'd stick with him. We were going through bad times, but the good times would come if only I could ride things out. I'd always given up too easily in the past. I'd lost my husband because I gave up on the marriage too quickly. I'd lost my baby because I wasn't strong enough to keep him and weather the bad times. It wasn't going to happen again. This time I wasn't going to give up, no matter what.

I decided to keep a list. I'd write down all the things that irritated Jack and try to see that they didn't happen. I couldn't change everything, but I could change the things that were my fault. I'd think of ways to make him happier and make his life easier, and I'd put those on the list, too.

Like the beating in Florida, the one in New Orleans was followed by a day or two of Jack's being especially kind and considerate. Knowing how tired I was of motels and hotels, and how badly I wanted a place of our own, he even suggested that we go apartment-hunting. I was ecstatic! He did plan to stay in New Orleans! We were going to have a home! We spent a day when we were both off work combing through newspaper want ads and looking at apartments. Jack didn't see anything that suited him, but I wasn't discouraged. We'd find something.

Since I worked on a regular basis and Jack didn't, he had more free time than I did. He never told me what he did with it, and I knew better than to ask. Even during the time I wasn't working, mornings and days off, he was away as often as he was with me. Since Wasyl was usually at work, I ended up spending a lot of time alone in the hotel.

I wasn't lonely. It was becoming easier and easier for me to withdraw into myself, to sit and play by myself in the growing fantasy world inside my head. I spent hours planning how I would decorate our first apartment, how I would arrange the furniture, what meals I'd cook for Jack. I looked through old magazines for recipes and decorating tips. When I saw something I liked I cut it out. I sat on the floor for hours, cutting up magazines like a child cutting out paper dolls.

I wonder how it can be that I never saw how nearly insane I was myself then, how far I was regressing, how close I was to losing myself altogether. If the thought ever did cross my mind, I must have pushed it away so quickly and so thoroughly that I don't remember it now.

One night when Jack was out and I wasn't working, I spent the evening in bed with my magazines. It was late, and I must have drifted off to sleep. The next thing I knew, Jack was standing over me, shaking me. Oh, God, I thought. He's going to hit me again. But as I came fully awake I saw that he didn't look angry or crazy. He looked scared. He looked like a little boy who'd done something wrong and been caught and was about to be punished.

He told me to get dressed and pack and to do it in a hurry. He'd cheated some guy in a card game, he said, and the guy was connected —Jack's shorthand for having friends in the Mafia. There could be trouble, he said. We had to get out of town right away.

I knew Jack tended to dramatize, but I could see that this time he was genuinely frightened. It made me frightened for him. Obediently, I dressed and packed as fast as I could. As I remember, we'd been in New Orleans a little less than three weeks.

chapter 10

After we left New Orleans our wanderings seemed to get even more disjointed and bizarre. The trip runs through my mind now like a movie made up of random bits of film, spliced together in no special order, with no meaning and no plot.

My first clear memory is of driving west again, through dry counties in Texas, trying to find a bottle for Jack. There was no liquor in the car, and he was frantic for a drink. I remember winding up and down across the state, thinking that all of Texas must be dry. Finally, Jack convinced somebody at a coffee shop to sell him some beer. We got a bottle of liquor later.

There were four of us in the car now instead of three. Somewhere along the line we'd picked up a young man with long blond hair and Levis. I think he may have been a friend of Wasyl's hitching a ride with us to Carson City, Nevada. I don't remember his name. He was just another kid on the road, like so many thousands in the mid-sixties. There was nothing especially memorable about him— except that he had a gun.

He sat in the front seat and Jack sat behind him in the back, next to me. Wasyl was driving. Jack and the hitchhiker were passing the gun back and forth, taking turns shooting out the windows at road signs. I tried to ignore it, but I couldn't. I was afraid of guns, and the sharp bursts of noise were terrifying. I remember Jack laughing at me: It was only a little gun, he said.

Then we were out of Texas and into New Mexico, and in some little town near Albuquerque we were stopped by the police. I don't remember why—maybe we were speeding. But once they stopped us, they searched the car, and they must have found the gun or the liquor. We had to go with them to a justice of the peace's office on a dusty road off the main highway, where we were held for several hours. The police ran a check on the car, and on all of us, while each of us was questioned separately. Who were we? Where did we live? Where were we going?

I don't remember what I answered, beyond giving my name. I didn't know where I lived now, and I didn't know where I was going. I was frightened. I'd never had anything to do with the police before. I kept imagining all sorts of things, none of them very rational. They were holding us for something to do with Jack's trouble back in New Orleans, when we had to leave so suddenly. They were going to arrest us. They were going to call my parents and tell them I was in jail. At last they simply let us go, and we kept on driving west. Nobody but me appeared to be upset by the incident. Nobody but me seemed to be lost on this lunatic trip.

I looked out the window at the flat, dry landscape. Out of New Mexico, into Arizona. Out of Arizona, into Nevada. Jack was talking a lot about Las Vegas. Las Vegas, like New Orleans, was his kind of town. There were lots of jobs there. There was lots of easy money. We may have stopped there. I don't remember. The next place we settled for any length of time was Carson City.

Carson City is memorable mainly because we rented our first apartment there. The night we got to town we dropped the hitch-hiker off, then checked into a motel as usual. But a day or two later we found a place a few blocks off the city's main street, and Jack paid a month's rent on it.

Wasyl was still living with us, and the apartment itself wasn't all that much—a living room, a bedroom, a kitchen, and a little dining area, completely furnished, right down to the pots and pans. It was, in fact, very much like all the motels. But it was presentable and clean, and I was overjoyed with it. It was, at last, a home of sorts.

Jack took me shopping for linens and other odds and ends to add to the furnishings. I got such a kick out of the shopping expeditions that even he seemed to have fun just watching me. My enthusiasm was too great not to be contagious. He bought me whatever I wanted, what little that was.

We stayed in Carson City about a month, and neither of us worked during that time. Jack never told me to get a job, and he never mentioned that he was looking for work himself. Yet there always seemed to be enough money. We ate out often (Jack's preference), and his fifth-a-day drinking habit was expensive. Still there appeared to be no shortage of ready cash. I didn't question it, but I worried about it. To have money you had to work. That was the only way of life I'd ever known. I'd worked off and on since I was fifteen years old, and I felt I ought to be working now.

With Jack's approval, I started looking for a job. I applied at several places, including a casino that was hiring cocktail waitresses. A few days later when I checked back with one of the casinos they asked me to come in for an interview. I couldn't wait to tell Jack, thinking how pleased he'd be.

He was furious. The casino had really been trying to get in touch with him, he said. He was the one they wanted, not me, but I'd butted in and stolen his job. It made no sense, and I tried to protest that I hadn't stolen his job, that I didn't even know he'd applied for work there. It did no good. He beat me up again, badly, and this time there were no tears and apologies afterward. He simply stomped out of the apartment.

I thought it over long enough to get it straight, which meant to adapt the truth to whatever version of reality Jack dictated. He was right. It was my fault. I'd stolen his job. I called the casino and said I wouldn't be in for the interview. I couldn't have gone anyway. By this point Jack was hitting me in the face as well as the body, and I was too bruised to make a very good impression on a prospective employer.

I don't remember much else about Carson City—only that Jack was drinking more than ever, and he was touchier than ever, and the beatings were getting worse and closer together. Then one day he said it was time to leave, so we packed up again and left.

The language of violence is so limited, and so casual. We hear it and use it every day. Joking with a friend, you say, "You want a punch in the mouth?" or a frustrated mother says, "I'm going to kill that kid," and it means nothing.

Before my trial I never told anybody in any detail about being beaten. I was ashamed, ashamed of my weakness and ashamed that

I could ever have let anybody use me that way. For a long time, also, there was nobody who would have cared nearby to tell, no family and no friends. Jack had seen to it that I had neither. And there was a third reason: I didn't think I could make anybody understand.

When, in 1983, I knew that I was going to have to sit on a witness stand and tell a jury about the beatings, I was terrified. I didn't have the words to make them see how it was. I could say, "He hit me," or "He kicked me," or "He choked me," but that only told what he did—not how it felt.

How do you tell somebody about the gut-squeezing fear you feel in that instant when you realize it's about to happen again, and it might be a bad one this time? How do you describe watching his hand start to move, and knowing you're about to feel an incredible shot of pain, and that it's going to go on, and on, and on? Most of all, how do you convey that sense of knowing that something terrible is about to happen to you and that you're utterly powerless to stop it? An irrational force is coming at you, and it's going to hurt you, and you can't reason with it or fight it.

Maybe nobody can truly understand it except another woman who's been through it. I just wrote that "the beatings were getting worse and closer together." That's an accurate statement of fact, but it's nowhere near the truth.

Out of Nevada, into California. It must have been early in 1966 by now, though I don't remember where or how we'd celebrated Christmas or New Year's, or whether we'd celebrated them at all. The three of us drove west again until we reached the California coast and there was no farther west to go. We got to Los Angeles and started looking in the area for a place to live. Before long we found one, a little furnished apartment right on the beach in the small coastal town of Hermosa Beach, south of Los Angeles.

Settling there was something that was, for once, more or less my idea. I'd asked Jack as soon as we got to Los Angeles if we could live near a beach, and he'd given his permission.

I loved the beach because it brought back good memories. It reminded me of when I was a little girl back in New York. Sometimes, on his days off, my father would take Mother and me to Jones Beach for the day. Daddy would play in the waves with me, and help me practice swimming, and oversee the construction of my elaborate sand castles. Mother would lay out a picnic on a blanket, and after we'd eaten, we'd lie in the sun, and maybe doze a little, and I'd feel warm and safe and loved.

My parents. They didn't know where I was now, or even if I was still alive. I hadn't talked to them since that terrible day I left New Paltz, but I thought about them. I was always going to call just as soon as I had good news to tell them. I was going to call from Florida just as soon as Jack was working, and we were settled in a house and planning our wedding. Then I was going to call from Louisiana, then from Nevada. Just as soon as there was good news. But the good news never came, and now I couldn't wait anymore.

A day or two after we rented the apartment in Hermosa Beach I went to a telephone booth. My mouth was dry as I dialed the number. What could I say? I knew what agony I had put them through, but I needed them now, needed those two people who would love me no matter what.

"Mother? Mother, it's Ginny."

Then my mother was crying, and Daddy was on the line and he was crying, and I was crying, too. I told them where I was and that I was fine. Everything was fine. California was beautiful. Jack was wonderful. We were settling down here, and maybe they could come out soon for a visit. And listening to the relief in their voices, I told myself that I wasn't lying. Not really. I was just being a little premature.

We hadn't been in Hermosa Beach long, no more than a month, when Wasyl finally left us to go back to New Paltz, where a draft notice was waiting for him. In all the time he'd been with us neither he nor I had ever mentioned what was going on between Jack and me. But right before he left, while he was packing a suitcase he'd borrowed from me, Wasyl said he thought it was just as well that he was leaving. He said he couldn't take Jack's violence anymore. I said nothing. Wasyl and I had never become friends, and I wasn't especially sorry to see him go. But for just a minute or two I envied him his escape.

If things had been bad in Carson City, they were worse in Hermosa Beach. Jack was drinking more than ever and his temper was on a hair trigger. My things-to-avoid-so-as-not-to-annoy-Jack list was getting longer and longer. I never knew what would set him off. Once he beat me because he didn't like the way I'd hung his shirts in the closet. Add to the list: Always hang Jack's shirts facing in the same direction. Another time it was because he saw dishes in the sink. Add to the list: Always wash the dishes and put them away as soon as the meal is over.

He was gone from the apartment a lot, and I thought perhaps

he was looking for work. If so, he must not have found it, because we hadn't been in town long before he told me it was time for me to get a job again. I found one easily, hiring on to work behind the bar at a beer bar in the town of Torrance, about a half-hour drive from Hermosa Beach.

The place was called the Velvet Hammer, and for the most part I enjoyed working there. It was a small, nicely decorated place that served only beer and wine. The owners were a couple in their forties, pleasant people, who were very nice to me. The Velvet Hammer was located in Torrance's business district, and the customers were mostly businessmen—friendly, polite regulars who never got out of line. The only thing I didn't like about the job was the hours. I worked the night shift and didn't get off until two in the morning.

When I first started working, Jack drove me to Torrance every afternoon and picked me up at night. Later, when he got tired of the commute, he allowed me to drive myself back and forth. This was a first. I'd never been permitted to use the car before. Of course, I still had to account for all my time except what I spent with him or alone in the apartment. If the bar was going to close late, I called and told him. I called again just before I left, so he'd know exactly when to expect me home. I knew better than to be late. Back in Carson City Jack had timed exactly how long it should take me to go to the laundromat. He knew how long it took to wash the clothes, how long to dry them, how long it took to walk there and back. Once I was five minutes off his estimate. That brought on a beating and a tirade about my being out whoring around. Add to the list: Never be late.

Hermosa Beach, like many Southern California coastal towns, had a main street that extended out into the ocean in the form of a pier. The street was lined with little beach shops, restaurants, and bars, most of which eked out a scanty living on a mixture of local and tourist trade. Jack spent most of his days in the bars. He struck up a friendship with one of the bar owners who shared his taste for nonstop drinking. On days when the proprietor got too drunk to work, Jack, if he was sober enough, took over the bartending duties on a relief basis. He told me that before long he'd be the permanent bartender.

I was glad to see him thinking about any kind of full-time work —maybe he wouldn't drink so much if he was working—but this new plan struck me as odd. Jack was usually so demanding and critical. For a small-town boy, he thought big. Yet the place where he was filling in was tacky and shabby, not to say a dive. It was a hangout for the local beach drunks.

If he was lowering his expectations for himself, however, he certainly wasn't for me. He was still demanding his own brand of perfection, and I was still trying to achieve it, and falling short, and having to pay for it.

One day I was getting ready to go to work, dressed as usual in slacks and a blouse. I was putting on my makeup, the same way I did it every day, when Jack came home. He was very drunk.

"Where're you going all painted up like that?" he wanted to know. I tried to stammer out some answer, and he started yelling. "You're going out all painted up like that because you're going to suck somebody's cock."

Then it was happening again, and the horror story that went with this beating was sicker than ever.

"I found this drunk on the pier," he was saying, "and I cut off his cock. I was going to bring it home, and you would've liked that, wouldn't you? You would, you whore, you would. Now you're going to do it to me . . ." He grabbed my head and started forcing it down.

Later, in his contrite phase, he told me he was upset because he loved me so much and he couldn't stand the thought that I was out at night in some bar with other men looking at me.

"I'll quit, Jack," I promised. And, the next night, I did. I can't believe it now, but I did.

A day job, preferably in some kind of office, proved harder to get than work as a barmaid or waitress. I went through a week or so of answering help-wanted ads without success. Then I saw an ad for people to work the phones at a telephone solicitation service. I didn't think it would pay much, but it offered day hours in an office, and the office was within walking distance of our apartment. I called and made an appointment for an interview. The next day I was hired on the spot by the owners—two of the most fascinating people I've ever known.

The first thing I noticed about Morton and Becky Brown was what a strikingly good-looking couple they made. Morton was tall, lean, and dark, while Becky had a milky complexion and fiery red hair. I was impressed next by how friendly and likeable they were. Morton was especially smooth and persuasive, and it occurred to me when we met that he could probably sell me the clothes on my back and charge me extra because I was already wearing them.

Morton's solicitation business had several clients, the main one being a local photography studio. The idea was to promote the client's wares over the telephone. We would offer cheap "prizes," or "gift certificates," that required a five-dollar "handling charge." It didn't take me long to learn the pitch.

I was so good at the job, in fact, that I won a quick promotion off the telephone. After only two or three weeks Morton made me his office manager, supervising six telephone solicitors. Now that I was a management type I spent more time with Morton, who was the boss, and with Becky, who kept the books, and the three of us got to be good friends.

Business was good and Morton was thinking about expanding. He wanted to open a new office in Huntington Park on the inland side of Los Angeles, and he asked me if I would get it started and manage it.

I wasn't sure, I said. It would probably mean moving, and I'd have to discuss it with my husband. (I always pretended Jack and I were married. It seemed so much more respectable.) My husband was looking for work as a bartender in Hermosa Beach, and he might not want to leave the area.

"Why don't I meet your husband," Morton suggested, "and then maybe we can talk about some sort of partnership arrangement where the two of you can work on a percentage."

I rushed home to tell Jack, and for once he was as excited as I was. We were going to be successful business people. Things were looking up.

That very evening I set off with Jack to introduce him to Morton and Becky. We'd been invited to their apartment, which turned out to be in a beautiful new complex in Torrance. Jack was very impressed. Brown must be doing all right, he said.

Jack hit it off instantly with both the Browns, and I could see by the way she looked at him that Becky was especially impressed. The partnership was discussed in general terms that night, and the next morning we all met in Morton's office to make final decisions and work out the details. Morton presented, and Jack accepted, a percentage plan in which Jack and I would become partners, if somewhat junior partners, in their company.

Morton and Becky helped us get the Huntington Park operation under way. We rented two adjacent apartments, one for an office and the other for Jack and me to live in. We put ads in the newspaper for telephone solicitors, interviewed job applicants, hired six of them, and got started.

Those first few weeks in business were good times for Jack and me. Being his own boss seemed to gratify him and give some direction to his life again. The beatings stopped and he drank less. For a time, he was almost as good-natured and loving as he'd been during the early days of our courtship.

Seeing the change in him, my own optimism was boundless. Jack was happy. Our relationship was on solid ground. We were together in a new business that might lead to even better things if we kept at it and worked hard. And, to top it off, we got word through a lawyer that Jack's wife had divorced him. He was free now, and I was sure that it was just a matter of time before we'd be married and emotionally and financially secure, with all the bad times behind us.

Jack and I decided that I would manage the office and he would deliver the "prizes." I was good at organizing things, we reasoned, and he was good at meeting the public. The arrangement started crumbling in a matter of weeks. On a slow day there might be only one or two delivery orders for Jack. With little to do he'd get bored, and when he got bored he drank.

The backsliding was gradual at first, but it soon picked up steam. Before long Jack was drinking up whatever cash he collected and bringing home nothing but the Green Stamps that customers were permitted to pay with. He brought home so many of them, in fact, that we were able to buy a large color television courtesy of Green Stamps. That was fine, but we were running low on cash, and Jack was coming home drunk more and more often.

Boredom wasn't his only problem. We were working some pretty rough neighborhoods, and Jack didn't care much for the clientele. It wasn't his scene or his kind of audience. Where were the swingers and high rollers and guys who were "connected"? Where were the people who used to love to hear him sing "Mack the Knife"?

Finally, he told me he wasn't going to make deliveries anymore. He wasn't going to go into any more smelly houses or talk to any more smelly people, he said. It was beneath him. He'd tell Morton to take the business and shove it. Or, if I didn't like that idea, I could make the deliveries myself, and he'd run the office. So out I went, knocking on doors in Bell and Huntington Park and Compton, trying to look confident and cheerful as I handed over the gift certificates to people who were often hostile or suspicious.

One day I called the office and nobody answered the phone. I called again and again. Still no answer. Thinking that the phones must be out of order, I decided to go back to the office and check. When I got there the office was empty. Its door was wide open. I went next door to our apartment and let myself in. There I found Jack in bed with a neighbor.

It would have been almost funny if it hadn't been so awful. Jack leaped up and grabbed me, apologizing and explaining even while the woman was throwing on her clothes and running for the door. He was trying to soothe me, but it was a long time before he could even penetrate my hysteria. I wasn't angry so much as I was crushed, inconsolable, totally unglued. Whatever else he might have done, Jack had never been unfaithful to me—at least, not that I knew of.

Still, he kept talking and I listened, and in the end I was able to rationalize even this injury. I was the only woman he could ever love, he said. That other girl was just some trashy whore. She didn't mean anything to him. How could I possibly be jealous of her? He didn't mean it to happen. He was feeling bad about himself because of the degrading work he'd had to do, and when she threw herself at him, his resistance was low. It never would have happened if he weren't in this business. But I was the one who'd wanted the business. I was the one who'd introduced him to Morton and Becky . . .

Looking back, I honestly believe that by the end of the day he had me believing that I'd all but pushed him into bed with another woman. It was once again all my fault. I tried to forget the whole thing and concentrate instead on how well Jack was treating me in the wake of the betrayal. All in all, things were still better than they'd been before we started the business.

As for the business itself, however, things were getting worse. Morton's whole soliciting operation, including our office, was slipping. The most profitable neighborhoods had been tapped and revenues were falling. He decided it was time to diversify.

He and Jack thought it might be a good idea to take advantage of Jack's expertise in running a bar. We'd buy a bar and the four of us would operate it as partners. Toward the end of 1966 Jack and Morton found a little beer bar for sale at a good price, in a working-class neighborhood in the town of Carson. It was called the No Regrets.

Morton put up most of the down payment. Jack paid a smaller share, but we were full partners because Jack would oversee the bar's day-to-day operations. Jack came up with our end of the initial investment by getting a loan from his mother.

Now that we were bar owners, all four of us had to apply for a license to sell beer at the No Regrets. This meant that Jack and I had to give our real names, thereby admitting we weren't married. Morton and Becky didn't seem to care one way or the other, but Jack apparently wanted to tie up the loose ends. Right after we bought the bar, he proposed.

"Since we've got to get that beer license," he said, "I guess we ought to get married."

It wasn't a very romantic proposal, but I was satisfied with it. I never questioned whether it made any sense to marry a man who had been brutalizing me. I never stopped to ask what in the world I was doing. On New Year's Day, 1967, we drove into Arizona and were married in the town of Winterhaven by a justice of the peace. We took Morton and Becky along as witnesses. For our honeymoon, we checked into a motel and spent the day watching college football bowl games on television.

chapter 11

The No Regrets was nothing fancy—just a little neighborhood bar with stools, a few tables, and a pool table. It was the kind of place where working men felt comfortable stopping for a few beers with their buddies after a long day, or bringing their wives for a night out. They could be sure of being among friends, since the bar's customers were almost all regulars. And they could be sure of a warm welcome from the new owner.

For Jack, in the beginning, the No Regrets might as well have been the Oak Room or the Polo Lounge. He'd always wanted to own his own bar, and this was, in however small a way, his dream come true. Morton may have been the senior partner financially, but he wasn't around much. It was Jack who, in the role of proud owner, hobnobbed with the customers every day, drank beer with them, shot pool with them, and cultivated a few of them as close friends. Being one of the boys was his true element, and he was back in it now. He greeted customers at the door, joked and swapped stories with them, organized pool tournaments. We had two regular bartenders, one for the day shift and one at night, but Jack liked to fill in for them occasionally, showing off his old flair behind the bar. Sometimes he even sang, just like in the old days.

He was as happy as I'd ever seen him, and that meant that I was happy, too. For the most part he was even-tempered and easy to live with. He confined his drinking almost exclusively to beer.

Along with our new business, we had a new home. We moved into an apartment in Torrance, near Carson and the bar. It wasn't nearly as grand as the big house the Browns had just bought in Torrance, but it was the nicest home Jack and I ever had together. It had two bedrooms and a big living room and a dining room. Both the living room and the master bedroom had sliding glass doors leading onto balconies, and the balconies overlooked a neighboring golf course with its clubhouse and swimming pool.

Sometimes Morton and Becky and I visited the No Regrets during the day, and I usually spent some time there at night just to keep Jack company. But I didn't work there. I was, at long last, a proper wife and homemaker, and I was content for the time being just to take care of the apartment, decorate it, fuss over its furnishings, keep it clean.

Everything was falling into place so neatly now. There was only one more thing I needed as a stamp of legitimacy for our marriage and our new life, a final benediction for the dream. I asked Jack if we might invite our parents out, and he agreed. In the spring, my mother and Jack's parents flew to California. My father, who hated to fly, begged off with a promise to come later.

Considering what a bad start everything had gotten off to a year and a half before, the visit went remarkably well. I knew from Jack that Mr. and Mrs. Sidote had thought of me at first as some kind of temptress who'd led their son astray. I think this was especially true of Jack's mother, who was the dominant figure in her family and the parent Jack was closest to. Nevertheless, the Sidotes and I were quite friendly with each other for the few days they were there. I called them Mom and Dad, and they were polite, if not overwhelmingly warm, to me. Jack was on his best behavior with my mother, showering her with little courtesies and attentions. And Mother, who'd detested Jack once, seemed determined to accept her new son-in-law with as much grace and affection as she could muster.

Everybody might have been walking on eggshells during the visit, but at least none of the eggshells broke. I suppose that all three parents, as well as my father back in New Paltz, figured that what was done was done, and everybody should make the best of it. No doubt it helped matters that the Sidotes and Galluzzos had such similar backgrounds, life-styles, interests, and beliefs. If they had their doubts about us, at least they got along well together.

After our folks left, I was at loose ends. There was only so much I could do around the apartment, and I had no real function at the bar except to play hostess occasionally as the owner's wife. Looking for a way to spend my energy, get more involved in the business, and maybe make a little extra money, I got together with Becky and we came up with a plan to hold a Family Day promotion at the No Regrets. Every Sunday the two of us would cook a special dish and take it to the bar. We'd sell all-you-can-eat meals for a flat rate, four dollars or so, and if there was any profit, we'd get to keep it. Jack and Morton thought it was worth trying, so I joined with Becky in what turned out to be my first venture into catering.

For our opening presentation we settled on spaghetti and meatballs. We got together enough ingredients to cook for a hundred people. We figured that two hundred and fifty meatballs would be about right.

I should mention here that Becky was a woman of strong opinions about almost everything, and I usually deferred to her judgment. I believed her when she insisted that you could use eggs in cooking without bothering to remove the shells. All you had to do was throw the eggs into a blender, she said, and the shells would get so pulverized, you'd never know they were there. She saw some guy do it in a demonstration on the Boardwalk in Atlantic City once, and it turned out fine.

We threw about five dozen eggs into the blender, six or eight at a time. Then we mixed the blended eggs into a huge tub of seasoned ground meat. We rolled the meatballs and cooked them in our spaghetti sauce. As soon as they were done, we fished one out and sampled it. It tasted like meat rolled in sand, Italian style. Even Becky's dog wouldn't eat it. We had to start over with new eggs and ground beef, and there went the profit margin.

We tried chili next, but it exploded all over Becky's kitchen. We had to pay her maid overtime to help clean up the mess. After that came barbecued ribs. Becky was quite sure that they had to be cooked on racks, and the only racks we knew about were the ones in her oven. We laid slab after slab of ribs on the racks, slathered them with barbecue sauce, and let them drip and sizzle. They tasted wonderful. We had to pay to have Becky's oven relined. The corned beef and cabbage proved to be a better-than-break-even proposition, but we ran out of corned beef early and had vats of cabbage left over.

We decided to give up. The promotion was bringing more families into the bar on Sundays, and they seemed to enjoy the food and drink a lot of beer. Unfortunately, Becky and I were getting too far into debt to afford all that success.

I guess I remember those silly, funny, disastrous days in Becky's kitchen so clearly and so happily because they marked the last good times before a new nightmare began.

We'd owned the No Regrets for only a couple of months when the neighborhood around it began to change. Samoans were moving in, and Jack and I welcomed them and cultivated their trade. We even threw a luau at the bar once in hopes of attracting more business from these big, outgoing people with their colorful clothes and the Polynesian lilt in their voices. But not everybody liked the newcomers as much as we did. Racial tension between the Samoans and the ethnic whites in the area was growing. Some of our regular customers moved, and others drifted away from the bar. Business was slipping, and we couldn't seem to do anything to stop it.

Morton was talking about pulling out. Though he'd never said so, I knew the bar had always been a little small-time for his taste, and there was nothing to hold his interest in it now that revenues were falling. In addition, the few telephone soliciting offices he still operated were running dry. Southern California was losing its charm for the Browns, and clearly it was only a matter of time before they decamped in search of lusher pastures.

With all this going on, Jack was getting discouraged and irritable and nervous, and—though he never would have admitted it—scared. His own dream had materialized just long enough to tantalize him, and now it was fading before he could get a firm grip on it. He was failing again and he knew it, and Jack couldn't stand to fail. I tried, as usual, to take the responsibility. I blamed myself for not coming up with new ideas to promote the bar and bring in new business. When I offered to work so we could lay off our bartenders and cut the overhead, Jack agreed. I took over the day shift, and he worked nights. But still the money got shorter and shorter, and he got more agitated. I knew what was coming.

It was the old pattern all over again. Jack started keeping a private stock of hard liquor at the bar and getting drunk almost every day. And sometimes even when he was sober he beat me.

There was nothing new in what was happening. The physical, sexual, and psychological abuse was the same. But one thing *was* different this time. *I* was. My reaction to the horrors was starting to change. Watching our lives disintegrate one more time, I felt the familiar terror, but this time I felt something new—a despair so bitter that it leaked like acid into the part of my mind that held the watercolor visions of what our future was supposed to be.

Through every bad time, I'd hoped that somewhere down the line my dreams would come true permanently. In the two or three months after we were married and things did seem to be working out, the hope grew large—so large, I guess, that it became a vulnerable target. But now, hard as I tried to deny it, some part of me knew that our life was *not* going to be all right. It would *never* be all right. Nothing I could do, no lists I could make, no humiliations I could endure and forgive would ever make it right. I still loved Jack, and feared him, and depended on him for my very existence. But I didn't hope anymore. I existed and endured, but I didn't dream.

I began to act differently too. I'd never offered any resistance to the beatings. Part of the pattern was that they always happened in the bedroom and always when I was naked, completely defenseless. And when Jack ordered me into the bedroom, or ordered me to take off my clothes, I did as I was told. Fighting back never entered my mind, but I was learning some of the basics of passive self-protection. I was learning to run and to hide.

I could usually tell by Jack's voice or by his attitude and mannerisms during the day whether he was likely to be violent by the time night came. On those nights, I'd go into the bedroom and barricade the door. I'd push the dresser up against the door and pile the mattress and box springs against the dresser. When he started raging I'd sit in a corner of the bedroom, shaking, praying that the door would hold, watching it shudder as he pounded against it from the other side. I knew that sooner or later, if the door held, he'd give up and go to sleep or pass out, and by the next morning the rage would be over. There were nights when he punched holes through the door with his fists, but he never got in.

Sometimes his violent moods were too sudden to prepare for, so I learned always to be dressed when he came home from work. That way I could run if I had to. Some nights I'd run out of the apartment building and across to the golf course and hide in the darkness there. Jack never chased me, I suppose because he was usually too drunk to run. I'd sit on the grass, at times for two or three hours, looking up at the lighted windows of our apartment about a hundred yards away. I could see him there, weaving around, smashing things or kicking the furniture, staggering over to look out the window. When I couldn't see him anymore, I'd go back to the apartment, tiptoe to the front door, and stand there for a while, listening. If everything was quiet, that meant he was asleep and it was safe to go in and go to bed.

Running probably saved me from some bad beatings, but it didn't spare me altogether from getting hit. Jack adapted to the tactic. When he saw that I wouldn't stand still and be beaten, he made sure he got in one shot before I could make it to the door. And he made sure that one shot was hard, and in the face.

There were nights when, instead of running to hide alone, I hid with other people. I still couldn't bring myself to talk to anybody about the beatings, but there were two people I trusted enough to run to for safety. One was Becky. The other was a neighbor whose apartment was close to ours, a man I'll call Sam Allen.

Sam was a tolerant, sympathetic, street-smart sort of man. If I showed up at his apartment at three in the morning, crying and bleeding, I didn't have to answer questions or draw him any pictures. He'd just mumble something about "What kind of a guy hits a broad?" and then he'd calm me down, talk to me, sit up with me, wait with me until things got quiet at home.

I knew Jack would never risk lowering himself in Sam's eyes by trying to drag me out of his apartment in the middle of the night, even though he often visited Sam alone. In Jack's mind Sam was the sort of "tough guy" that he admired so much and tried so hard to be. He used to drop in uninvited and try to impress Sam with stories, real or imagined, about his own crimes. He liked to tell Sam about all the important Mafia people he knew back in New York, hinting that he'd worked for them. And the more he talked, the more appalled Sam became.

"That sonofabitch is always dropping names," Sam complained to me once. "Christ only knows where he'll drop mine. I wish he'd just keep his ass out of here." I think one reason Sam got to be so protective of me was that he disliked and distrusted Jack so much.

There were times when I'd call Becky late at night from a public phone on the golf course. Usually she took me to her house to spend the night. Twice, when it looked like I might have a broken nose, she took me to a hospital emergency room. I wouldn't tell her any details about what had happened to me, but of course I didn't have to. It was obvious. In the mornings, protesting, she'd take me home.

"I can't believe you're going back there," she'd say. "Why do you stay with that bastard?"

Why did I stay with him?

I must have been asked that question a thousand times by now.

I must have asked it myself ten thousand times. The trouble is, there's no easy answer. Or rather, there's no *one* answer. There are a lot of different explanations that apply to different times.

I stayed with him, at first, because he made me feel good about myself. I stayed because I loved him, because leaving would have meant another failure, and I was terrified of failing again. I stayed because I believed him after the first beating, or the second, or the third, when he said it would never happen again, and when he begged my forgiveness. I stayed because I accepted the blame for having provoked him.

I stayed because I had nowhere else to go and I didn't know what else to do. I stayed because I was afraid of being alone and because I was ashamed. I stayed, eventually, because I was afraid of what he would do to me if I left. At the time I had no way of understanding what was happening to me. I thought that I was being beaten because there was something wrong with me, some shameful flaw in me, that brought it on. That had to be true, I thought, because other women, good women, weren't being beaten by their husbands or lovers. Oh, maybe it happened in the slums sometimes, to poor, degraded people who couldn't help themselves. But it didn't happen to people I knew, to the women who lived next door, or down the street, or back in New Paltz. It was happening only to me. I was guilty, for some reason, and I was alone.

I couldn't know, then, that there were millions of women just like me, exactly how many no one is certain even today, since spousal abuse remains one of the country's most underreported crimes. One conservative estimate is that forty million American women will suffer a serious beating by an intimate partner at some time during their lives. And two thousand to three thousand women die each year at the hands of a husband, a lover, or an ex-partner.

During the time I lived with Jack Sidote, there wasn't a single shelter for battered women in the United States. The battered woman's plight was ignored, or worse, she was blamed for causing her own beating, or labeled hysterical, or a "habitual problem," by those she turned to for help—the police, emergency room staff, her marriage counselor, social worker, or clergyman. There were no stories in newspapers, no magazine articles, no television movies or talk shows about domestic violence. Women were being tortured and even murdered by the men they lived with—just as they are today. But "Are you still beating your wife?" was just a punch line to a joke, and everybody laughed.

"Battered-wife syndrome" was a term I'd never heard. Researchers weren't using that phrase yet, and very few of them were even investigating the problem. It wasn't until the growth of the second wave of feminism in the early 1970s that women began defining the issues that affected them. When they brought to public attention the seriousness and the prevalence of domestic abuse, humane services were created and women demanded from institutions protection from battery.

So I had no way of knowing, back in 1967, how precisely my own situation fit the classic profile of domestic battering. (In fact, until I read Del Martin's book *Battered Wives* I didn't realize that that is what I was.)

Here are some of the things that experts say about that profile today:

Wife beating isn't confined to the ghetto. It cuts across all social, racial, and economic lines. It can happen to the woman next door or down the street, and it makes little difference whether her husband is a doctor or minister who went to Harvard or a grade-school dropout who digs ditches. It occurs in marriages where partners abuse alcohol and drugs and in homes where they don't. Violence may begin early in a relationship, even before the wedding, or it may not show up until years later.

Incidents of wife abuse, or the abuse of any woman in an intimate relationship, have a three-phase pattern. There's a tension-building phase, during which the man may get increasingly agitated, or may withdraw. Sensing this, the woman tries to please him and to anticipate his every whim in hopes of changing his mood and warding off violence. Or she may just try to stay out of his way. Either way, she fails. The second phase comes—the beating itself, which may include psychological abuse and sometimes sexual abuse. Then there's the final phase, when the man is loving and contrite and says it will never happen again, and the woman forgives him and lives in hope that he will change, that the beatings will stop. But they never do. The studies show that, unless help is obtained, the violence escalates, the cycle continues.

There are many complicated reasons why a woman stays in a relationship where she is battered. She may love her husband or lover and believe that every beating is the last one. She may be emotionally and financially dependent on him. She may fear being on her own even more than she fears being beaten. She may be afraid that if she leaves, he'll come after her and possibly kill her. She may be ashamed to admit to anyone that her marriage is a failure, or ashamed because she's submitted to so much degradation already.

Obviously, I was in no way unique. Jack Sidote was a man who needed to shift blame elsewhere for every inadequacy, every mistake, every failure in his life, and I was a woman who was all too willing to accept that blame. And so we joined in our neurotic, destructive dance together, and neither of us could seem to stop.

No, I was not alone. *But I didn't know that then.* The horror of wife beating would at least begin to come out of the closet and into the public light at a later day. There would be a name for what was wrong in my life, and a description of it, and theories about how it happened, and to whom, and why. There would be dedicated, brilliant people—though never enough of them—who understood it and could help women through it. But it would all come a little too late for me.

Had it come soon enough, maybe things would have been different. Maybe I would have been stronger or gotten out sooner. There's even the chance I wouldn't have gotten involved with Jack Sidote in the first place. But the speculation, hindsight, and wishful thinking can't erase the pain or change what happened.

I did stay with him and watched as the bar continued sliding downhill. Morton offered Jack the Browns' share of the partnership in the No Regrets and Jack borrowed more money from his mother to buy it. I also borrowed money from my parents to help keep the bar going. Morton and Becky, my best friends, left California for some promising new venture in the Midwest and I felt more alone than ever.

Jack's drinking got worse and he started arriving later and later to relieve me at the bar. Sometimes he came in drunk and sometimes he didn't come at all, so that I had to work double shifts.

One hot night in August I was sleeping, fully dressed, on the sofa in the living room, expecting a bad time when Jack came home. Then he was shaking me awake.

"I killed somebody," he groaned.

It was another one of the horror stories that always went with the beatings, and I pulled away from him, ready to run. Then I saw that he was crying. I looked at him closely, and on his face was that guilty, scared, little-boy look that I'd seen only once before—on that night in New Orleans when he told me we had to leave town. And suddenly I was afraid that this particular horror story might be the truth.

chapter 12

That Friday had been bad from the start.

I was exhausted, for one thing. I'd been working double shifts at the bar for days, opening at about eleven in the morning and working through until closing at two. The only other choice was to close the bar, since Jack was in no condition to help. He'd been drinking himself into a stupor almost every day for several weeks.

Along with being tired that Friday, I was sick. All through the double shift the day before I'd had chills and fever and aches. I knew that I was coming down with the flu and that I just couldn't make it through another fifteen-hour day.

I tried phoning Jack at about three that afternoon, asking him to come in early. The first few times he told me to "fuck off," he wasn't coming in at all, and he hung up. I kept calling. I knew I was making him furious, but for once I didn't care. I could hardly stand up and had to go home and go to bed. Finally, we had a terrible fight on the phone. I told him that if he didn't come in, I'd have to close the bar. Friday was one of our busy nights, and we both knew that we couldn't afford to close. Swearing and yelling, he said he'd come in about eight o'clock. The place had better be open and I'd better still be in it. When he did come in around nine he was angry and sullen, but he looked sober enough to work. He didn't even speak to me. I went home and fell into a deep sleep on the living-room couch.

The next time I saw him was when he woke me later that night, crying and frantic, saying that he'd killed somebody. The story he was telling was barely coherent. Some Samoan kids had come to the bar and threatened him, he said, and he shot at them. One of them was hit, there were witnesses, and the police knew about it. He said we had to go back to the bar. People were still there, the doors weren't locked, and he'd left money in the cash register. I had to go back with him and help him talk to the police when they came. Maybe we'd tell them he wasn't even at the bar when the shooting happened, he said. I could tell them he was home with me.

On the way to the No Regrets I tried to calm him as best I could, while at the same time fighting down my own terror. Jack was in desperate trouble. If only I hadn't made him go to work. Now he might have to go to jail, and I couldn't live if that happened. I could never survive without him.

People were still milling around the bar when we got there. When the police came, I watched in pure dread as they started asking questions: "Which one of you is John J. Sidote?" "What can you tell us about a shooting here earlier tonight?" The questioning lasted only a few minutes before Jack was arrested and taken to the police station.

Because people had seen the shooting, the story Jack finally told the police that night went like this: A young Samoan in the bar was being obnoxious to one of the other customers and Jack asked the boy to leave. The Samoan left at about a quarter to two and Jack locked up and began to clean up, while six or seven customers finished their pool game and the last of their beers.

There was a knock on the side door, and when Jack asked who was there, he didn't recognize the voice that answered. He was afraid there might be trouble, so he went out the front door to see who was knocking, and started walking toward the alley that ran along-side the bar. At that point, he said, four Samoans tried to grab him. He ran back inside the bar and asked his friends for help. Jack and three or four other men went back outside and walked into the alley. As they did, three more Samoans ran out of the alley and toward the street in front of the bar. All the Samoans started piling into a station wagon. Jack ran to a car that was parked in the alley. It belonged to a friend who was in the bar, and he knew there was a gun on the front seat. Grabbing the gun, he ran for the street and saw the station wagon pulling away. The boys were yelling profanities and promising that they'd be back, Jack said. He called out for them to stop. When they didn't, he fired a shot "into the air."

He told police that he was afraid they might have been trying to rob him. He was frightened at the thought of what might have happened if they'd come into the bar when he was alone there, or when I was. He was afraid they might come back another night. He fired the shot only as a warning. He wanted them to stop the car and come back so he could talk to them and get to the bottom of the problem.

But that warning shot that Jack fired "into the air" had gone through a car window and into the head of the Samoan teenager who was driving. Another boy took the wheel and the car drove off. The Samoans went directly to a hospital, where the wounded boy was admitted in critical condition and taken immediately into the operating room.

After Jack was arrested, his friends at the bar decided to go back to our apartment with me and wait for more news. I was hysterical. Throughout the night we called the hospital again and again for reports on the boy. About eight o'clock in the morning, a nurse told us that he had died.

The rest of that Saturday is a blur. Somebody called a doctor, who came and gave me a sedative. I fell into a kind of restless half-sleep, but I kept waking up screaming. I struggled with the thought that Jack had actually murdered somebody. My husband had put a bullet into the brain of a young boy, a total stranger to him, a person who'd done him no harm. The thought was more than I could comprehend or cope with, so I kept telling myself over and over that the shooting was an accident. It was an accident. The police would see that, and they'd let him go.

Of course, that's not what happened. After the Samoan boy died, Jack was charged with murder. The charge was reduced later to involuntary manslaughter. Jack was tried by a judge and found guilty. About nine months after the killing, in May of 1968, he was sentenced to serve from six months to fifteen years at the California Institution for Men at Chino.

The Monday following Jack's arrest he was arraigned and bail was set. I telephoned his mother and my parents and told them what had happened. Both families were shocked and grieved, but both accepted my explanation that the shooting was accidental. Mrs. Sidote wired money for Jack's bail, and I went to the jail to get him out. Jack looked haggard and frightened that day, all of his usual bravado gone. Seeing him that way scared me even more.

His mother flew to California a few days later and stayed with us for a while. I remember very little about her visit except that she and I were beside ourselves with worry. I felt that she blamed me for what had happened. I know I blamed myself.

Life with Jack was unusually placid for the first few weeks after the shooting. I think he knew that he was going to prison and he was too afraid to be angry or violent. Instead, he seemed intent on clinging to me, as though I could protect him from punishment somehow. He wanted constant reassurance from me—reassurance that I loved him, that I'd wait for him, that there would never be any other men in my life. I promised all those things, over and over. But as he recovered from his initial shock at what had happened, and as his trial date got closer, he started once again to express his fear as rage. And of all the bad times I'd been through with Jack up until then, this period was by far the worst.

There were some beatings, but they weren't nearly as bad as the constant, frenzied sex, and what went with it. He'd keep me in bed for as often and as long as he could possibly manage, pounding furiously at me. There was no love in it. There was hardly even any sanity.

Threats also became a part of my daily life. "You'll be able to come to see me in prison every weekend, and you better not miss a day," he'd say. "I'll have guys keeping tabs on you, and I better get good reports. You better not be whoring around. If I hear you're fucking some other guy, I'll kill you!

"And if I don't kill you," he'd say, "*I'll see you rot in jail!* You remember that whore I killed? Remember those drunks in New Orleans? Remember that drunk I found on the pier and cut his cock off? I'll tell 'em you did it. You killed all of 'em. And they'll believe me. They will, Ginny! You're nothing but a whore anyway. They'll believe me."

I lived this sickness with him, numb with fear. I was terrified of him, but that was nothing compared to my terror of losing him. I didn't know how to be alone or how to make decisions anymore. I hadn't handled my own money since I got together with Jack, nor met people, nor made friends. I didn't know how to survive without him. He told me I could never love anybody else and I believed him.

I was also afraid that he might do exactly what he threatened to do. I knew his power, how persuasive he could be and how single-minded in his rage. He might say all those things he threatened to say about me—and somebody might believe him.

We never reopened the No Regrets. Neither Jack nor I could face going back there after the shooting, and within a week or two we no longer had that option anyway. The bar had been mortgaged to the hilt. We couldn't meet the payments and we lost it. A few weeks later our car was repossessed. We were deeply in debt to our parents and we were both out of work. Jack's lawyer advised him to get some kind of job before the trial because it would look better to the judge if he was employed. He went to work as a laborer in a local shipyard but I stayed home. I was too frightened, defeated, and depressed to think about working.

Then the trial came. Jack waived his right to a jury and pleaded self-defense before a judge. After finding him guilty, the judge delayed sentencing pending a probation report. Jack was to go to Chino for a presentencing diagnostic evaluation, which could last up to ninety days. In the meantime, he was continued free on bail for about a month, so he could get his affairs in order.

The intense brainwashing continued—the occasional beatings, the constant sex and threats. Every day, over and over, he warned me about what would happen to me if I didn't toe the line while he was away.

Amid all this, we tried to make plans. I would have to move out of the apartment and find a smaller, cheaper place to live. I'd have to find work. I got a job with Pacific Bell as an information operator. The pay was about seventy dollars a week, enough to get by on if I was careful. At the telephone company I met another operator, a woman named Angie, who said she had relatives with an apartment to rent in their house. They lived in the same town where I was working now, the coastal fishing village of San Pedro, south of Los Angeles. The relatives were nice Italian people. Jack had met them and approved. I moved into the small apartment in their basement.

Then Jack was gone. I hadn't come to terms yet with the actuality that he might be gone for years. There was still the possibility that the diagnostic evaluation would end with a recommendation for probation, and then he'd be free in just a few weeks and back home with me. I clung to the hope that that would happen.

Part of the evaluation was an examination by a psychiatrist. After the examination, Dr. Jack Levitt, then a psychiatric consultant at Chino, recommended that Jack be institutionalized in a facility that offered a psychiatric program. While Jack seemed repentant, the doctor said, he didn't seem to fully understand or appreciate that what he'd done was wrong. Levitt's diagnosis read: "Personality pattern disturbance, schizoid personality with acute schizophrenic reaction at the time of the offense." The report described Jack's motivation for the shooting as "markedly bizarre" and his reasoning on the night it happened as "weird."

"The sequence of events by which he reached the conclusion to fire the shot sounds very much as if he were in a schizophrenic state at the time, although the diagnosis cannot be made at present," the report went on to say. "The diagnosis of schizoid personality would seem most appropriate. Because of the seriousness of the offense and his failure to appreciate his own bad judgment, this examiner would be reluctant to release him into the community at the present time."

The report was dated May 10, 1968. Shortly after it was delivered to the court, the judge handed down the sentence of six months to fifteen years. At the time, I didn't know what to make of the psychiatric diagnosis. "Schizoid personality" meant little to me, though I hoped vaguely that some professional had been able at last to pinpoint the cause of Jack's crazy spells. Maybe that meant that while he was away Jack would get some kind of help that I'd never been able to give him. What I did understand clearly now was that he was going to be gone a long time and that I was going to have to find a way to survive alone.

It's ironic that Jack drew me to him in the first place by giving me some sense of self-worth at a time when I had very little. During the time I lived with him he stripped me of whatever thin shreds of dignity I did have left. He saw when he met me that I despised myself, and he used what he saw. I couldn't heal myself, and he systematically isolated me from anyone who might have helped me. The only assessment I had of myself was the one he gave me. He was my mirror, and this is what I saw: Stupid whore. Worthless slut. Dumb cunt.

It's ironic, too, that he used to tell me in those heady days when we first met that I was everything he'd always wanted. I was his ideal woman. By the time he left for prison, that's exactly what I was. I was a beaten, spiritless *nothing,* totally passive, almost mindless. I was Jack's ideal woman—a robot he could control completely, the ultimate testament, if the only one, to his power.

He had taken everything from me. Now, though I didn't know it yet, I was about to start the long, slow fight to take it all back.

chapter 13

My career at the telephone company was dismal and short. I started out working a morning shift, but I was never on time. Dragging myself out of bed every day was a struggle I often lost. I was threatened with probation more than once before a sympathetic supervisor decided to transfer me to the night shift. Under the new schedule I worked from two in the afternoon until nine in the evening, and that was a little better. Still, there were days when I just couldn't make it in to work.

I'd been an operator for only two or three months when I had some sort of breakdown one night on the job. I started crying hysterically and couldn't stop. That incident prompted the company to give me a mental disability leave. I'd be paid a fraction of my salary, and I'd attend group therapy sessions at a free mental health clinic. A phone company supervisor would check on me periodically to see if I was sane enough to go back to work.

The therapy sessions were useless, probably because I took no interest in them. I simply sat through them, never talking, never even thinking about what my problems were or how I might try to solve them. I didn't want to think at all.

I was in profound depression, seldom venturing out of the

apartment. I went to work, when I was working, to the therapy sessions, and to the store to buy food—mostly cat food. I had some Siamese cats, they multiplied, and soon I was living with sixteen cats in my basement apartment. The place was a mess and it didn't smell too good. The cats were my only close companions—except for Jack.

Every Saturday morning I got up early and prepared a hot meal, all the dishes Jack liked best. I packed them in a picnic hamper and drove to Chino, arriving about nine in the morning. I don't know what I'd expected a prison to look like, but Chino certainly wasn't as bad as I might have imagined. Despite fences and guard towers, it looked something like a large school, with an administration building and a lot of dormitories and work buildings. It was out in the country, and parts of the grounds were really quite lovely.

The prison bureaucracy was much more depressing than the physical facility itself. I'd stand outside the administration building in line with other visitors, sometimes for as long as three hours. Once I was inside, a guard would rummage through the picnic basket and search my purse. Then I'd be allowed out into the picnic area to find a table and wait while a visiting pass was delivered to Jack.

During our first few visits Jack looked drawn and thin, as though he were shrinking away somehow. Maybe the forced sobriety had something to do with it. Even his personality seemed flattened and subdued. He wasn't angry with me very often, but he didn't appear to be especially glad to see me, either. He wore prison-issue clothes—jeans and a work shirt that were too big for him. They were so different from the natty clothes he'd worn before, just as he was different from his usual overpowering self. I felt terribly sorry for him and I felt angry. It was a gross injustice, I thought, that he had to be in jail at all. Couldn't people see what kind of a man he really was? Now, I say to myself, Couldn't I? Why couldn't I?

The early visits fell into a routine. As soon as he joined me in the picnic area, I'd unpack the food and we'd eat. Rather, he'd eat. I had no appetite. He'd gobble the food in silence, commenting on it only if there was something he didn't like. When that was the case, I'd apologize and promise to do better next time. Then I'd repack the basket and we'd stroll around the grounds and talk. Guards were stationed here and there, but we had an amazing amount of privacy. Jack was in the minimum security part of Chino, and minimum security prisoners pretty much had the run of the grounds during visits.

We talked mostly about him, about prison life. He complained a lot—about the food, the guards, the other prisoners. Still, as the visits continued I could see that he was adapting rather well. He was settling in to being one of the boys again. Good at befriending the other inmates, Jack also caught on quickly to the knack of cultivating the guards to get little privileges for himself—extra food, more free time, choice work assignments. In short order he would become a master at manipulating the penal system.

When I visited he would ask a lot of questions about my life. Some had to do with whether I was making enough money to keep things going until he got out. (I'm trying, Jack. I'm doing the best I can.) Most had to do with where I went (almost nowhere) and whom I saw (almost no one). Visits ended in the late afternoon, and I'd drive back to San Pedro, feed the cats, and go to bed.

On the few occasions I did go out in those days, I went to the drag races with a couple who were friends of Jack's. The cars ran on a track shaped like a figure eight. The outcome of the races depended largely on which drivers proved gutsiest when meeting oncoming drivers at the central intersection.

I enjoyed the racing—the noise and speed and heat and dirt, the smell of sweat and gasoline, the shouting crowds. There was something vital about it and intensely alive. I started going down to the pits and got to know some of the drivers and pit crews. Later, I began to pitch in, in a small way, to help the mechanics modify cars for racing—stripping out the interiors, juicing up the engines. I'd learned a lot about cars from my boyfriend Fred when I was a teenager, and I still remembered enough to make myself useful.

One night one of the mechanics asked me why I didn't join the league for women drivers at the track and take a crack at driving. The idea seemed outlandish at first, but the more I thought about it, the better I liked it. Why not? I went to a few meetings and then I badgered drivers to loan me their cars. I'd end up totaling three of them in my brief but spectacular career.

The thrill of my first race was indescribable. Roaring around the track with a powerful engine under my command, I pushed the accelerator all the way to the floor and kept it there. I felt a rushing, reckless freedom and power that I hadn't felt for years. I was too excited, too exhilarated, to be afraid.

I couldn't wait to tell Jack about it the next time I saw him at Chino. I guess I should have known how angry he'd be. He told me I had to stop. I was never to set foot in one of those cars again. He said he was afraid I'd get hurt, but he didn't need to bother translating. What he meant was that he didn't like my being in a place with a lot of men around. He didn't like my doing something pleasurable without him. He didn't like my doing anything on my own.

He was punching the old familiar guilt button again and at first it almost worked. I had no business going out and enjoying myself while poor Jack was stuck in jail, I told myself. He was right. I'd have to quit. *But I didn't.* I kept going to the track and I kept driving. I finished out the racing season but just didn't tell Jack about it. I lied to him, if not outright, then certainly by omission.

I didn't realize at the time what a momentous thing I was doing, or what it might mean. I'd never disobeyed Jack before. Now I was slipping gradually but easily into deception. And the aim of the deception, whether I defined it to myself or not, was to allow me to start living more fully, with a minimum of interference from him. I was still accounting to him for my life, just as he demanded, just as I always had. But now I was avoiding trouble not through my customary total obedience, but by doing what *I* wanted to do and editing out the parts I knew he wouldn't like.

I was beginning to pull away from him. I was doing it unconsciously, but I was doing it.

My first few visits to the racetrack coincided roughly with my return to work. Money was too short to afford me the luxury of a complete breakdown, so after about a month on disability leave I pulled myself together and went back to the phone company. I might as well have stayed home. Only a week after I got into the swing of thumbing through phone books again, the Communications Workers of America went on strike. I belonged to the union, so I found myself out of work again and walking a picket line. That was another luxury I couldn't afford. I began to look for another job.

An Italian restaurant in San Pedro hired me as a cashier, but handing out pizzas over a takeout counter was no real answer to my financial difficulties. The salary was tiny, there were no tips, and I wasn't earning enough to make ends meet, much less to pay off old debts. The two thousand dollars I'd borrowed from my parents when the No Regrets was sinking preyed on my mind. They couldn't afford it, yet they'd given me the loan out of love and trust, no questions asked. I wanted badly to pay them back.

About the time my money worries were peaking, Angie's father paid me a visit at the restaurant. Angie had introduced both Jack and me to her parents, the Colettas, after she befriended me at the phone company. Mr. Coletta had sympathized with Jack and had promised to help look out for me, and now he was making good on his word. How was I doing, he wanted to know. Did I need anything? I was too desperate to be subtle. Yes, I said. I needed another job. I needed to find work somewhere where I could make some real money.

I don't think I expected any magic solution from Vincent Coletta, but I got one. "I've got a friend named Dick Masters who runs the bar and manages banquets over on the *Princess Louise*," he said. "Do you know the *Princess Louise?*"

Of course I knew the *Princess Louise*. Everybody in the area did. It was a showplace. The *Princess Louise* had been a cruise ship that sailed between Southern California and Alaska. When her sailing days were over, she was converted into a floating restaurant, docked in the port of San Pedro. Her three decks housed a huge restaurant and cocktail lounge and eight banquet rooms, the largest of which could seat eight hundred people. The *Princess Louise* served excellent food and drinks in an elegant atmosphere, so it had a large and faithful clientele. And it was so well managed that the personnel turnover was said to be almost nil. People who went to work there usually stayed. They were treated fairly and paid well and the waitresses could count on generous tips. I told Mr. Coletta that I'd appreciate anything he could do to help me get a job on the *Princess Louise*. A few days later I was interviewed by Dick Masters and hired.

Banquet cocktail waitresses didn't work full-time schedules on the *Princess Louise*, but rather came in on an assignment basis. I started off working banquets on weekends. At first, I had no real idea what I was doing. For all my work experience in bars, I'd never worked in a place that demanded any standard of professionalism from cocktail waitresses. All I'd ever had to know was how to write down orders on a slip of paper, hand the paper to a bartender, deliver the drinks, and pick up the cash. On the *Princess Louise*, we never wrote anything down. We had to memorize orders according to a complicated system.

I found myself learning pretty fast, and I enjoyed my own progress. I think I may still hold the record for the longest order, having once memorized, ordered, and served forty-four cocktails without a mistake. Dick Masters began complimenting my work and adding to my banquet assignments. Before long I was also working some club meetings during the week, as well as a few shifts in the main bar.

The money seemed almost too good to be true. I could take home a hundred dollars in one night in tips alone. That meant that, working only two or three nights on the ship, I was earning more than twice as much as I had working full-time at the phone company or the pizzeria.

But money wasn't the only attraction the job held for me, or even the main one. Working on the *Princess Louise* was like being part of a family. I started making friends there, and they were *my* friends, not Jack's, not people who tolerated me because I was his wife or, like Becky and Morton, people I was allowed to be with because they'd passed his inspection. For the first time in years there were women to talk to and confide in.

Nevertheless, the most important thing in my life was still Jack. Nothing interfered with the weekly visits to Chino, even though those visits were getting more and more unpleasant. Jack was becoming abusive again, as well as suspicious. He didn't like my working at the *Princess Louise* at all. He said I was just "hanging out with a bunch of whores and pimps" and that I should go back to the phone company. I didn't understand it and I couldn't believe it. I was doing so well and making so much money that he should be happy for me, for both of us. When he got out, I'd be able to afford to give him all the time he needed to find the right career for himself. He could start his own business or maybe buy another bar. We could buy a house.

But all my arguments about the advantages of my working on the ship only made him more irritable. His dissatisfaction with me seemed to grow in direct proportion to my increasing success. I'd better not get some big idea that I could make it without him, he said. I'd better not be that dumb. Then there were the accusations about "whoring around." I couldn't be doing so well on my own, he said. Some guy had to be keeping me, maybe more than one guy. During several visits he worked himself into rages with such fantasies, and nothing I could say would calm him down.

He started hitting me again. He'd drag me around corners, into buildings—anywhere out of sight of the guards—and punch me a couple of times. Nothing that would show or get him into trouble, just enough to remind me who was boss, to punctuate the new round of threats. He'd kill me if he caught me fucking around, he said. He'd see me rot in jail.

Late in 1968, my mother and father came to California to visit and went with me on one of the trips to Chino. Jack and I went for a walk by ourselves that day, there was an argument, and he lost control and hit me in the face. My parents saw the marks.

Daddy didn't mention what had happened until we were driving home. When he did bring it up, I could feel his sadness in the very simplicity of his words. "Leave him, Ginny," he said. "Come home."

I started to cry. In that moment, the temptation was so strong just to throw over the whole thing, to forget that I was ever married to Jack Sidote or even knew him, to accept the offer of refuge and rest. But I didn't.

"I can't leave, Daddy," I said. "I love him. I have to stand by him. He's not really like what you saw today. It's just that his life is so awful right now."

I was silent for the rest of the trip. I was trying to figure out what was going on in Jack's mind. What was wrong with him? Why was he so angry?

Now I know what the experts say: that in a battering relationship, dependency is a two-way street. The woman is more obviously dependent, but the man's dependency is just as real. Ironically, the woman he tortures is also the one who holds him together emotionally. He's so insecure that his control over her is the only sure validation of his own worth. That's why he's so jealous and possessive and seems to love her the most right after he's hurt her. It may be the sickest kind of love, but there it is.

Jack was always a shrewd guy. I think he realized, long before I knew it myself, that he was losing his hold on me.

chapter 14

I remember the months Jack was in prison as a time when I counted days. In the beginning, I counted the days because I couldn't wait to have him home again. I was lonely and incomplete without him. Toward the end of his sentence I still counted the days, but for a different reason. I dreaded the day he'd be free. I'd begun to hate him.

It's hard to say exactly when I realized I was changing. There was no sudden leap from point A to point B. It was a gradual thing, and it had less to do with my feelings about Jack than with my feelings about myself. With him gone, I started recovering some sense of who I was. And the more I learned to like myself, the less it was possible to love him. The stronger I got, the less I feared him. It was a slow process, but somewhere along the line I started to see Jack as he really was, and I despised what I saw.

If I had to pinpoint a single moment when I recognized that I was changing, it would be the night we gave the banquet on the *Princess Louise*. My two best friends at the time were young women named Clara and Bobbie, who worked with me as cocktail waitresses on the ship. One day we got to talking about how few people we knew among the hundreds in the area who worked in nice restaurants in the beach communities near Los Angeles. We decided to throw a party, selling tickets to pay for it. We'd invite all the waiters and waitresses and chefs and maître d's to a banquet on the *Princess Louise* so that everyone could meet. The ship's management gave us enthusiastic backing and we started making plans. This would be no simple get-together but a dinner and dance with all the trimmings. We made up invitations and worked on decorations. We solicited door prizes from other restaurants, planned a menu, and hired a band. I ended up coordinating most of it.

When the big night arrived, about five hundred people showed up. The ships's main banquet room was filled with people who ate, drank, danced, and laughed. Nobody went home early. By any standard, the evening was a great success.

Toward the end of the evening, Dick Masters went to the microphone and asked for everybody's attention. He thanked the people who'd worked on the party, and then he called Clara and Bobbie and me to stand beside him at the microphone. He thanked us individually, me last of all.

It was such a special moment. I stood there, with bright lights shining on me, and I could see hundreds of people smiling and applauding. But I couldn't hear them. I couldn't hear any more of what Dick was saying. All my thoughts were turned inward: I'd tried something on my own, for once, and it had worked. "Ginny Sidote," Dick had said when he thanked me. Sidote? That sounded wrong, somehow. That wasn't who I really was. I was another person, somebody in my own right. I didn't have to be a weak, beaten-down slave who depended on someone else for my very survival. I was not just existing anymore. I was on my own and I had survived!

When I saw Jack at Chino the following Saturday, I told him about the party. I had the silly notion that he might be proud of me. He wasn't, of course. He ranted again about how I was wasting my time with nobodies, with pimps and whores, doing things I had no business doing. Listening to him, another novel thought occurred to me: Jack was full of shit. It was an astonishing thought, but I let myself pursue it. He was talking about my friends. Maybe they weren't his kind of high rollers, but they weren't pimps and whores, either. They were decent, caring, hard-working people, and I liked them. He didn't even know them. What right did he have to put them down? What right did he have to put *me* down? I sat there and watched him raving, and I felt a peculiar detachment, as though I were watching a monkey in a zoo. You bastard, I thought. You crazy bastard.

So much was happening in my life. I'd moved, for one thing. I was beginning to feel stifled by the kind but constant attention I got from the family whose house I lived in. I wanted more privacy. So I found new homes for my tribe of cats and moved into a shared rented house in Redondo Beach.

At work, things were getting better all the time. Dick was giving me new responsibilities, and the more I took on, the more confident I became. By now I was helping to train new waitresses on the ship, and I was learning more about the business end of running a restaurant. Even on days when I had no work assignments, I often spent time on the *Princess Louise.* I volunteered to help in the banquet office, fascinated by all the work that went into producing a banquet, from the day it was booked to the day it was served. I wanted to know more about marketing and promotion and about food and wine. A new world was opening up for me, and I was eager for it.

But the visits to Chino grew steadily worse. There were no good ones anymore, no intermissions between rounds. There was only the endless battle. It seemed as though my life away from Jack had become a wonderful parade, with bright balloons and brass bands. The parade marched for six days out of every seven. But on that one day I spent at Chino, the parade vanished and the music stopped. Where once I'd lived through the week just to see Jack on the weekend, now I dreaded Saturdays. The time eventually came when I stopped cooking a big meal each and every weekend. Sometimes I'd just stop along the way and buy cold cuts instead. And sometimes I showed up late.

When I couldn't face going there alone, I'd ask Clara to go with me, and good friend that she was, she always said yes. She went, even though she couldn't stand Jack and he couldn't stand her. She knew, just as Becky had known months before, what Jack was doing to me. But again, I couldn't bring myself to talk to her about the situation in any detail, and when she'd ask me about leaving Jack, I'd give her the same old answers: Jack had left everything to be with me. Now I had to stick by him. I couldn't leave him when he was down. I had to be there for him.

But what I couldn't yet say to her, I was beginning to admit to myself. It was over. Maybe I couldn't leave him while he was in prison, but I would leave him. It was just a matter of time. I could never go back to the ugliness of life with Jack Sidote. I could never again let a man treat me the way he did.

In the summer of 1969, Clara and I were talking about getting a place to live together. One night after apartment-hunting we went to the movies and stopped off afterward for a drink at the *Princess Louise.* Dick Masters joined us. He was glad we'd come by, he said, because a new manager had just come on board, and Dick wanted us to meet him.

He pointed to a man standing across the room on the ship's starboard side, talking to someone at the hostess station. He was tall, at least six feet, and very slim, with dark, wavy brown hair and a small mustache. Even from a distance, I could see that his clothes fit him with hand-tailored precision.

He was handsome, but he was more than that. There was something about the way he stood, the angle at which he held his head, the way he walked toward our table. Heads turned. Eyes followed him. He had great presence, and . . . what was the word? Elegance? Yes, that was it. This guy, whoever he was, certainly had elegance.

He glided up to the table and said good evening. His voice sounded funny and it took me a minute to realize that I was hearing a crisp British accent. Dick got to his feet to make the introductions.

"Ladies," he said, "I want you to meet the new restaurant manager of the *Princess Louise,* Raymond Foat."

Foat talked with us awhile, exchanging pleasantries. He was as suave and charming as he looked, and I didn't like him at all.

"Isn't he good-looking?" Clara asked after he left.

"He's okay," I said.

I was slow to see it, but Ray Foat was much more than okay. At the time we met, my frame of reference hadn't expanded enough for me to appreciate him. The unfortunate view I'd grown up with was that "man" meant macho. A real man was hard and tough and commanding. He advertised his power. He was hip and streetwise and at least a little rough around the edges. He sweated and swore. Real men weren't gentle and polite and considerate. They didn't have perfectly barbered hair and manicured nails. They didn't have odd, prissy accents. Real men didn't charm women, they ruled them. Ray Foat just wasn't my type.

I didn't warm to him much in the weeks that followed, though everybody else on the ship seemed to love him. I found everything about him false and slick. I used to watch with amusement the elaborate, gallant way he greeted women customers coming on board.

He'd bow to kiss the hand of some matron: "You must tell that husband of yours that he's keeping you away from us far too much. I have to insist that from now on you visit us at *least* once a week."

The woman would float off in a happy fog, and Ray would repeat the performance, with some variations, for the next one in line. I'd like to see him try that routine in Brooklyn, I thought to myself. Good lord, what a phony.

In fact, there was nothing phony about him. Ray Foat was a man who genuinely loved women. He understood them, respected them, valued them, found them fascinating. He liked to make them feel good about themselves, and he was terrific at it because it came naturally to him. He could find something beautiful in the plainest woman and something interesting in the dullest. He was smooth, polished to a high sheen. But all that charm wasn't forced. It was just Ray.

He was married, but separated and in the process of getting a divorce. Sensitive as I was to marital difficulties, even I started feeling a little sorry for him after a while, but I had troubles of my own to focus on.

If I ignored Ray, it could never be said that he ignored me. He seemed to look for excuses to seek me out. He asked for my opinions on all sorts of little things having to do with the ship—opinions I knew he didn't need, but which he listened to with respectful attention. I often found him standing on the *Princess Louise*'s deck watching as I came to work, as though he'd been waiting for me. Sometimes he'd make a joke of piping me aboard. He'd get on the public address system that boomed all over the ship and say, "Good evening, Ginny. Welcome to the *Princess Louise.*" On nights when Clara and Bobbie and I left the ship to have dinner somewhere else, he had a way of finding out where we were going. When we got there, we'd find a special bottle of wine waiting, compliments of Ray.

His attentions were never heavy, but they were persistent. Not liking him was getting to be hard labor. He seemed to be a nice person, and after all, you couldn't blame a guy for his accent. Of course he sounded British. He *was* British.

And so, in time, we got to be friends. We spent time together, talking. We even cried a little on each other's shoulder. He came to understand that my marriage was in trouble, though I never told him exactly why, and he talked to me about his problems with his wife. He'd recently moved into an apartment of his own.

Ray knew Clara and I were looking for an apartment, and he

told us about a building in his own block. The apartments were beautiful, and Clara and I signed a lease. Ray helped me move and even kept a couple of boxes of my belongings in his place until Clara and I could get things arranged.

When I remarked to Clara on how thoughtful he was being, she said, "Certainly he's thoughtful. Can't you see that he's falling in love with you?"

I laughed it off. His life was almost as messed up as mine. Nobody was falling in love with anybody. Who had the energy? Who had the time?

One night Clara and I were working late at a banquet when we got a phone call from Ray. We had to come to his apartment as soon as we finished work, he said. Something terrible had happened.

We got there to find that someone who was a fine hand with a razor had broken in. Methodically, completely, and very neatly, the intruder had destroyed every piece of clothing in the apartment. His underwear had been taken out of its drawer, the crotches were cut out of every piece, and then each one was folded and put it back in place. His suit jackets had been slit up the inside of the sleeves and up the back and were once again hanging in his closet. The pants had been sliced along the inside seams of the legs. The toes were cut out of all his socks. Even his handkerchiefs had big holes in them. The destruction was absolute, but you had to look hard to see it. At first glance, everything in the apartment seemed perfectly normal— except for the smell. Some of his clothes, as well as my two boxes of odds and ends, had been drenched with chlorine. The whole apartment reeked of it. And on closer inspection, I found that some of Jack's letters to me were missing from one of my boxes, letters that had his return address on the envelopes. At the time, I couldn't understand why anybody would take them.

It was hard not to admire the vandal's thoroughness. It was also hard not to laugh. But Ray looked so sad and bewildered, so pathetic and devastated by it all, that my heart went out to him. I guess it was that night that I began to love him. On my next trip to Chino, I found Jack in a terrible rage. Ray's wife had written to him. She'd said that her husband and his wife were having an affair, and Jack must put a stop to it.

It wasn't true, and I denied it. No, I wasn't fucking my boss. I wasn't fucking anybody, for God's sake. I wasn't. I hadn't. I wouldn't. No, no, no, no, no . . .

As always, the denials were useless. Jack would just have to calm down in his own good time—or not, for all I cared by then. I was sure now that the only thing I wanted from him was to be rid of him. I was just as sure of that as I was sure that I loved Ray Foat. Ray's wife had been less wrong than premature in her accusations. Before another month had passed, we were, in fact, having an affair.

Now it was 1970. Jack had been gone for almost two years and would be getting out of jail soon. Though I tried not to think about it, I had to decide how I was going to handle him, what I was going to tell him, *when* I was going to tell him. It seemed to me that until he was out of jail and had had some chance to remake his own life, I was committed to keeping up at least the pretense of a marriage.

I felt guilty about sleeping with Ray. Jack was still my husband, he was in jail, and I was cheating on him, breaking the rules. At the same time, it felt *right* for Ray and me to be together, better than anything ever had in my life.

Our relationship was full of tenderness, courtesy, respect, and caring. I remember that when he asked me, as he often did, how I felt about one thing or another, I'd be amazed. No man had ever cared how I felt or been interested in my thoughts. I'd been a child in my first marriage and not much more than a confused adolescent with Jack. But Ray and I loved each other the way adults do, or the way they should. With Ray I grew up.

Because of who *he* was, Ray was able to give me a special gift, one I treasured in those days. To him, I was a *lady*. With Jack I was always a whore. I could never get past being a whore. I could have worked for years to earn my lady stripes and still I would have been a whore. But Ray Foat treated me like a lady from the night we met. Not a convict's wife, not some lowlife from nowhere. A lady. He treated me that way for all the years we were together, and I think he still thinks of me that way today. I had pulled myself out of the slime of my marriage to Jack before I ever met Ray. I climbed the mountain without him. But being able to see myself the way Ray saw me may well have been what restored me.

I spent as much time with him as I possibly could. But on Saturdays I still went to Chino. In more than two years, I never missed a week.

Ray and I had been lovers only three or four months when, for the time being, the affair ended. A new floating restaurant, the *Princess Louise II,* was opening in Vancouver and Ray was going to manage it. It hurt to see him go, but not as much as it might have. We knew we'd be together again, though we never talked about it. Either he'd come back to California, or I'd join him in Canada. His divorce was about to be final. Now it was up to me to clear up my own situation. It was just a matter of working out the details.

Early in July, when Ray had been gone for about a month, Jack became eligible for a work-release program. Though he wouldn't be paroled until August, he was able to leave Chino every morning to go to work at the body shop owned by a friend of his named Bart. Bart was lenient about Jack's work schedule and so, most mornings, Jack had an hour or more to spend with me. He also got occasional passes to stay home for the weekend.

On his first weekend pass, we went to lunch at a beautiful restaurant. I picked the place, ordered the food, chose the wine, hoping to pamper him into a good mood, keep him calm, buy time —until August. Halfway through the meal, I knew I'd never be able to wait that long. Jack complained about everything. The service was crummy and the food was slop. The menu wasn't even in English. The wine was too expensive.

I was sick with disgust. Was it possible that I'd never really seen him before? Could I actually have loved this man? Could I really have been a slave to him for five years? Awful as it was, I stretched the meal for as long as I could. I was terrified of being alone with him. He'd want to go to bed with me, and I didn't think I could stand it.

That night, and the next night, and the dozen or so mornings and nights that followed, were pure hell. I tried to hide the revulsion I felt for him, but I couldn't. He knew and he was in a frenzy, bounding back and forth between wild extremes. Sometimes he was gentler with me than he'd ever been. I'd gone without a man for two years, he said. It was hard for me to readjust. He could see how that was. At other times he beat me and took me by force again and again.

There were times when I told him I was leaving, but he didn't believe me. Telling him brought on beatings so savage that I was in mortal terror. Could I ever muster the courage to *make* him believe me? And what would he do when I did?

The day finally came when I found out.

"You've got to go and make a life for yourself," I told him. "I can't live with your sickness anymore. I'm leaving."

He knew that this time I meant it and he began to scream. "You're never going to leave me! You're never going to leave me! If you ever leave me, I'll kill you or I'll see you rot in jail. . . ."

He brought up all the old horrors, all the old threats.

"Jack," I said, "I'm going."

That's when he tried to kill me.

He started punching me, in the face, in the body, everywhere. I could feel my own blood slick across my face. Then I was on the floor and he was kicking me, over and over, as hard as he could. He lifted me up and threw me across the bed and whipped me with his belt. Then he climbed on top of me, still screaming. He hadn't stopped screaming. I felt his hands close around my throat. I knew, then, that this time he didn't just mean to hurt me. He meant to kill me.

I blacked out, I don't know for how long. The next thing I knew Clara was there, screaming, shouting at Jack to get out. And Jack was yelling, "I'm coming back tomorrow, and that whore better be here. I'm gonna kill her! I'm gonna kill her!"

Then Jack was gone. Clara was still there. She said I had to see a doctor. I was hurt. No, I said, I had to get out of town. That maniac was going to come back sooner or later.

Clara cleaned me up as best she could and helped me dress. I was hurt, but nothing seemed to be broken. I was well enough to travel, and I was going home. Clara called my parents. Then she called her boyfriend John and the two of them took me to the airport and put me on a plane for New York.

My father met the plane. He took one look at me and burst into tears. Then he put out his arms and hugged me to him, and I couldn't stifle a scream of pain. Every part of me hurt. I couldn't stand to be touched.

Daddy drove me home to New Paltz, and that night I slept in my own room, in my own bed, three thousand miles away from Jack Sidote. I was safe. The ugliest part of my life was finally over.

chapter 15

I stayed in New Paltz six weeks. It was long enough for the bruises to fade, at least the ones that showed. It was a time of recuperation and renewal for me, and of soul-searching and some long-overdue self-assessment.

I remember thinking how different this homecoming was from the time I returned to my parents' house after having the baby. I was confused and aimless and very immature then, caught up in old mistakes, looking outside myself for answers, waiting for some man to rescue me, take charge of my life, solve my problems. Now I knew better, in my head if not yet entirely in my heart. Some part of me may still have wanted the prince to come, but I didn't expect him and I certainly wasn't going to sit by the hearth and wait for him to show up—especially since I strongly suspected that he was a fraud. If I was disillusioned, I was also smarter and tougher for the experiences I'd had. I was determined to go forward and make something of my life, on my own if need be.

This homecoming I had no secret to keep and my mother and father had no questions they were afraid to ask. What had happened to me was there on my face for anyone to see. The sight of it brought out all their protectiveness, of course; to them I would always be a daughter who needed protecting. But now I was also something of an adult among equals, a woman who'd gone through some bad times and come out more or less intact. So there was a new honesty and openness among the three of us, and a closeness I'd never felt before. This time I had no guilt to shoulder, and my parents had no blame to cast. The disintegration of this marriage was *not my fault.* They saw it that way, and even I began to get a fragile grasp on this novel idea. I'd left Jack Sidote not because I couldn't make a marriage work, but because no woman should have to stay with a man who needed to hurt, or even to kill, to prove himself.

I wish I'd spent more time back then thinking about that question of guilt. If I had, maybe I could have forgiven myself, not for leaving Jack, but for having been with him at all, for having permitted my own degradation. I might have allowed the wounds inside, the ones that didn't show, a chance to heal. But instead of confronting them I simply turned away from their ugliness. It was enough that every morning I looked into the mirror at my swollen cheek and lips, my black eye, the purple ring of bruises around my throat. They were graphic reminders of a life I meant to put behind me once and for all. I had all the pain I could handle without looking inside for more.

I turned to practical matters. The first thing I had to do was to get Jack completely out of my life. I wanted a divorce, certainly, but even more urgently I had to make sure that he wouldn't come after me as soon as he got out of jail. He'd tried to kill me once. I was convinced he'd try again, especially after I asked for a divorce.

Shortly after I got home, while all the bruises were still fresh, my mother and father suggested that the three of us visit Jack's parents. If they saw what he'd done to me, maybe they'd see that it was in their son's best interest to stay away from me and concentrate on rebuilding his own life. I didn't think the visit would do any good. I'd always felt that the Sidotes didn't like me, that they blamed me for Jack's leaving New Paltz in the first place and for all the problems that followed. But I was scared enough to try anything.

It was a short, unfriendly visit. The Sidotes were obviously shocked by the way I looked, but the more we tried to explain what had happened, the more hostile and defensive they became. How did they know it was Jack who'd beaten me up? Maybe somebody else did it. And if it was Jack, I must have done something really awful to deserve it.

A few days later, I spoke to Jack on the telephone. The conversation started off politely enough before degenerating into name-calling and threats. He'd kill me, he said. He'd kill my whole family if I tried to get out of the marriage. I was shaking so badly I could hardly hold the telephone, terrified not so much by the threats, which were not new, as by hearing his voice again. His release from jail was only days away. I had to stay in control of myself and concentrate on two objectives: keep Jack calm for the time being, and arrange things so that there were thousands of miles between us.

I wanted to put our marriage back together, I told him, counting on his egotism to make him believe such a lie. The best hope for us in the long run was to start fresh, I said. We should get a divorce. It was the only way to wipe out all our past troubles and start over. He should have his parole transferred from California to New York. That way we could see each other on old, familiar ground and work toward getting back together.

It sounded crazy even to me, but I prayed Jack would buy it. I didn't know yet where I'd settle permanently, but I knew it wouldn't be New York. If I went back to my job in California, I didn't want him there. Getting him back on the East Coast seemed to be the best way to keep my options open. Talking about divorce made him furious, but I'd expected that. Maybe when he calmed down he'd think it over and put in for the parole transfer. In any case, there was nothing more I could do for the moment.

Where to go and what to do were the next items on my agenda. If Jack returned to New York I could go back to Southern California. I had good friends there, a place to live, and a job on the *Princess Louise* that offered a reasonably secure future and a good living. But I wasn't thinking just in terms of a job anymore. I didn't want to be a cocktail waitress all my life. I wanted a career. Volunteering in the ship's banquet office had taught me a lot about the food and beverage business, and Ray had helped me learn even more. I felt I had most of the skills I needed to move into management, and what I didn't know I could learn. I wanted a chance to advance, and that chance wasn't likely to come along on the *Princess Louise.* There were no openings.

Ray and I had already talked about my going to Canada to be with him and perhaps work on the *Princess Louise II.* I had reservations about that plan because I thought it could be a real hindrance to Ray. He was the top executive of the *Princess Louise II* and hobnobbed with the ship's owners. Most of them were monied, powerful Canadians, socially prominent and socially conservative. What would they make of Ray's living with his girl friend?

For that matter, what would I make of it? Ray and I loved each other, but we were both just out of disastrous marriages and wary of rushing into new commitments. My years with Jack had undermined all my ideas about marriage. I wanted to be with Ray but I wasn't ready for any binding arrangement, and I was afraid that going to Vancouver might force me into one. From a practical standpoint, going there meant living with Ray, at least at the beginning.

After a month or more of letters and phone calls back and forth, Ray and I decided to leave it at this: I'd fly to Vancouver in mid-September for the grand opening of the *Princess Louise II.* I'd stay with Ray for a while, long enough to see how I liked the city, the restaurant—and the living arrangements. If I decided to stay I'd look for work there. The job of catering and banquet manager on the ship was still open, and Ray would be glad to recommend me for it.

Going to Canada was one of the better decisions of my life, as it turned out, at least in terms of who I was and what I wanted at the time. I was changing, but not altogether changed. For the developing part of me, determined to make it on my own, Canada opened up a new and promising career. And for the old part of me that no amount of bitter experience had been able to kill altogether, the part that still stubbornly hoped for Cinderella solutions, Ray seemed a viable prince and Vancouver looked remarkably like a fairy-tale kingdom.

The city was set in a flat basin beside the Pacific Ocean. It was fresh and clean, charming in an Old World way, cosmopolitan, but with a sort of genteel English colonial air. I never got tired of exploring it, and Ray was a wonderful guide. We might go for a walk in the lovely seaside park near his apartment and watch the cricket players, and Ray would explain the game to me. We'd walk down Robeson Street, an avenue lined with little shops selling food delicacies from all over the world. Ray would tell me about the exotic items I was seeing for the first time, and we might buy a few and take them home to sample. Sometimes we'd borrow a boat and go for a day's outing up the British Columbian coastline, where towering mountains covered with evergreens rose straight up out of the blue ocean. Or we'd ride the ferries that ran from the city to the Vancouver islands. We'd stand on the deck in the clean salt air, holding hands, talking about how nice it would be to live on an island one day.

It was all very romantic and there were so many things to see and learn, so much room to grow. There seemed to be no limits. I could come and go as I pleased, with Ray or alone. I never had to explain to anybody; nobody was watching me, timing me, threatening me, hurting me. Living this new way, I found it easy to forget that Jack Sidote had ever existed. At least, it was easy to push him farther and farther out of my conscious thoughts.

Ray made it even easier because he was so different from Jack. As gentle and considerate as I'd remembered him, Ray was always supportive and glad to be with me. "Princess," he called me, and he treated me like one. He had a way of teaching me things without ever condescending to me or laughing at me. He didn't restrict my freedom; he was part of it.

Wonderful as he was, wonderful as this new life was, it wasn't easy for me to trust again, to believe it would last or even that it was entirely real. The few times we argued, if Ray raised his voice I'd find myself flinching, waiting for a blow to come. If I stayed a long time at the laundromat or the supermarket, I might have a minute of panic before I remembered that no, nothing bad was going to happen when I got home. A phantom followed me. It was no bigger or more substantial than a wisp of dust in the corner of a room, but it was there, and I watched for it. A tone of voice, a violent scene on television, a snatch of some old song, and I'd see it—just for an instant and only from the corner of my eye, but it could still make me cringe.

The grand opening of the *Princess Louise II* was quite a social event. A large delegation of city officials attended, along with local sports and media celebrities and leaders of Vancouver society. The party was impressive, from the guest list to the ice sculptures to the hors d'oeuvres. And the ship itself was lovely. She was a three-deck cruise ship, a little older than the first *Princess Louise* and not quite so big, but just as elegant. I liked her, I liked her staff and crew, and I liked the owners and their wives. I decided almost at once that I wanted to work there.

Getting the job went quite smoothly. I got a government work card. Ray talked to the owners, and I was interviewed and hired. Within a month after my arrival in Vancouver, I was the new banquet and catering manager of the *Princess Louise II.* I had my own office toward the bow of the ship, and clients would meet with me there to outline their needs and ideas. I'd show them our facilities, make suggestions about food and wines, flowers and music, the general ambience of the party. Once the banquet was sold I'd work with the ship's chef and other department heads, hire the band or other entertainment, call the florist, and do whatever else was needed to stage the event. The night of the banquet it was my job to be there and make sure everything went as planned.

It was challenging work, and at first I made my share of mistakes, most of them from an excess of enthusiasm. If a client said he wanted a floor show of waltzing St. Bernards, I tended to say sure, fine, and worry later about how to make the dogs dance. It wasn't uncommon for me to meet with the chef, the bar manager, and Ray, the ship's manager, and say something like, "The good news is that I've booked a banquet for eight hundred people. The bad news is that we don't have a room big enough to hold it." Fortunately, my colleagues were usually more amused than angry, and they always bailed me out. I think they liked me and knew I was trying to do a good job. Besides, I lived with the boss. I can't deny that helped.

As time went on and I mastered the basics of the job, I started promoting the ship's banquet business instead of waiting for it to come to me. I got a directory listing all the major civic clubs in the city—the Kiwanis, Rotary, Lions, Optimists, and so on—and checked into where they held their luncheon and dinner meetings. I put together packages of information about the ship and mailed one to each club, then followed up with phone calls to appropriate club members. When I saw how successful this tactic was, I used it with corporations that held regular lunch and dinner meetings. Business got steadily better. Ray was as proud of me as a doting father, and I was pretty proud of myself.

Working on the ship carried with it a certain life-style, more because of Ray's position than mine. We were expected to socialize with the ship's owners, their families and friends, and that meant that we moved in some pretty lofty social circles.

The ship's owners also owned mines, lumber mills, land, sports franchises. Ray and I found ourselves watching football games from a special box. We went to yachting parties and on ski trips. All the owners belonged to an ancient, exclusive golf club in West Vancouver, and Ray, a good golfer, was often invited there to round out a foursome. We were invited to dinners and parties there, and to parties at a number of West Vancouver mansions.

I was born to none of this, of course, but I found myself fitting in surprisingly well. I got to be friendly with the women in this favored circle. I went to the same hairdresser they did, shopped where they did, lunched where they did. After a time I dressed, spoke, and acted very much the way they did.

It wasn't that Ray and I were social peers of these people. We weren't and we knew it. They were lords of the manor. Ray was more on the order of a faithful retainer, and I was the faithful retainer's faithful retainer. We might go to the golf club often, but we would never have been invited to join, nor could we have afforded to. We were asked to lavish, seated dinners at the mansions, but seldom to small, intimate gatherings. Ray was, after all, an employee—even if a particularly handsome, presentable, and charming employee. He was in much the same category as the football coach, the hockey coach, some star players, and maybe a favored factory manager or two. Still, we enjoyed the whirl.

We did, however, present a problem to our fashionable friends. We weren't married. We were the only live-in couple in the clique, and our domestic arrangement didn't go over especially well. It wasn't, I believe, a question of moral disapproval. It was just that there was a certain formality among these people, and we constituted a socially awkward situation. They didn't know quite what to do with us. We'd get invitations addressed to "Mr. Raymond Foat (and Ginny)." Hostesses would stumble over introductions: "This is Raymond Foat and his, uh . . . friend, Ginny." (Bad enough to have to explain who this employee is, let alone the girl friend, for heaven's sake. Why does it have to be "Mr. Peon and his peon" when "Mr. and Mrs. Peon" would be so much more sensible?)

Ray, especially, hated this sort of thing. The son of a working-class family, he'd left home at sixteen to go to sea, working his way up on British merchant vessels from mess boy to cabin boy to steward before joining Cunard Lines and traveling the world in style. He had gained his considerable polish the hard way. He knew and respected social protocol, and he loved being accepted. The awkwardness of our situation went very much against his grain. I didn't like it much either.

We started talking about marriage. It was possible now, if we wanted it. My parents had forwarded to me an interlocutory decree of divorce from the State of California. Jack had filed for divorce as soon as he got out of jail, and he'd gotten his parole transferred from California to New York, as I'd suggested. When he got home, it was to find me gone. It wasn't until years later that I got some indication of how furious he was at the time. My parents told me that he wrote them a letter, threatening again to kill me, promising to get even if it was the last thing he ever did. They, of course, did not tell him my whereabouts.

In any case, Ray and I now were free to marry—to conform to

the social pressure, of course, but also because we both were still fairly conservative: Ray with a certain British primness and I with my Italian Catholic upbringing. Living together wasn't quite right. Besides, if we got married we could have children. We'd talked often about how much we both wanted that.

And so, Ray proposed and I accepted, and in May of 1971 we were married aboard a yacht off the coast of British Columbia. The wedding was spectacular.

chapter 16

Since Margaret Sinclair married Pierre Trudeau in Vancouver a couple of months before Ray and I got married, our wedding was easily outclassed as the season's most socially significant event. But no one could say we were upstaged for style. The Trudeau wedding was a small family affair, simple and more or less secret. Ours was all glitz and pure Hollywood.

We started off mildly enough by getting engaged in the old fashioned way. Ray gave me a ring that we'd had made up by a prominent Vancouver jewelry designer. Wedding rings, his and hers, were designed to match. As soon as word of the engagement got around, congratulations poured in from our friends, whose relief was obvious. At last, no more problems with introductions or invitations. Everyone was delighted and anxious to help. One couple threw a big wedding shower for us and we were deluged with expensive gifts—crystal, silver, china. One of the owners of the *Princess Louise II* offered to let us have the wedding on his sixty-foot yacht. That sounded perfect and we began making elaborate plans.

We juggled the guest list to keep it small enough for everyone to fit comfortably on the boat, yet big enough to cover our social obligations. We ended up with twenty-five names, and I noted with satisfaction that some of them were the names that appeared in the society columns. Clara would come up from California to be my maid of honor.

I designed my wedding dress myself, with some help from friends. It was pale blue crepe lined with white satin and sewn with seed pearls. The dress would have been fairly traditional except for the fact that its long skirt was split all the way up the front to display hot pants underneath. Hot pants were very "in" at the time, if not necessarily for wedding gowns, and I thought the dress was the last word in *haute couture,* so much so that I had a miniature of it made to go on the bride doll that stood beside the groom doll on the wedding cake.

My makeup for the wedding would be done by a woman from an exclusive West Vancouver salon. The champagne, liquor, and gourmet hors d'oeuvres would be catered by the chef from the *Princess Louise.* Looking back, I guess the whole affair was pretentious and self-indulgent, not to say downright decadent. On the other hand, it was the best party I ever went to, before or since.

May seventeenth, my wedding day, dawned warm and clear. The guests, the food, and the drinks were loaded aboard, and I swept onto the main deck to the strains of the "Trumpet Voluntary," featured at Queen Elizabeth's coronation. Ray had thought that would be fitting for his princess. When it came time in the Protestant service for Ray and me to sign the marriage registry, the tape was of Simon and Garfunkel's "Bridge Over Troubled Waters." The song meant a lot to us. Ray and I had helped each other through some bad times, and our love was based on our friendship, the closeness and sympathy that grew out of shared difficulties.

By the time we were to leave the yacht for our honeymoon, the music was considerably less sentimental. We made our exit to Lynn Anderson singing "I Never Promised You a Rose Garden." It was my own particular selection, though I had no idea how prophetic it would turn out to be. I chose it mostly as a cute bit of comic relief, something to pick up the mood of the party for the return cruise and give our friends a laugh. But I don't think that's all I meant.

There on that sleek yacht, at my elegant wedding, I couldn't stop the short, sharp stabs of memory of another wedding day, spent in a cheap motel room watching football games on television. Mingling with our chic friends, I could still see myself standing in the visitor's line at Chino, that and other things, much worse things. About to launch a life with my gentle, handsome, wonderful new husband, I knew how bad things could be with a man and how wrong a marriage could go. Any marriage, even this one. Nobody with any sense should expect a rose garden.

Still, I never would have married Ray had I not thought that we had a very good chance to make it. I was banking on the fact that he was a very different from the men I'd known before, and especially different from Jack. What I failed to realize or fully consider at the time was how different a woman I was becoming from the one I'd been. Not that I could call myself "liberated" in any sense. I wouldn't even have known what the word meant then. I still defined myself in terms of a man, and I didn't see anything wrong with that. I deferred to Ray, catered to his whims, relied on his guidance, accepted his judgments. I adopted his interests and cultivated his friends. I kept myself attractive and our apartment neat for him. I did all the little "womanly" things that I assumed were required to make his life comfortable and happy. And he *was* happy. This deferential, submissive woman was the one he'd fallen in love with and married. For me, the deference was old habit, dating back not only to Jack but well beyond him, back to watching Grandma Ida cater to the men in the family.

But for all the outward deference, I really wasn't that woman anymore. I'd learned that men, the users, could also be used. I could use a man to establish myself. I could take what he gave me, use what he taught me, for my own self-improvement, my own welfare, and my own future. I could make sure that no matter what happened to him or to the marriage, I would survive. This attitude was brand-new to me. With my first two husbands I'd always worked toward the common goal and the mutual good, as defined by the man. The unit, the marriage, came first. Now I came first. I loved Ray genuinely, but not at my own expense. I was no longer willing to love anybody at my own expense.

After a four-day honeymoon Ray and I returned to Vancouver and went back to work. Married life seemed to suit us. We settled down in a new apartment in a beautiful high-rise in West Vancouver and were very happy. That summer my parents came to see us, and they liked the city and were absolutely delighted with Ray. By the time they went home they were more content than I'd seen them in years, and I knew why. Their daughter, the one with all the problems, had finally gotten her life straightened out. She was married to the right man at last, and everything was going to be fine from now on. They could rest easy.

I was anxious to meet Ray's family as well, so when we heard that his sister Meg was going to be married in the fall, we decided to go to England for the wedding. It would be my first trip to Europe and I could hardly wait.

It took me several days to catch on to the Sussex accents of the Foat clan, but once I did, I warmed to the family quickly, and they to me. Ray's father was a little like my own—short, balding, a little paunchy, and very sweet—and Ray's jolly mother reminded me delightfully of actress Margaret Rutherford. Ray and I went sightseeing in London for several days before the wedding, then returned to Brighton to help cater the event. Afterward we spent two beautiful weeks in Mallorca and then went back to England. We traveled around the northern countryside, visiting old castles, going to the races at Ascot.

The trip was a euphoric time for us, but when we got home to Vancouver just before Christmas we were in for a rude shock. The *Princess Louise II* was closing. We'd known the ship was having financial problems but we hadn't realized how serious they were. The owners had decided that the best way to salvage their venture was to move the ship down the coast to California, possibly to reopen her there later. Ray and I were both about to be unemployed.

Early in 1972 there was a lavish, bittersweet closing party, and afterward the *Princess Louise II* was towed to a drydock south of Vancouver to be checked for seaworthiness for her voyage down the coast. There was an awful eeriness about that short trip. Under tow instead of her own power, she moved silently through the water with only four people on board—Ray and I and two other managers. The ship had always been alive with people and laughter and music, and now she was silent and hollow. Our mood was somber, mine especially.

I remember our being more sad than panicked by the situation. We expected we'd be able to find new jobs fairly easily. I'd spent less than a year and a half on the ship, but it had been a time of enormous personal growth, and not only in my relationship with Ray. My knowledge of my profession, my social poise and sophistication, and a wider acquaintance with the world had all developed. I'd even begun picking up the threads of some old ambitions and interests of my girlhood. I'd enrolled in some night classes at a local university, getting a real taste of college life at last. I'd studied accounting and management to help me in business, as well as literature just for the pleasure it gave me. And for the first time since 1963, I had felt at least a slight stirring of my commitment to social and political activism.

At school I'd made friends with a young American woman whose husband was an American draft evader. Through her I learned of the problems the draft evaders in Canada were facing. Many were almost totally isolated from their families and friends in the States. They were reluctant to communicate with anybody back home for fear of giving away their whereabouts. There was a pervasive dread at the time of being kidnapped by United States agents and taken back across the border for prosecution. Underground networks had sprung up to help make communications possible and safe. Letters and packages could be mailed to safe addresses of sympathetic people in Canada, to be relayed to their true recipients. Phone messages could be relayed to and from the draft evaders the same way. I ended up mailing and receiving letters and relaying phone calls, mostly from the *Princess Louise.*

I don't pretend that I was deeply involved in these activities or that I was making some major statement against the Vietnam War. It was just that I was homesick for the United States and felt that I was missing a historical time there. I was beginning to realize how much I needed commitment to a cause, working to change things and trying to make them better, feeling I could make a difference, however small. All those years with Jack I'd paid no attention to what was going on in the world. I'd had too much grief and violence of my own to worry about anybody else's. Now, slowly, I was reawakening.

I never told Ray much about what I was doing. I was afraid of his disapproval and somehow I was sure he'd disapprove. Among our West Vancouver friends, the draft evaders were just so many cowards and hippies, and the sooner Canada got rid of them the better. My helping them would have been an unthinkable social gaffe to Ray, something that was "unladylike" and "just not done." I did it anyway, but quietly.

By the time the *Princess Louise II* went into drydock Ray and I both had new jobs. I was delighted with mine. Through a friend I'd learned that a Vancouver hotel, the Georgia, was looking for someone for the newly created post of catering sales manager. I applied and was hired on the spot. The Georgia was a fine old Victorian hotel with a large and competent staff. My duties were to solicit catering business, help create banquets and other food events for conventions booked there, and oversee the production of those events. I had an excellent salary, my own secretary, and good cooperation from my colleagues. I did very well at the job.

Ray, on the other hand, was dissatisfied with the job he had taken managing a chain of coffee shops, and he was looking for a change. One night we were having dinner at an excellent restaurant called the Three Greenhorns when the restaurant's owner joined us at our table. He said he'd just signed contracts with a hotel-motel chain in America to open a Three Greenhorns in every new hotel that Quality Inns opened. The first one was about to open in Anaheim, two blocks from Disneyland. Would Ray be interested in going there to manage it, perhaps with an eye toward overseeing other new operations as they opened?

It was a wonderful offer, and Ray was very interested, as was I. I liked my job and I'd been happy in Vancouver, but I was homesick for the States in general and for Southern California and my friends there in particular. The only problem was that I wanted to keep working. After talking it over, we decided to offer the Three Greenhorns owner a package deal. Ray would go as restaurant manager if I could go as catering manager. The owner agreed, and in June of 1972, just in time for my thirty-first birthday, we left Canada and went home to California.

chapter 17

I look back on my job at the Georgia Hotel as a kind of watershed. I didn't work there long or accomplish anything spectacular, but it was the first time I'd gotten a job on my own in a field I'd worked toward ever since I was a cocktail waitress. I did it through my own talent and my own reputation in the catering business, and with no help from Ray or anybody else. I felt now that nobody could take away my independence again.

For all the pride I took in that accomplishment, however, it had its down side. Once I'd gone out on my own, Ray and I, who'd been such a good team professionally, never really worked well together again. At the Three Greenhorns in Anaheim there was friction from the start. It wasn't that I mounted any big rebellion or defied him openly or insisted on my own way. It was just that little by little I stopped asking for his advice. I had my own job, I knew how to do it, and I did it. He wasn't my boss anymore, or my teacher. No more lofty Professor Higgins and guttersnipe Eliza. Ray missed his role as mentor, and I think he was uncomfortable with my growing self-assurance. It seemed to diminish his somehow, and he no longer took the pride in me that he had during the days when he'd felt that I was more or less his own creation. There were small arguments, then bigger ones, and then arguments that carried over from our work to our personal lives. It was, I suppose, the beginning of the end of the marriage, though it would take years for the process to play itself out.

Nevertheless, when we first moved back to California we were happy enough. There was a big welcome-home party for us, and it was wonderful for me to be back with Clara and Bobbie and my other friends again. Ray and I set up housekeeping in a nice apartment in Anaheim. I took up golf, and we played together occasionally on our days off. I became active in the Food and Beverage Association, a local trade organization. And so life went, fairly placidly, through the rest of 1972 and 1973.

Ray and I were working hard to make the restaurant a success, but neither of us was satisfied professionally. We had philosophical differences with the owner about how to run a restaurant, differences that made the differences between Ray and me seem comparatively mild. Early in 1974 Ray took a job as food and beverage manager of the Disneyland Hotel. He was much better off, but I was caught in the backwash of his move. The Three Greenhorns owner, miffed at being stuck with the wrong half of his package deal, started taking his anger out on me; and a couple of weeks after Ray left, I followed.

I decided to stay home for a while. After all, I'd worked almost nonstop since I was a teenager—I, who grew up with the doctrine that the man was supposed to work while the woman stayed home. Ray was making a more than adequate salary, so I'd be a traditionalist and give full-time housekeeping a try.

Within two weeks I was bored to the point of coma. I found that there was only so much cleaning and cooking I could do before everything was spotless and everyone was full. I missed the structure of a regular work schedule, the contact with other people, the work itself. I couldn't get used to the relative inactivity and I wasn't inclined to try.

I suppose it would have been different if we'd had children, but there weren't any and it seemed there never would be. I'd started trying to get pregnant as soon as we married, and when months passed and nothing happened we went to a doctor to find out why. It turned out that there was a medical problem, a more or less minor one that probably could have been remedied. We'd been on the verge of pursuing a solution back in Canada just before we found out that the *Princess Louise II* was closing. We decided to postpone things until a better time, and somehow the better time never came.

. . .

About the time I was bottoming out as a bored housewife, a business friend called with some interesting news. A new hotel was opening in the area and it needed a catering manager. Within a week I was back at work. It would quickly become one of the more miserable jobs of my life, but it would also be the occasion for another milestone.

The problem was my boss. In those days I was unfamiliar with the term "male chauvinist pig." Otherwise, he would have had a label. A construction foreman by trade, he was making his first foray into hotel management. He knew nothing about it, and he hired several department heads who knew only slightly more than he did. I was the one who routinely worked sixteen-hour days and who came up with workable proposals for bringing more business to the hotel, but I was also the only female department head. Therefore, I was the lowest-paid and the only one expected to do her own typing.

I was the only one there with any significant experience in catering banquets. Yet on the rare occasions when the hotel manager booked a major convention, I had almost no say in decisions about how the banquets would be produced. The owner would call a meeting of the department heads and I would sit there, almost as though I should be taking notes, while everybody else decided. If the owner was feeling benevolent, I might be allowed an opinion on what color the flowers should be.

We fought and bickered constantly, and when I quit, only a few months after I started, there was no polite farewell or formal notice. In the middle of yet another battle about an upcoming banquet, I stormed out, after assessing my boss's business ability in distinctly unladylike terms.

All in all, though, I probably owe that particular MCP a word of thanks. Because of him I was able to say to myself for the first time, "You're getting crapped on here *because you are a woman.*" When I was a girl I knew that boys had more freedom, more avenues for development than I did. But that fact was so evident, so much a given, that I accepted, internalized, and all but forgot it, never really questioning the right or wrong of it, never protesting. I think if anybody had asked me before 1974 if I'd ever been discriminated against because I was a woman, I probably would have said no. Yes, I'd felt discrimination, but I'd never consciously connected it with gender. If I couldn't go to college, or if I had to work so my first husband could go, it was because that's the way things were—not because I was a woman. If over the years I'd felt put down or patronized, it was because I wasn't smart enough, or educated enough, or rich enough, or good enough, because I was from the wrong ethnic group, or religion, or social class—not because I was a woman. If I lived with a man who beat me, it was because I was dumb, or weak, or didn't do things right, or deserved no better— not because there are sick men who like to torture women.

Now, finally, I was beginning to make the connection. At the hotel I knew my job and I *knew* that I did it well. If I was being underpaid or criticized or ignored or stifled, it wasn't because of any inadequacies of mine. It was because I was a woman. I thought, too, about how far I'd come in my career, and how long and hard I'd worked to do it. And now, where was I really? Where could I expect to go? I was never in charge, never the one with the decision-making power, and it didn't seem that in my profession I ever would be. I couldn't rise to be food and beverage manager or hotel manager, not because I couldn't do the job—but because I was a woman. Realizing all this, I felt inadequate all over again, this time for taking so long to catch on, for not seeing it sooner.

It didn't occur to me then to think about the problem of sexism in any global sense, to consider that women all over the world were suffering because of their sex, some of them far worse than I was. What I saw was that I, Ginny Foat, was suffering because of mine. But that was a start, at least. The field for my growth as a feminist had been plowed, and now, by fortunate coincidence, somebody was about to come along and plant the first small seed.

One frustrating day, while I was still at the hotel, I had a visit from an imposing woman in her late sixties. She said she was a longtime member of a national women's community service organization called the Soroptimists, which was sponsoring the formation of a new chapter in the area. She wanted me to be one of the founding members. Membership was by invitation only and was limited to executive and professional women.

I felt immensely flattered, as though my long, hard climb was somehow being validated. I had achieved something after all, and it was being recognized by my peers. "My peers" was a new concept in itself, one that I could hardly comprehend. I'd never known other "executive and professional women," or thought of myself in such exalted terms, or expected to be recognized as such. I gave my visitor an enthusiastic yes to her invitation and quickly became one of the most active members in the new chapter.

With the Soroptimists I organized projects to raise money for a home for retarded people. I worked on projects to aid senior citizens. I helped organize and run the S Club, an organization for young women in high school, involving them in our service activities, holding after-school seminars on topics like citizenship and community responsibility. Within a few months I was a Soroptimist officer, taking on more and more responsibilities, gratified and grateful for the confidence my fellow members showed in me.

The Soroptimists certainly was not a feminist organization, although there might be occasional discussions at meetings about economic discrimination against women or sexism on the job. Its main thrust was to bring the talents of women to bear not on women's issues specifically, but on problems of general community concern. I didn't derive much in the way of feminist theory or feminist self-discovery from the Soroptimists. What I did find with them, for the first time in my life, was role models of strong women who were successful as something other than wives and mothers.

Before, even my closest friendships with women had centered on men. Men were what we talked about most of the time: how to attract them, how to dress for them, how to manipulate them, how your relationship was going with a particular man, what troubles you were having with men. Ever since grade school, it seemed, other females were either competitors or conspirators in the constant quest for men. Now, I was with women who didn't seem overly concerned with the constant quest and who didn't define themselves exclusively according to what men wanted or expected or allowed. Stepping back, at last, from the arena of competition and alliance, I began truly to appreciate women as companions—not against men or in preference to men, but simply apart from men. I began to value feminine strength and gentleness and wisdom for their own sake. I felt a new unity and intimacy with women, along with a new responsibility and loyalty to them. Up to that time, my habits hadn't changed much since high school, when breaking a date with the other girls was what you did automatically if your boyfriend called with a better offer. Now, I'd keep commitments I'd made to these women, even when Ray was available and wanted me to be with him.

Ray was tolerant and even approving of my Soroptimist activities. My fellow Soroptimists were sound, respectable, substantial women, and we did sound, respectable, substantial things. He even enjoyed being included. At the formal dance to install new officers, he was a suave and handsome escort, charming as ever.

At about that time, I started a little sideline as a stationers' representative, selling invitations and stationery. I called the operation Occasionally Yours, and after I left the hotel I expanded it, working out of our apartment, planning and coordinating small parties. If I was hired to do a wedding reception or a bar mitzvah, I'd find a place, hire a caterer, help plan the menu, order the invitations, hire the band, and call the florist. Essentially, I put the party together as a package, then contracted the actual work out.

I'd been working at my new enterprise for a couple of months when I heard from Danny Marcheano, an old friend from my days at the Three Greenhorns. I'd hired him as banquet bartender and found him a bright, good-looking, outgoing guy who got along with everybody. Now Danny was calling to say that he too had gone into business for himself, as a caterer, working out of a tiny apartment. He suggested we join forces and start a catering business together. We had no working capital, no backing, no contacts, no facilities to speak of. But we did have my knowledge of catering, Danny's great talent as a salesperson, and our considerable combined chutzpah. That, we decided, was plenty. We'd call ourselves Affairs Unlimited.

If our prospective clients had known what a shoestring operation we were, they probably wouldn't have hired us. But they didn't know, and the accounts started coming in. We did the cooking out of my kitchen—which was a disaster for poor Ray, who'd come home from work to find his apartment covered with food and his wife harried and elbow-deep in canapes. Still, the three of us managed to struggle along with the arrangement until Affairs Unlimited got its first big job.

Whirlpool Corporation was having a grand opening in a nearby industrial park, and we were hired to do a week's worth of catering for one thousand people. For most of the week we were only doing light lunches—sandwiches and other things that could be prepared easily ahead of time. But there was a final party for staff and important dealers that would require prime ribs, baked potatoes, and all the trimmings for about three hundred people. We could get ten to twelve portions from one rib roast, which meant that we were going to have to cook about thirty roasts in my apartment-size oven. We could fit in three at a time, and they had to cook for upwards of three hours. We started cooking the day before the party and cooked throughout the night, setting our alarm clocks at three-hour intervals and catnapping between shuttling the roasts in and out.

The party turned out fine, but it was the last straw at home. We shopped around and found a little takeout Mexican restaurant. It didn't look like much in front, but in the back there was a big stove, refrigeration, trays—everything needed for a really professional catering company. The price was low, but it was more than Danny and I had at the time. We decided to try for a bank loan.

We chose a banker who'd handled business for Ray and me at the Three Greenhorns. He gave us the application papers, and we filled them out and returned them. The next day we went back to the bank for a decision on the loan. Everything was in order, the banker said. There was no problem. All he needed was Ray's credit information and Ray's signature on the application.

I was astounded and furious. Why did Ray have to cosign for me when nobody had to cosign for Danny? What did Ray have to do with it? It was my business, not his. The bank would be taking a chance on me, not him. I was an established businesswoman with a good reputation in the community, and now I was being told that I couldn't proceed with my own business unless I turned to my husband like a little girl who needed Daddy to hold her hand while she crossed the street!

There was a hot argument, but the bottom line stayed the same. If we wanted the loan, Ray would have to cosign for me. As we left the bank I was still steaming. Incredibly, Danny was laughing. He thought the whole incident was very funny. So did Ray when we told him about it later. He'd be happy to cosign, he said. What was all the fuss about?

There seemed to be no way to explain my anger to them, and that made me even angrier. Why were they so obtuse? Certainly any woman in my position would understand how I felt. It was later that same day, leafing through a newspaper, that I saw an advertisement for an all-day seminar that the National Organization for Women was holding in Anaheim. I decided to go.

chapter 18

The next day I got up early to get ready for the seminar. I dressed in the usual way. First came the makeup, heavy on the eyeliner, with false eyelashes applied hair by hair. A subtle touch of eye shadow, some black eyebrow pencil, some blusher, dark lipstick. I checked my inch-long false fingernails to make sure my manicure was neat. Then I pinned my fine, thin hair close to my head and put on a long, black, gypsy wig, the kind that fluffed out around the face and cascaded halfway down to the waist in the back. It was my favorite of my many wigs. Very bouffant and stylish, I thought. Sexy. Finally, I climbed into my usual costume for daytime, a trim polyester pantsuit.

I drove my long black Cadillac to the building where the seminar was being held and went inside—and suddenly felt like a totally unprepared Alice being yanked through the looking glass. All the women looked so strange! Most of them had short hair and wore no makeup. The prevailing uniform appeared to be T-shirts worn underneath coveralls, though some women were wearing Army fatigue pants and work shirts. Here and there a rare woman had on tailored pants and a blouse, but these women looked a little uncomfortable. I wondered if they might be harboring their own polyester pantsuits back home in their closets. Some of the women carried little flashlights and plastic gizmos it took me a minute to identify. Specula. That's what they were—those gadgets that gynecologists use to examine you. What were they for?

One thing was for sure. None of these women looked remotely like me. And if I was confused by them, they were at least equally startled by me. When I walked in conversation stopped. People turned and stared. Almost nobody spoke to me, not then and not the rest of the day. My mind flashed back to a horrible memory. My God, I thought, it's the Bucknell homecoming dance all over again. I'm dressed all wrong. I'm utterly out of place. I saw the same contempt in eyes staring from above T-shirts and coveralls that I'd once seen above floating silks and chiffons. Contempt and something else. Wariness. These women were looking at me in much the same way a roomful of dope addicts might look at an obvious narc.

I figured I had two choices. I could turn around and run, or I could shake off my embarrassment and plunge ahead. I decided to plunge. I'd come to learn and I was going to learn. The whole scene was alien to me, but there was an air of determination and purpose about these women, as though they knew exactly who they were and what they were doing. I felt that they had some answer, some solution, that I *needed* to understand.

The day's formal activities started off with a plenary session that featured some excellent speakers. Listening to them, I felt myself holding back little gasps, sometimes of recognition, sometimes of surprise. There was a discussion of the Equal Rights Amendment. (Funny, I'd never thought about the ERA before. I wasn't even sure I knew exactly what it was. Could changing the law really change our lives?) There was talk about reproductive rights (Yes! What if there had been more options that time I was pregnant?), about discrimination against women in education (I wasn't the only one denied college because of my sex), about homemakers' rights (Wives actually had rights other than the right to serve husbands?), about lesbians (Were there really women who didn't need men?), about women and political power (Was it really possible that women could have an impact on government, that exclusive province of men?).

I was still pondering the speeches when the general session broke up and we divided into workshops. I decided to go to one on the ERA. It included some discussion of discrimination against women in business, and though it didn't answer any of my questions about credit, it was an eye-opener in other ways. I wasn't the only

one to squirm under the thumb of male management. I wasn't alone
—again, that wonderful knowledge. Later that morning I went to
a workshop on women's music. There were women playing and
singing music written by women, about women, for women. (This
is beautiful, I thought.)

That afternoon I went to a workshop called "Self-Examina-
tion," and it was there that I found out what the specula were for.
The Feminist Women's Health Center was sponsoring this session, which was supposed to help demystify female sexuality. We
were going to familiarize ourselves with our own bodies by throwing a little public light on what most of us grew up calling our
private parts. The idea was that men know all about their genitalia
and have all kinds of intimate and intricate emotional involvement
with them—even to the absurd point of defining their masculinity
by the size of their penises—while women don't even know what
their genitals look like! A couple of women volunteered to be models. They climbed onto tables and spread their legs. (How could
they!) Specula were inserted and flashlights turned on. The rest of
us were invited to come up and take a look. (This is really kinky,
I thought. On the other hand, I really *don't* know what I look like
down there. I've never seen a cervix, mine or anybody else's.) I
went up and looked, and it didn't seem so kinky after all. It
seemed instructive, natural, healthy, emotionally neutral, and re-
freshingly honest.

A woman from the Health Center gave a lecture. If you know
what your cervix looks like, she said, you don't have to kill a rabbit
to find out if you're pregnant. You can tell just from noting the
changes in your cervix. If you have a yeast infection from time to
time, as many women do, you don't have to pay a gynecologist fifty
dollars to cure it. You can cure it yourself, in many cases, with a
carton of yogurt. The lecture ended with an invitation for those of
us who were interested to come back during the day and examine
ourselves. I was getting more enlightened all the time, but not to the
point of shedding years of embarrassment and repression about my
own body. I decided to pass for the time being.

Still slightly flushed and flustered from that workshop, I was
floored by the next one. It featured a self-proclaimed witch, an
exotic-looking women in robes, accompanied by a large German
shepherd. She talked about the matriarchal religions and about the
goddesses who were worshipped long before the patriarchal deities
came along to supplant them. She described how women had been
persecuted for centuries in the name of organized religions that

branded them as seducers, destroyers, and perpetrators of "original sin." This was a far cry from anything I'd ever heard in catechism class. For an instant, I felt a creeping, atavistic fear that I was probably going to be struck by a lightning bolt just for listening to this. I thought both the witch and the dog looked pretty ferocious and the topic was more than a little bizarre. On the other hand, didn't I feel the truth of what she was saying? If women were equal in the sight of God, as I had been taught, they were still undoubtedly inferior in the sight of many of God's male servants.

My last memory of the seminar is of a speaker at the concluding session. She didn't give a speech; she merely announced the date of a meeting. It was for volunteers working on the battered-women's shelter. My reaction tells a lot about how far I'd progressed in dealing with my past. What were battered women? I wondered. I decided that somebody must be trying to build a shelter for women who were mugged or beaten up on the streets. That was nice, I thought, but I never knew it was that big a problem in Anaheim.

There was supposed to be a dance that night and I was eager to go. I could go home and unearth some jeans and change so I'd feel more in tune. Then Ray and I could come back. I asked one of the women about the party. She took one look at me and was instantly hostile, but she answered my questions. Yes, the dance was open to the public, she said. Anybody could come. You didn't have to be a NOW member. I said I was going to try to make it if my husband could get off work. She looked at me with icy disdain. "It's for women only," she said.

To my great disappointment I missed the dance; I slept through it. I went home from the seminar exhausted and fell immediately into a long, deep sleep. For the time being, my mind had absorbed all it could handle. I was in turmoil. In one day my whole life had been turned upside down. Almost everything I'd been taught as a child, everything I'd ever thought about myself as a woman and a wife, had been challenged.

The next day was a Sunday and I spent most of it alone, thinking. I hadn't gone to the seminar looking for upheaval. All I wanted was some help in figuring out why some bastard at a bank made my husband cosign a note for me. I was into credit, not covens and cervixes. Yet once I got there I had stayed all day, despite feeling out of place, despite my bewilderment and embarrassment. I was hungry to see and hear everything. And if I was confused and upset, I was also excited and exhilarated by what I saw and heard. I'd stumbled into a world that, for all its strangeness, seemed saner than the one I lived in. But if that world made sense, then most of the rest of my life was nonsense. It was as though I'd always been homesick for a place I'd never been, and at last I'd come home.

I tried to talk to Ray about the seminar and my feelings, but it was a mistake. I don't remember exactly what he said, but there was some light, disparaging remark, perhaps to the effect that apparently I hadn't learned much about banking. I was left with the impression that he thought I was wasting my time and being silly.

The next day I went out and bought *The Feminine Mystique, Sisterhood Is Powerful, The Second Sex,* and several other feminist classics I'd heard mentioned at the seminar. I read them all within a few days, staying up late at night, unwilling to put them down. Every page seemed to bring a new revelation. In December of 1974, at the first regular meeting the Anaheim chapter held after the seminar, I joined NOW.

When I look back at those early days—the Days of the Speculum—it's with a mixture of amusement, nostalgia, and pride. We were excessive sometimes, sometimes ridiculous, sometimes as rigid and judgmental as the society we wanted to change. We made mistakes, certainly. We insisted, for instance, that everybody conform to our own brand of nonconformity, in the way we dressed and what we said. We were trying to make a political statement with the way we looked. We wanted to overturn some old, destructive, divisive stereotypes about women, to divorce feminism from men's fiction of "femininity," to protest that our value was more than ornamental. We were trying to show that women shouldn't be categorized on the basis of their appearance, but we ourselves lost track of the fact that a woman can look any number of ways and still be a feminist. Even in a polyester pantsuit, she can believe in women's rights and, more important, have faith in the special qualities shared by women that have the power to make the world better.

In our defense, we *were* still in the infancy of the latest wave of feminism, pioneers feeling our way, casting around for a new way of looking at things. We had inherited the wisdom and experience of the suffragists and our other foremothers, but we had to learn to adapt them to our time. We were searching for our own code words and symbols, our own sources of power, our own methods and means of cohesion. There weren't many of us, and there were many against us, and we felt a great urgency to act fast and decisively to bring change. Like most revolutionaries, we were innocents.

Those of us who lived through those early days, who became

witches or sat around exploring our inner mysteries with mirrors and specula and penlights, can look back and laugh at it now. We can even invite younger women to laugh. But it seems to me they should also try to understand how much they're able to take for granted today because of us. If they're confident of getting into a good law school or medical school that doesn't discriminate on the basis of gender, it's because of us. If they have any meaningful access to the political process, it's because of us. If they have a rightful say over when and whether to have children, it's because of us. If they're less apt to have a boss who calls them "honey" and pinches their backsides—if they're less apt to have a boss *at all*—it's because of us. If they grow up with more options, more pride in themselves, fewer restrictions on their ambitions and talents, it's because of us.

Feminism has come far and fast, even though, sadly, we've mislaid some of our commitment and passion along the way. Maybe we've become victims of our own incomplete achievements, co-opted too early by our own success.

We went to some extremes, yes, but we were right. And nothing and nobody, no dissension within the women's movement or reactionism outside it, can ever minimize or detract from what we did.

I joined NOW, but I wasn't welcomed immediately into the fold. I went to my first meeting in my customary garb—eyelashes, fingernails, wig, polyester. Old habits die hard. I didn't understand yet about personal dress and political statements. After all, we achievers at Soroptimists had speakers who told us "How to Dress for Success" and "How to Pack So Your Skirts Don't Wrinkle" and "How to Bring out Your Best with Makeup." Surely the rank-and-file NOW women couldn't be all that different. They were. Again, I ran into a lot of scrubbed faces, cropped hair, denim, and fatigues. And again, nobody spoke to me.

I wasn't discouraged but I was convinced it was time for a change. After I left the meeting I went directly to an Army surplus store and bought some men's T-shirts and fatigue pants. At the next meeting I still had the hair and nails and makeup, but at least I was dressed right. I began to make some friends. I don't know whether the other women talked to me because I was looking more politically correct or just because by now they were getting used to seeing me around, but the climate was definitely warmer. I was even asked out for drinks with some of the other members after the meeting. Things warmed up so much, in fact, that at my fourth meeting I was elected chapter finance officer.

That was the beginning of my "meteoric rise" in feminist circles. Of course, I didn't know my rise was meteoric until I read that description in newspapers years later. The reporters made it sound as thought I'd enjoyed a miraculous ascent, effortless and inevitable. In fact, my career as a feminist was nothing like that.

NOW was only eight years old when I joined. It was still a very fluid organization, still evolving, struggling to build up strength and solidify its own philosophy and methods. In that kind of environment anybody willing to work is likely to advance fast, and I was relentlessly willing to work. I worked hard and constantly and with total commitment. No job was too small or menial and no detail was unimportant. I was always available, always ready. There would be one short hiatus, but almost from the day I joined NOW, the women's movement was my life, and I brought to it the passion of a convert.

By the time I was elected to a chapter office in Anaheim I'd been to only four general meetings, but I'd attended committee meetings and subcommittee meetings and any random ad hoc meetings I could find. I went to the newsletter meeting, for instance, and when I couldn't find any better way to make myself useful I collated pages. I wanted to be part of everything. Missing anything at all might mean missing something vital, something necessary to my new existence. Feminism was a fountain where I was finally being allowed to drink. I couldn't get enough of it.

I listened. If someone was talking about feminism and global politics, I listened. If someone was talking about how to staple the newsletter, I listened just as hard. I was avid to learn. There was so much lost time to make up for, so many years of not seeing things right in front of me that were obviously wrong. I listened much more than I talked, because at first I was afraid to talk. I didn't want to sound stupid and I knew that I hadn't learned all the jargon yet and didn't have the theory down pat. But I had never in my life done anything, right or wrong, halfway. Once I discovered feminism I sprinted from the starting gun, running flat out.

chapter 19

I joined NOW at a time when the organization itself was undergo-
ing a major upheaval. NOW's founders in the mid-1960s were
mostly middle-class and upper-middle-class career women, who kept
politely to economic issues that were comparatively respectable and
safe, and shied away from controversy. But as NOW grew and its
membership became more diverse, internal dissent grew as well. For
example, a large issue arose over lesbianism, and a number of lesbian
women were forced out. A group called the Majority Caucus began
pushing for decentralization of the organization, for more input and
power from the grass roots, and for involvement in "radical" issues
that affected women on all economic levels. Equal pay for equal work
was still important, of course, but the Majority Caucus wanted
NOW to act on lesbian rights, abortion, racism, and violence against
women. Led by Ellie Smeal, the Majority Caucus was able to take
control of NOW in 1975 after a bitter fight. Its slogan was "Out
of the mainstream, into the revolution."

As it turned out, it wasn't long before NOW found its way back
into the mainstream. But feminism as a revolution was what I
believed in when I joined and what I believe in today. I was "trying
to save the world," my father would have said, and he would have

been right. I'm still trying and I suppose I'll die trying, still believing that it's possible.

There were lots of outlets for revolutionary zeal in the NOW of 1975, and I got involved in as many as I could find. One of my first projects was to help with the local planning for "Alice Doesn't Day." Taking its name from the song and movie "Alice Doesn't Live Here Anymore," it was to be a nationwide general strike by women to show the country the impact that women have on the national economy. Teachers, secretaries, doctors, homemakers—all women —were supposed to refuse to work on that day. In our chapter the day was going to be celebrated with a fair. We'd arranged to use a local park and to set up food booths, poetry readings, and music. We were offering the striking women a place to congregate and express their solidarity. I helped plan and promote the event in Anaheim, and Danny and I catered the fair and donated the food.

That was the first Alice Doesn't Day and, unfortunately, the last. In our chapter alone, three women were fired from their jobs for taking part in the strike. Others, including a number of women who had children to support, were threatened ahead of time with unemployment and chose not to participate. It was the same all over the country. The day turned out to be a statement of sorts, but it fell far short of the impact we'd hoped for. If it failed as a protest, however, the opposition to it succeeded in further radicalizing many of us. We regrouped and looked for new avenues of protest.

That year we mounted a lot of what we called zap actions, which were peaceful but confrontational protests against antifeminist institutions. For instance, on Mother's Day we demonstrated outside a Catholic church that was a vocal center of antiabortion sentiment and that had denied Communion to two of our chapter members just because they were wearing NOW pins.

As chapter finance coordinator, I planned and organized a variety of fund-raising events. I went to regular meetings and to various committee meetings and did some writing for the newsletter. I was getting to know women from other NOW chapters and was becoming especially friendly with the leadership of the Los Angeles chapter, the largest and most powerful in California and the one in the vanguard of the organization's new radicalism.

For all my frenetic public activity, I think the single thing that was most important to my growth as a feminist in those days was the private and highly personal experience of belonging to a consciousness-raising group. In NOW's consciousness-raising program eight to ten women met once a week for ten weeks. For all the ridicule it's since occasioned—maybe from people who were most threatened by it—consciousness-raising performed at least two vital functions.

First, it opened your eyes to the personal and political significance of attitudes and practices that you might never have questioned before. It helped you examine them and helped you deal with what you found. Almost every feminist knows how it was to feel those clicks of recognition, those "aha!" moments of discovering the source and nature of some particular form of sexism that hit home.

There was a session, for instance, on the power of language. What was society saying about us, and doing to us, when a fifty-year-old woman could be called a girl? Was the practice any less derisive or contemptuous than calling black men boys? How did it make us feel about ourselves? How did it help keep us powerless? Why mustn't a "lady" ever get angry? Who and what would be threatened if she did? Could the use of such terms ever be innocent? No, we learned. "The personal is political" was a leading motto of the movement.

There was a session on violence. How does pornography degrade and endanger women? Who invented the myths about rape and who needed to believe them? How could men say of a woman who'd undergone the most brutal and terrifying ordeal that she "asked for it" or "wanted it" or "probably loved it"? What was rape? Did it have to be at knife point at the hands of a stranger? Or was it any sexual experience, even in marriage, in which a woman is taken without her consent? The answers seem so obvious now, but they were new to us then and enormously enlightening.

The second vital service of consciousness-raising was to end our isolation. We found out we weren't alone, and that was the beginning of power. If I had felt like a willful and wrongheaded oddity in my own family, so had other women. If I'd felt ashamed and guilty about my desires and ambitions, so had other women. If I was slow to recognize the fallacies in the dreams we were spoon-fed as children, or too fast to buy into a system that regarded me as second-class because of my sex, I wasn't alone. The more we shared with each other, the more we felt united, and the more we empathized with all women.

There was one very emotional session devoted to our relationships with our mothers. We found that all of us were resentful and distrustful of our mothers to one degree or another. We all had felt stifled or neglected or misunderstood or denied. But had we ever looked at our mothers apart from us, as women in their own context?

What dreams had they had as young women, and which of those dreams had vanished? What were they allowed and what were they denied, and how did the constraints of their own time and place make them what they were? I think it was at that session that I first began to know my mother, and to forgive her for never really knowing me, and for all the other deficiencies and slights, real or imagined, of my girlhood.

There was a deep feeling of trust within most consciousness-raising groups. You could share your feelings or not, but no verbal abuse was allowed against women who did choose to speak. Each member of the group took an oath at the first meeting never to talk outside the group of anything personal that was said there, and I've never heard of that oath being broken. With the members of my group I was able to share my most intimate thoughts, doubts, and secrets—or most of them. And for all the betrayals that later would come to me at the hands of other women in the movement, the confidences I shared in that group were never betrayed.

Liberating and cleansing as consciousness-raising was, it might have given me a way to exorcise my old demons and make peace with my past. But it didn't. Instead, I used it, as well as other things I was learning as a feminist, as my last, best vehicle for denial. In the consciousness-raising session on violence there was some discussion of battering. I thought to myself, How terrible that things like that can happen to women. Never once did I think, How terrible that it happened to me. I found out where the battered-women's shelter was, and Danny and I often donated food to it. He would make the deliveries. For reasons I refused to analyze, I always managed to be too busy to go myself. Still, I was glad that I could help "those poor women." Those poor women. Never me. I could deal with the issue of battering only if I objectified it. I could not and did not identify with other battered women. On the contrary, I used them to help keep the issue abstract, to put a distance between their agony and mine. I could help them; therefore I was not one of them. The personal may have been political, but in some areas I couldn't afford to make the political personal. It never occurred to me to judge or blame other victims of battering. At the same time, it never occurred to me to forgive myself.

For me, by now, Jack Sidote didn't exist and had never existed. I'd succeeded in erasing him. I'd also succeeded in erasing her, Ginny Galluzzo, that woman who lived with him and collaborated with him in her own humiliation and shame. She was gone now, and unconsciously I knew that she must never be allowed to come back. If I ever had to face her I'd choke on my hatred for her. Weak, passive, stupid bitch that she was, I hated her more than him. I hated her most of all.

There I was then, in 1975, immersed in a dozen different NOW activities, and comanaging a catering business that was becoming busier and busier. When I had a spare moment, there was also the matter of my marriage.

Before my activist days, and before Affairs Unlimited became a success, all my spare time had been devoted to Ray. Now we hardly saw each other. I would come home at the end of my day exhausted and fall into bed. Ray, who was working long hours at Disneyland, often got home after midnight to find me fast asleep. I'd be up and gone again the next morning before he was even awake.

On days when he did get home early he'd often arrive to find his living room filled with women who met his courtly charm with indifference at best and hostility at worst. I'd taken over a NOW task force called Women in Transition, helping women who were going through difficult divorces or trying to re-enter the job market after years as homemakers, and I usually held the meetings in our apartment. In all his experience Ray had never met women like these, and he didn't like them at all. At first there were some fairly mild comments, like "Do you really think these people are your sort?" But the complaints and value judgments progressed rapidly to "How can you associate with those unfeminine women when you're so feminine?" It was as if he thought the abandoned false eyelashes, wig, and hairpieces were what had made me feminine.

If he didn't like my friends, he didn't like me much either. What had happened to his princess, the sweet, adoring, submissive woman he'd married? It was as though somebody had snatched her away and left this hard, angry stranger in her place. This new Ginny didn't even look the same. Gone were the false eyelashes and fingernails, the wigs and hairpieces. I got by with my own hair now, though I still dyed it, and my makeup was more subdued. All Ray could do was wait and hope for the return of his original wife. Understandably, he was confused. He was quietly and patiently bewildered at first, but before long he was outright angry.

And I was furious—at him, at almost everybody and everything. Consciousness-raising was healing on some fronts, but on others it tapped subterranean lakes of undiscovered rage and gave you permission to express it. A "lady" *was* allowed to get angry, and by God I was mad! I couldn't connect with my rage at having been abused by a maniac for years, but I could get mad at society in general. How had "they" dared fuck with my head and my life the way they had? How could they have made me believe in that sappy dream about princes and happily ever after? Why had they fed me lies and tried to make me weak and keep me ignorant? All that loss and waste and pain! And men, the filthy bastards! They were all users and takers and oppressors, all worthless. It was an affliction to have to live in the same world with them.

I became almost a caricature of a feminist. I was going through that phase that most feminists know, the one where you allow yourself to luxuriate in your wonderful newfound anger before the world settles back into a saner perspective.

At the same time, I was trying to keep one toe in the camp of middle-class respectability. It wasn't easy; I couldn't discuss my feminism with nonfeminists without yelling and screaming. I was always correcting people, jumping on them for the slightest infractions of my new rules, scorning such useful qualities as humor and tact. I was about as tolerant and diplomatic as Torquemada. I was a royal bitch. Ray, and Ray's golf buddies, and the golf buddies' wives, began to look at me as though I were a lunatic.

I still made a halfhearted stab at cooking and cleaning, but for the first time in my life, I was inclined to let the housekeeping slide. And Ray, accustomed to gourmet meals and an immaculate apartment, was now confronted with cold dinners and dirty socks. For a time we tried ignoring each other, then we quibbled, then argued, then fought. So it went through 1975 and into 1976. Ray took a job managing a restaurant in Los Angeles, about fifty miles from where we lived. He came home only on his days off, which was fine with me, since it meant I could have meetings that lasted until all hours without worrying about shooing everybody out before my husband came home.

Ray was totally involved with his job; I was totally immersed in the movement. By the time I realized how far apart we'd grown, the marriage was almost beyond rescue. Confronted by the fact, I panicked. I wasn't ready to lose Ray. We had our problems, not all of them political, but he was still the sweet, gentle, patient man I'd married. I was the one who'd changed. He'd been so understanding and so loving for so long, I guess I took it for granted that he'd be understanding and loving forever. He'd accept the changes. Finding out otherwise left me hurt and scared.

The feeling wasn't much different from the way I felt when

Jack was sent away to Chino. What would I do if Ray left me? How could I make it on my own? Of course, by now I'd proved a hundred times over that I *could* make it on my own, and still I was scared. I finally had the whole dream—the nice home, the nice husband, even a nice Cadillac and a nice poodle. What more could a good Italian girl from New Paltz want? Maybe I'd learned as a feminist that the dream was a lie, but the dream had guided my life for more than thirty years and feminism for fewer than two. When the crunch came, I chose—for the moment—to throw out the feminism and keep the dream.

Anyway, what had feminism done for me? Expanded my world, saved my life, made me more loving and caring and aware and involved, a more rational Ginny might have answered. But it had also made me angry and intolerant and bitchy and tired. I was worn out with it. My life in crisis again, I simply wanted to go back to a time when everything was simple and happy. I wanted everything to be nice. I wanted Ray.

I pulled back from feminism with the speed of a reflex action, like a threatened turtle flinching into its shell. I'd overstepped my bounds again, done things I wasn't supposed to do, gotten involved where I didn't belong. I'd almost blown my marriage. Well, things were going to change. I was going to stay home and take care of my husband, assuming he'd let me.

Ray and I had some long talks and decided we both wanted to save our marriage. Coincidentally, all this was going on at a time when Danny and I were having a lot of business differences. I'd leave not only the women's movement but catering as well, I decided. I'd stay home and be a full-time wife. Danny bought out my share of Affairs Unlimited, and Ray and I used the money as the down payment on a house.

Ray had been transferred to a restaurant in the suburban Los Angeles community of Woodland Hills in the San Fernando Valley, and the house we bought was in the adjoining neighborhood of Canoga Park. It was the dream's finishing touch, this home of my own, the all-American tract house, Southern California style. A three-bedroom rambler, it had a large back yard with a patio and the inevitable swimming pool and Jacuzzi. It was nothing if not nice.

I threw myself into a massive redecorating project—picking new carpeting and wallpaper, buying furniture, painting, building planters, hanging drapes, installing a bar. When I finished we had a huge housewarming party. That was fun, I thought when it was over. Now what? In the following weeks I settled into a daily round of minor housewifely chores and spent a lot of time by the pool working on my tan. Within two months I was bored witless.

Ray didn't seem to be very happy either. I was focusing all my attention on him now, and he was finding it more a burden than a pleasure. He'd been a virtual bachelor for months, and suddenly he was expected to be home for meals on time, to take his wife out at regular intervals, to behave like a devoted husband. He was supposed to be pleased when I dropped in unannounced at his restaurant to have lunch with him, or decided to surprise him by picking him up at work. Instead, he appeared to find this new life-style restrictive. In any case, we started arguing again and the marriage slipped off its temporary plateau and started back downhill.

One thing we did agree on was that I needed an outside interest again. Ray told me that a tennis club near his restaurant was looking for someone to manage its bar and snack bar. I could run things there and at the same time start up my catering business again, using the club as a base. And that's what happened. Meg and Mickey Austin, Ray's sister and brother-in-law, came to live with us and the three of us went to work at the Warner Center Racquet Club.

I revived Affairs Unlimited as a Los Angeles County venture separate from Danny's Affairs Unlimited in Orange County. Business was good. The work eased my boredom, but by no means did it fill my life. I felt as though some part of me had been carved out, leaving behind a nagging, growing emptiness.

On one of my days off I was puttering around my garden when a woman stopped by who was running for the California State Assembly from our district. We talked for a while and I leafed through her campaign literature, impressed both by her and by her politics. I asked if she was getting any help from the Valley chapter of NOW, and when she said no, I promised to look into it for her.

I'd stopped going to NOW meetings but I'd never given up my membership. Surely one little meeting couldn't hurt. The last time I'd gone overboard, I told myself. I'd tried to do too many things and I'd let myself get overly emotional. I was beyond most of my anger now, and I'd learned to pace myself. Just a few meetings here and there, to fill up my time.

So it was that for the first time in several months I found myself at a NOW meeting. Nothing much happened. I talked about the candidate a little bit and then listened while the chapter discussed its usual business. Yet of all the thousands of feminist meetings I've been to, that one stays in my mind because of the way it made me feel. I was happy and complete, content and at the same time immensely excited. God, how I'd missed it! Listening to the women talk about changing things, doing things, I closed my eyes for a minute and thought: What am I going to leave for the women who come after me? That I made history? Or that I made a great lasagna? I don't know where it comes from, this need to save the world that my father diagnosed so many years ago. But there's no denying anymore that it's basic to my very identity. It's who I am.

A woman was saying that the chapter didn't have enough leaders for consciousness-raising groups. Would anyone like to volunteer? I hesitated. Ray wouldn't like it. Well, I thought, that's tough. Surely one little group couldn't hurt. I raised my hand.

At first, it was only a meeting now and then. But soon there were a lot of meetings, and committees and subcommittees. There were women in Ray's living room again whom he endured with gritted teeth. It was clear that he thought I'd deserted him again, and he saw signs of defection in everything I did. When I cut my hair short he saw the act as a kind of symbolic last straw, the final proof that I'd "lost my femininity" forever.

By now we were fighting almost all the time, caught in a downward spiral that neither of us could stop. While his relatives lived with us a cold politeness had prevailed around the house, but once they'd moved there was nothing to restrain the screaming matches. We went into counseling, but that only brought more bitterness to the surface. Ray criticized my friends, my appearance, my housekeeping. He blamed me for abandoning him for the women's movement. In short, he blamed me for changing. For my part, I thought he was inflexible and chauvinistic for refusing to let me grow, for trying to keep me in a mold I no longer fit. The harder we tried to stay together, the more obvious it was to both of us how far apart we'd grown. Early in 1977 we separated and Ray moved out of the house. I think that if he could, he would have sued for divorce on grounds of adultery and named as corespondent the National Organization for Women.

We were both angry and frustrated by the time we split up, but at the same time I was terribly sad. Ray had meant a lot to me and done a lot for me, and I wasn't so much changed that I didn't acknowledge the debt. There had been a time when the marriage seemed to work, but it was, finally, not good enough to accommodate two full and equal partners. Once I was whole and independent, no longer "the little woman," the marriage foundered. It seemed that the price for keeping it afloat was for me to deny my own identity. I just couldn't do that. I would have been happy to be his partner and equal, his friend and lover and wife. But I couldn't be his pupil and his creation. I couldn't be his princess anymore.

After all my terror at the thought of being without a man, I surprised myself with how easily I adapted to it. It was a relief to end the emotional uproar that living with Ray had become. I felt more at peace and I had more time and freedom for my feminist work and for other aspects of my life as well. I developed a closeness with my women friends that I'd never allowed myself time for before. My operation at the tennis club was running nicely and my catering business was prospering. Danny and I had become friends again. From time to time I'd drive the hundred miles or so to help him out with a catering assignment in Orange County, or he'd come up to help me.

Once I got past the first shock of the separation from Ray, those first few months of 1977 were unusually productive and happy. I had the feeling that I was coming to the end of a long, erratic, painful search for who I really was and what I wanted. Life would be much smoother from now on. I was sure of it.

chapter 20

It was one of those mornings when you feel like whistling, a beautiful, sun-drenched day toward the end of May. Danny had come up the night before to help me with a party and he'd stayed over at the house. He was still asleep and I was getting dressed for an appointment with a client. I put on my favorite daytime outfit, a cream-colored three-piece pantsuit and a striped silk blouse. I was almost ready to go when the doorbell rang.

Four men in business suits were standing at the door when I opened it. I'd never seen any of them before. One of them said, "Are you Virginia Galluzzo?"

His using my maiden name didn't register at first. The only thing I could think of was that these men might be trying to serve me with some kind of papers. Ray must be up to something. I'd filed for divorce and I was half-expecting him to contest it or cross-file. I didn't intend to get served with anything until I could find out what was going on.

"No," I said, "I'm Meg Austin." That was Ray's sister's name.

"Well, can we come in?" asked the man doing the talking. "We're from the Los Angeles Police Department." It was then that

I felt the first stirring of uneasiness. This couldn't have anything to do with the divorce.

"Are you telling me that you're not Virginia Galluzzo?" the man demanded.

"No," I admitted, "that's who I am."

"Is John Sidote your ex-husband?"

I felt rooted to the floor. Just the sound of his name, with all it implied, left me too confused and frightened to speak. I didn't know what was going on, but if it involved Jack it had to be something terrible. The four men were staring at me, waiting.

Then they were asking more questions, but I could hardly follow what they were saying. Nothing seemed to make sense. Jack Sidote had just been a bad dream, hadn't he? He wasn't real. Then this couldn't be real. But now one of the men was saying . . .

"I want you to come downtown with us. We need to talk to you about John Sidote saying that you murdered some people."

Everything blurred. I remember walking into the room where Danny was sleeping, waking him, and telling him there was some kind of trouble with the police and he had to call a lawyer. I remember leaving the house with the four men and getting into a car. I had no idea where they were taking me.

Then we were all in a room at a police substation in Van Nuys. I understood by now that only two of the men were from the Los Angeles Police Department, a Detective Warren Eggar and a Sergeant Vince Scott. The other two, Gary Minter and Mike Harper, were investigators from the Douglas County Sheriff's Department in Nevada. That confused me even more. I didn't even know anybody in Nevada. The four of us—Eggar had left—were sitting at a table that had a large tape recorder on it. One of the men asked if it was okay with me if they taped the conversation and I said yes. I glanced at a clock on the wall. It was 9:55 A.M.

Minter read me my rights and I confirmed that I understood them. I did understand them, but I was too frightened to exercise them the way I should have. I felt like a child alone in the dark. The irrational thought kept running through my mind that I had to be a good girl and give these men what they wanted, whatever that was, and they'd let me go. I'd answer anything they asked and tell the truth, and then they'd understand that all this was a mistake and they'd let me go home. After all, I hadn't done anything wrong. I wished my lawyer were there. When I first got to the substation I'd tried to phone him, and tried to phone Danny to make sure he'd called him, but I couldn't reach either one. I decided to talk anyway. I didn't want these men to think I was being uncooperative or trying to hide something. I wanted them to see how willing I was to do the right thing.

Harper was talking now, his voice not unkind.

"See, what we're interested in, Virginia, is this. If Sidote's lying to us, if John's lying to us, flat-out lying to us, we want to hear your side of it. If you're not involved in any of this, fine."

I didn't know what "any of this" actually was yet, so I started trying to tell them what I did know, starting with my leaving New Paltz with Jack and Wasyl. But then Harper was putting a paper in front of me and saying I should sign it so they could talk to me. I guess it was a waiver of some sort. I didn't question it. I just signed.

"Then if you'll just tell us, Virginia, when you left from New York, stuff like that, maybe that'll help clear this mess up," Harper said.

"I—I—I don't remember," I stammered. "That part of my life was a real bad part of my life because he was really such a horrible person, I mean, you know, terrible with me, as far as, you know, he used to hit me, and . . ."

I knew I had to make them understand how it had been with Jack, but I didn't know if I could. They didn't seem to want to hear about it. They wanted to know dates and places. Where had we been? When? Where did we live? Where did we work?

I told them about driving to Florida and then Baton Rouge and then New Orleans. Or was it New Orleans first and then Baton Rouge? I couldn't remember. It had been twelve years ago. I'd tried so hard to forget, and I'd succeeded all too well. The more I talked, the more jumbled everything became.

Did we get to Carson City in the summer or winter? they asked. Was our apartment on the Reno side of the main street or the Lake Tahoe side? I wasn't sure. Did we drive all the way to California, or did we leave New Orleans by plane? We drove, I said. I thought we drove. Did Jack say we flew?

Harper and Minter were insistent but pleasant and polite, even considerate. They were, I surmised later, the good cop half of the good cop–bad cop routine. They were the ones I was supposed to trust and confide in. Scott, who said very little during the first part of the interview, was the bad cop, the heavy. The rest of us had been talking for about ten minutes when he first spoke.

"Virginia," he said, "I did run you through the National Crime

Information Center, and there is a warrant for you in Louisiana, and they will extradite you."

"What is the warrant for?" I begged. "What did I do in Louisiana?"

"The warrant's for murder," Scott said.

I started pleading with them then to tell me what was going on. Who was I supposed to have killed? Where? When? How did all this start? Did Jack just go to the police and make up these things?

Basically, what I learned was this: Jack had gone to police in upstate New York and told them that I'd helped him commit two murders. In Nevada I'd supposedly lured a man out of a Lake Tahoe casino so Jack and I could rob him, and during the robbery I shot him. In New Orleans, as Scott told it, "you and Jack picked up a guy on Bourbon Street, a sailor, enticed him to some location and, when you tried to roll him, apparently there was one hell of a fight, and one of you picked up a tire iron and did his head in." The Louisiana murder supposedly took place in November of 1965, the Nevada murder the following month.

Later there would be variations, many of them, in the accounts of the crimes. Scott, for instance, was wrong about the New Orleans victim, who turned out to be not a sailor but a wealthy middle-aged businessman. Jack himself would change important details every time he told his story. But on May 25, 1977, sitting in that police station, what I knew for sure was that I was being accused by a vengeful, vicious maniac of two terrible crimes that I knew absolutely nothing about. Somehow Jack Sidote had reached out and was holding my life in his hands all over again, and again I was helpless to fight him. I'd never gotten away from him at all.

Desperate now, I tried again to tell them about Jack. He was crazy. He was jealous and possessive and violent and sick. He'd sworn to get even with me for leaving him, and that must be what he was trying to do now. He must be saying these things to hurt me. Again, they didn't seem especially interested. They wanted to know if I'd ever filled out a job application in Lake Tahoe. Had I worked there? Where did I buy groceries in Carson City? Did Jack like guns? Was he a hunter? Was I? Had I ever shot a gun? Where was the laundromat I used in Carson City? Did Jack gamble in Nevada? Where did he get the money? How much rent did we pay? Was I ever a go-go dancer?

I had the feeling of running slow-motion through a nightmare. I kept trying to answer the questions, but some of them didn't even make sense. Why were they asking about hunting? Where did they ever get the idea that I was a go-go dancer? And the details they wanted. All those facts and dates. I couldn't remember. What if they thought I was lying? I looked at the clock again. It was a little after eleven.

Now Scott was talking, saying that Louisiana authorities were going to come to California and arrest me. "And down in Louisiana, from my experience with the South—I've been down there after people—they do not fool around with you down there.

"You know," he went on, "you tell a very convincing story, and you haven't convinced me one bit."

"I don't, I can't convince you," I said, stumbling. I was crying now. I was as terrified as he meant me to be.

"Listen to me," Scott spat. "You know quite a bit about this, and for God's sake, if Jack forced you to do this kind of stuff, now is the time to lay it out. If he made you—"

"I don't know—"

"—do this stuff—"

"—what this is all about."

"Yes, you know what it's all about," Scott said flatly.

"No, I'm sorry, I do not."

"You've been with the man, you've admitted all that," Scott bored in, listing again the stops Jack and I had made on that hateful cross-country trip, the stops that I'd now confirmed that we made.

"Because I have nothing to hide in this," I tried to explain. I tried to stop crying, to pull myself together. "I mean, this is, this is what happened when I was—"

"You were with the man constantly," Scott said.

"I was not with him constantly," I protested. "Yes, I was with him across country, I was, I was with him—"

Scott broke in, talking about depositions that Jack had given. "He turned himself in in New York because it was bothering him about these murders," he said. "Everything that he's told these people from Nevada and New Orleans, you've verified everything he's said . . . I may as well tell you, you're under arrest for murder on a fugitive warrant from Louisiana. They're sending me the tele-type right now, and you're going back to Louisiana."

Then Minter said that Jack planned to testify against me in court.

"How can he testify against me?" I whimpered. "I mean . . . I don't . . . how can he testify against me? I don't know anything about this . . ."

"Listen to me." It was Scott again. "A man turns himself in

— 161 —

in New York City [*sic*] and lays out a couple of murders. He surrenders himself and he's going to take the stand against you. With whatever evidence these gentleman have, and with the evidence they have in Louisiana, I'm telling you, I wouldn't want to be in your shoes right now. Unless there's something . . ."

"I am really getting very scared," I said, "because I feel that I have no way of defending myself in this situation."

"Well, you have one way of defending yourself," Scott snapped, "and that's telling us the truth. If this man forced you in some way—"

"I would . . . I would like to speak with an attorney," I said. (Finally! After babbling for more than an hour, and for all I knew giving them a whole arsenal to use against me, I finally insisted on seeing a lawyer.)

"If you're innocent what do you need an attorney for?" Scott sneered. But he was too late with that ploy. I'd been talking because I thought innocence was defense enough, and obviously I'd been wrong.

"If you haven't done anything wrong . . ." Scott was saying.

"Because you just, you just answered my question," I said. "You don't believe me, and so if you don't believe me—"

"There's too much evidence," Scott said. "You have a stacked deck against you right now."

"Then I need help," I said. "Don't I?"

My attorneys would eventually get a copy of the tape that was made that day, and I've listened to it many times. I can hardly recognize the voice on it as mine. It's a soft, hesitant, terrified, pleading voice. It belongs to a younger woman, younger than I am now and younger than I was on the day the tape was made. It's Ginny Galluzzo's voice.

After the taping was over, I was taken to another room for questioning that was even more bizarre than what I'd already been through. Scott asked me about one murder after another, all committed in Los Angeles County and still unsolved. Maybe it was some sort of routine the police went through with anyone accused of murder, but I couldn't imagine why he was doing it. I could only comprehend that things were getting crazier and crazier.

When Scott was finished with me I was booked. There was no fingerprinting or photographs, only more questions, this time for a clerk filling out paperwork. It was a struggle just to recall my address and height and date of birth. By now the disbelief, disorientation, and fear were so great that I couldn't focus my thoughts. Nothing penetrated the daze until the strip search.

A matron took me to a cell and we both went inside. She ordered me to take off all my clothes, face away from her, and bend over and spread my cheeks. It was my first strip search, and I didn't know why it was being done. I'd never heard about dope being concealed in the rectum or vagina. How would I have known about things like that? All I knew was that I was being stripped and degraded for no apparent reason, stripped not just of my clothes but of my dignity and my very humanity. I was being treated like an animal, and I didn't even know why. I started to cry again, the tears squeezing out from under my clinched eyelids. I couldn't look at the woman. On some level I knew that I was being victimized and that I should be outraged, but I wasn't. Instead, irrationally, I felt over-whelmingly ashamed. I thought of dying. I wanted to die.

The matron told me to put my clothes back on and then she left. When I was dressed I looked around the cell. It was a barren little closet of a room with double-deck cots, a toilet, and a sink. The door was made out of steel bars. I sat down on the lower cot and stared into space a few minutes, my mind a blank. Then it occurred to me that I'd be spending the night in this place. I'd wakened this morning a perfectly ordinary woman, comfortably middle-class and secure, looking forward to a nice day and a nice life. In the few hours since then, without warning or reason, my life had disintegrated. Tonight I'd be sleeping on a cot in a jail cell. The awful reality was beginning to reach me. Suddenly I found myself sobbing, shrieking hysterically, not with any hope of relief but with sheer animal terror. I was still that way when Bob Tuller arrived.

A respected criminal lawyer, Bob is a big, gruff, gray-haired man, rumpled and fatherly, who wears baggy suits and large red suspenders. Danny and I had done some catering for him and the three of us had become friends. When I saw him I calmed down a little, enough to tell him what had happened, how insane it all was, how confused and scared I was. I was desperate for answers and solutions, but I could see that Bob was more than a little shocked and confused himself. He and Danny had been looking for me for hours, he said. They didn't know whether I'd been taken to police headquarters downtown or to a substation, and it had taken a long time to pinpoint this particular substation. He hadn't had time to assimilate what had happened, but he said I should try not to worry. Obviously, this was all a mistake, and we'd get it straightened out. Everything would be better in the morning.

The next morning I went to court, hopeful that at least I'd be able to get bail. I could go home and sit down with Tuller in a quiet, familiar place and start trying to get to the bottom of all this. Instead, I found that I was being taken to Sybil Brand, the county women's prison. I was being held as a fugitive on a murder warrant, the judge said, and there could be no bail pending extradition. I would stay in jail until I agreed to be extradited or until the governor of California signed an extradition order. That's all I heard before I fainted.

chapter 21

There was a sharp odor from something being waved under my nose. Smelling salts? I opened my eyes and realized that I was stretched out on a bench in a small room behind the courtroom. People were standing around looking down at me. Now Bob was bending over me and saying, "Don't worry, we'll find out what this is all about. It'll be okay." I nodded. I could see and hear, but I had only the dimmest impressions of what was happening. I was withdrawing deeper and deeper inside myself, escaping.

I was in a car, and then in a hospital, the county hospital. Somebody was taking my blood pressure and shining a light into my eyes. I was in another car, and it drove through a gate between high walls and stopped. I was in a place that looked like another hospital and people were examining me again. But it wasn't a hospital. It was the infirmary at Sybil Brand.

Talking, cursing, crying, brassy laughter . . . I was in a noisy place now, a holding cell, with ten or fifteen other women. Hookers, dopers, and vagrants. The hookers looked like huge, fantastic birds of prey. Long red nails, stiff beehive hairdos, gold lamé shorts, spike heels. The others were small, drab birds, bedraggled and tattered. They all looked at me suspiciously, then ignored me. Dressed wrong again, I thought crazily. I still had on my beige pantsuit and silk blouse. I didn't fit in.

Women in uniforms herded us three at a time into a room with showers and told us to take off all our clothes. It was another strip search, no more bearable or less shameful than the one I'd been through the day before. We handed our clothes to a trusty, who folded them and put them into plastic boxes labeled with our names. When the search was over we were told to straighten up and face the showers. I stood naked and shaking, my eyes tightly shut again, feeling a clammy mist crawl over my skin. The trusty was spraying us with what I later learned was delousing liquid. We had to stand for a few minutes to give the spray time to work. Then we were told to shower. When we were clean and dry we were handed back our own underwear, in my case only my panties. My bra had underwires and that was against the rules, a guard said. The wires could be taken out and used as weapons. We put on our underclothes and were given our prison-issue uniforms, our little-girl pinafores, knee socks, and tennis shoes.

We were taken to another holding tank, where we stood around waiting for the prison booking procedure to begin. I was finger-printed and photographed, and then somebody handed me an envelope with money in it. We were allowed to keep any money we brought into the prison up to ten dollars. Anything over that would be put into an account that we could draw on to shop at the commissary for items like toothpaste, shampoo, cigarettes, or candy. The envelope had my name on it and a number. My prison number. I was told to memorize it. I nodded obediently, but with whatever was left of my rationality and will, I made myself a small promise. I wouldn't let myself become a number. No matter what happened, I would never memorize that number. I never did.

The booking over, we were put into another holding cell for assignment. There were many parts of the prison, I would learn—cell blocks and dormitories for different categories of prisoners. There was a section for women awaiting trial or extradition, a section for women who'd been tried and convicted, a section for women who for one reason or another couldn't be integrated into the general population. Those included high-publicity cases, snitches, and women accused or convicted of the worst crimes of all, in the eyes of the other inmates, crimes against children. There was also the infirmary. I was assigned to return to the infirmary. The prison authorities had apparently concluded, correctly, that I was having some kind of mental breakdown.

I was in the infirmary maybe a week, maybe two or three. I'm not sure. Time meant nothing because I spent most of it either raving or in a drugged twilight. When I was in touch with reality I would get hysterical, and hysteria disrupted prison order and routine. So I was given Thorazine, a strong tranquilizer, as much and as often as I wanted. I wanted a lot of it. On the drug I could float above the nightmare, detached and safe.

I was hardly conscious of my surroundings, though I knew I was lying in a narrow bed in a ward with other narrow beds. I knew there was an incredibly ancient black woman in the bed next to me. She talked all the time, muttering to herself, sometimes screaming. I was afraid of her. I was afraid of the staff, too. I was dimly aware of being taken one day to a small examining room for a pelvic examination. It was done by a cold, silent man who, I learned later, was called "Dr. No Touch" by the prisoners. He administered "Pap tests," a euphemism for venereal disease checkups, and he was nicknamed for his extreme aversion to touching the inmates, or even speaking to them. I was afraid of him, of the guards, of the other inmates, of the prison itself, afraid of the past, the present, and the future. But when I felt the fear start to swallow me I could ask for more Thorazine. I'd take it and drift away into a merciful nothingness where there was no fear, no time, where I was neither happy nor unhappy, where I hardly existed.

It would have been a luxury to go completely insane, but I was afraid of that, too. If I was sane and all these horrors were happening, what would happen if I went mad? They might put me away in some institution for the criminally insane and leave me to die there. Some part of me insisted on survival, and therefore on sanity. I had to bring myself back to reality, no matter how awful the reality was. I couldn't afford to be a vegetable. I stopped asking for extra Thorazine and took only the dosage prescribed. The fits of hysteria stopped and I became quiet and docile. Before long the infirmary staff decided I was well enough to join the general population.

I was transferred to a cell block where inmates ordinarily go when they're first booked in. There were about twelve hundred women in Sybil Brand at the time, twelve hundred in a jail built for eight hundred. The overcrowding meant that there were three women in every cell meant for two. Each cell had bunk beds with an extra mattress shoved beneath the lower cot. At night the mattress would be pulled out into the middle of the floor for the third inmate. The guard who locked me in said I was to sleep on the lower bunk, but once she left, one of my new cell mates told me I'd misunderstood. I was going to sleep on the mattress on the floor. I didn't argue. It didn't matter.

I never got very friendly with my cell mates. It wasn't that they were especially hostile, but we had communications problems. They spoke a street language that was foreign to me, and sometimes they'd ask me questions that I couldn't answer because I couldn't understand them. Possibly they interpreted my bewilderment as aloofness, so the misunderstanding was mutual. I was an oddity. They were wary of me and I was afraid of them. I kept quietly to myself as much as possible, partly out of fear and partly because I was still on drugs.

I was on the list for what was called "medical line." Periodically the names would be called of inmates throughout the prison who were on medication. We'd all go to a long corridor outside the cell-block area and line up. The line stretched the length of the corridor, but its width was confined to an area measuring about three feet between the wall and a line running parallel to it along the floor. We had to stay between the wall and the line. It was forbidden to lean against the wall. It was forbidden to talk. We'd inch our way along until we reached the end of the corridor and the little window where drugs were dispensed. A nurse would give each of us a pill and a cup of water. We had to take the pill there and then. Standing next to the window was a guard whose job it was to make sure the pills were swallowed. He'd make us open our mouths and then he'd peer inside, sometimes probing under our tongues or between our cheeks and teeth. Refusing medication was forbidden. Hiding it or throwing it away could mean punishment, possibly a stretch in solitary confinement.

Along with the drugs, part of my "treatment" was to pay weekly visits to a psychiatrist who worked part-time at the prison. The sessions were a joke. He was bored and preoccupied and I was afraid to talk to him about anything remotely personal. Bob Tuller had warned me against talking to anyone about anything that could pertain to my case in any way, so with the psychiatrist, as with everyone else at Sybil Brand, I kept conversation to an absolute minimum. It sounds like paranoia, except that my fear that somebody was out to get me was no fantasy. Somebody *was* out to get me, and as a result I was learning to be on guard with everyone, all the time.

Tuller visited me almost every day to keep me abreast of my legal situation, which was a tangled mess. I'd been jailed on a fugitive warrant from Louisiana, but there was also a murder charge pending in Nevada. We didn't know which state, if either, would finally

— 168 —

extradite me. Nevada seemed the more likely bet because Sidote had been extradited from New York and was in jail there. But Bob had to be prepared on both fronts. He had to find criminal lawyers in each state licensed to argue my case, if it came to that. He also had to fight extradition to give himself and the other attorneys time to prepare a defense. He seemed to be on the phone constantly to one state or the other, trying to determine something about the nature of the charges against me. What was the evidence? How strong were the cases? It appeared so far that there was no evidence in either case except the word of Jack Sidote. To me that was incredible, the most insane part of the whole insane situation. Was it really possible that all this was happening to me on the basis of nothing more than the unsubstantiated word of a schizoid, alcoholic ex-con?

It *was* incredible, but it was true. As the days passed I began to grasp the full magnitude of my predicament. Somebody was listening to Sidote's lies and believing them, and I could be in jail for a long time. I was still in only my first month of imprisonment, but ninety days were allowed for a state to extradite. It was beginning to appear likely that I'd be in for the entire three months. If I was going to survive, I was going to have to acclimate myself to prison life better than I'd done so far. I couldn't keep sleeping on the floor and shying away from contact with other inmates. I needed to learn the ropes.

Ordinarily, the women on my block weren't confined to their cells for the entire day. The cells opened onto a barred corridor, and we were allowed to go into the corridor and mingle if we wanted to. I started mingling. I listened and tried to learn. One thing I found out was that I could improve my living conditions somewhat if I could get a prison job. Women who volunteered to work got to live in what was called the "working dormitory," a big room like a barracks, with perhaps sixty beds in it.

I applied for and got a job in the prison visiting room, making sure prisoners got to the right windows. The work got me a bed in the working dorm, along with such luxuries as my own metal closet next to the bed and a small towel rack of my own. It also got me a change of pinafores. There were different-colored pinafores for inmates assigned to different parts of the jail. The women in the working dorm wore blue.

About the time I moved I also stopped taking the Thorazine altogether. I was still required to go to medical line, but I usually managed to drop the pill into a pocket of my pinafore and only pretend to take it. It was risky but I understood that making myself alert and aware again might be a first step toward getting out of the mess I was in. At least, that's the way I felt on my more optimistic days. During the down times, and there were still many of those, the pills took on another kind of significance. I was collecting them, saving each one and adding it to a growing stash hidden in the back of my closet. I wasn't sure I wanted to live in a world so chancy and irrational that the word of Jack Sidote could destroy my life. If I couldn't go on, there were the pills. The thought of dying frightened me, but so did the thought of living.

Eventually, I discarded suicide as an option. I knew the guards sometimes conducted random searches of an inmate's living area. They'd pull up mattresses, rifle through closets, and even tear pictures off the wall. If they found my pills I could be sent back to the cell block, or worse. Finally I flushed them down a toilet. By then, I was in the new surroundings as well as drug-free, and my will to live had reasserted itself.

Life in the working dorm was fairly tolerable much of the time, especially in light of what I'd learned as a feminist. I realized I was on a more even emotional keel when I stopped thinking of my fellow inmates as thieves, prostitutes, murderers, or forgers—as criminals—and started thinking of them as women, women pretty much like me. I got to know them and, more often than not, to like them. I listened to their stories and usually found in them more pain than malice, more desperation than vice. Most of the women were shrewd and tough, tough enough to have survived on the streets. For all my own varied experiences, I wasn't sure I could have made it in the malignant world that many of them had to live in, and I respected their tenacity, their capacity to endure.

Once I came out of my shell a little I found most of the women willing to be friendly. They shared bits of useful information on making daily existence a little more civilized—how to make bobby pins from foil in cigarette packs, how to make hair rollers from the cardboard cores of toilet paper rolls, how to glue pictures to the wall with toothpaste—all the helpful household hints of jail. In return, I shared what skills I had. After a while some of the women seemed to regard me as a kind of consultant. They'd come to me for help in looking up information in law books, or to sound out legal strategies, or just to talk about their kids, lovers, or husbands and about their plans for how to live once they got out.

At first I supposed that my role as jailhouse counselor had to do with my being a little more educated than the other women and a little more experienced in what they regarded as the "straight" world. But I learned there was another factor. There was a certain status in jail that had to do with the crime you'd been accused or convicted of committing. Most of the women felt, probably rightly, that theirs were crimes of survival, products of necessity more than of greed or cruelty. "You do what you gotta do" was a phrase I heard a lot. Women who did what they had to do were respected for their toughness, and the more dire the necessity—the more serious the crime—the more respect they commanded. I was charged with two murders. That was real class.

I don't suppose that it occurred to any of my fellow inmates that I was innocent, any more than it occurred to me that they might be. Nobody cops a plea in jail. Nobody's guilty of anything. Everybody got a bad rap, or a bad couple of raps, or a bad ten raps. The protested innocence is so universal that it's never believed. If you're in jail, it's because you're guilty. Inside prison, just as on the outside, there's that presumption of guilt. The difference is that inside it doesn't matter in the same way. The "straight" standards don't apply. You take people as you find them and, with few exceptions, nobody passes judgment.

I found a certain comfort in the camaraderie of the working dorm. There were times when I could almost convince myself that I was living a sort of collegiate dormitory life, a protracted slumber party with my friends. Then a guard would yell, "Line up, ladies," or "Locker check, ladies," and I'd remember where I was.

Inmates at Sybil Brand were allowed one visit a day, whether from one person or a group. Visiting wasn't easy. The visitor might stand in line for two hours to reach the admittance window, only to be told that the woman he or she came to see had already had her visit for the day. Despite the rigors of the system, I had a lot of visitors.

Ray came to see me often, all bitterness between us tabled for the time being. He'd been flabbergasted by my arrest, but right after it he moved back into our house and took over the management of my business. It was no time to talk about reconciliation or the future, but he was loving and supportive throughout the ordeal and I was grateful. Knowing how concerned I was about mounting legal bills, he tried to reassure me. "We'll do whatever we must," he'd say. "If we have to sell the house, we'll sell it. The important thing is to get you through this and back safe at home."

Danny visited too, often with Bob Tuller. He was indignant at the police and outraged over the whole affair and, I think, very afraid for me. But when he saw me he tried to keep up a brave front, making little jokes, kidding me about my dowdy pinafore, offering as much encouragement and support as he could.

There were visits from women in NOW, from members who'd opposed me on some issues as well as from friends. The organization wasn't doing any formal solicitations, just passing the hat at chapter meetings, but about a thousand dollars had been raised for my defense. Along with financial support the NOW members brought me news of the movement. The talk at the time was all about the International Women's Year conference, which was upcoming in Houston. I tried to be an enthusiastic listener, but it was hard. I'd worked on IWY planning and I was to have been a delegate to the conference. So much was passing me by.

Faithful as always, two of my most constant visitors were Bobbie and Clara, my friends from the old days on the *Princess Louise*. Clara took over scheduling duties, organizing my visitors so that everyone who wanted to see me would be able to without conflicting with somebody else. Bobbie masterminded a fund-raising project to help pay my legal bills.

My thirty-seventh birthday came a week after my arrest, and Bobbie staged a birthday party for me in the Sybil Brand visiting room. She and Clara were there, along with some other close friends. Drugged and sick as I was at the time, I couldn't help laughing at the sight of Bobbie, now pushing fifty herself, dressed as a birthday cake. She and Clara had brought me a present, a little gold necklace with my name on it. I couldn't take it at the time, or even touch it. Inmates and visitors were separated by panes of glass. But as soon as I got out of jail they gave it to me and I put it on. I've never taken it off.

If the visits lifted my spirits at times, they also had a way of sending me into bleak depressions. They underscored my pain at being separated from my friends and deprived of my normal life. Sometimes at night I'd get permission to use a pay telephone in the prison and I'd call Ray or Clara or Danny or Bobbie. When they'd answer I'd find that I couldn't even talk. I'd just cry, on and on, while they tried earnestly and futilely to console me. Eventually I'd hang up, go back to the dorm to lie down, then try to sleep and fail. I'd stare into the darkness and see in my mind the flushed, wild face of Jack Sidote bending over me and hear him screaming, over and over, "I'll see you rot in jail."

One night in August I woke from a fitful sleep and looked at the clock on the dorm wall. It was four-thirty in the morning. I tried to go back to sleep and couldn't, and the next time I looked at the clock it was still four-thirty. I felt disoriented. Was I only imagining trying to sleep? Was I really asleep and having some strange dream? Finally I did sleep, but when I woke up the next morning the clock still said four-thirty. Obviously, it had broken during the night. For some unaccountable reason the incident left me uneasy. Later that morning I was called to the visiting room and Clara was there, and I could see from her face that something terrible had happened. She told me that Bobbie had been murdered. She'd been killed sometime after midnight and her body was found in the morning, wrapped in a rug in the garage of her suburban Orange County home. The police didn't know who killed her.

Whacky, irrepressible, goodhearted Bobbie, who'd first shown me the ropes on the *Princess Louise,* who'd mothered me and nagged me and stood by me through the terrible times with Jack and through all the times that followed. The news of her death toppled me all the way back to the bottom of my emotional ladder. For several days I was hysterical and incoherent, as bad as I'd been when I was first jailed. There seemed to be no end to pain, no limit to it.

August was coming to an end and so was the time I could be held in Sybil Brand pending extradition. Yet there was no definite word on whether I'd be extradited. During my three-month jail stay I'd been called into court a number of times for hearings on delaying extradition, but they were tactical legal maneuvers, filled with technicalities that meant nothing to me. The hearing scheduled for my ninetieth day of incarceration was special, however, and as I was loaded onto the prison bus bound for court that morning I felt a stomach-churning mixture of anxiety and hope. If neither Nevada nor Louisiana was prepared to extradite, I'd be free. The hope died as soon as I walked into the courtroom and saw a man and a woman dressed in uniforms of the Douglas County sheriff's office. Nevada was going to extradite.

In court that day were about a dozen of my friends. They listened to the news that Governor Jerry Brown had signed the extradition papers, then watched helplessly while I was led out of court in handcuffs, which were attached to waist chains, and leg shackles.

The six- or seven-hour car ride to Nevada would have been funny had the situation been less grim. After leaving court the deputies decided to stop at a store in Van Nuys that sold uniforms. They wanted to go shopping! I sat in the back seat, trussed up in my various chains while they took turns going into the store. When they were finished we started driving northeast, but we hadn't gone far when they decided to stop at a McDonald's. They asked if I wanted anything and I said yes, I'd like a hamburger. It was about four in the afternoon and I hadn't eaten since breakfast some ten hours before. They detached my handcuffs from my waist chains so I could eat without doubling over, and after lunch they reattached the things and we drove on.

By the time we made our next stop, this time for coffee, the woman deputy and I had struck up a conversation about crocheting. She crocheted, and I'd taken it up to pass the time in prison. We talked about various stitches, about what she was making, what I was making. After a while I noticed that she and her partner were exchanging questioning looks, as though something peculiar was going on. It occurred to me then that they'd probably come to California expecting to pick up a crazed killer, and what they got instead was a subdued, polite housewife who was talking about her needlework. They were right. It was peculiar.

When we stopped at a restaurant for the deputies to fill their coffee thermos, things got odder still. They said it would be easier to keep the thermos in the back seat, where there was more room, and to let me serve the coffee when they wanted it. To do this, I'd have to have my hands free. "We're not supposed to take off the handcuffs," one of the deputies said, "but if we do, do we have your word that you're not going to do anything?" It seemed like such a silly question. What was I going to do? Make a break for it in leg shackles in the middle of a desert? Or maybe brain them both with the thermos bottle. That's what a crazed killer might do, all right —unless, of course, she gave her word that she wouldn't. I promised not to make any desperate moves and they took off the handcuffs for the rest of the ride, locking them again only when we pulled into the driveway of the jail. They took me inside and saw me through the booking procedure.

It was an old, tiny jail in the little town of Minden, the Douglas County seat. I was photographed, fingerprinted, and booked on a charge of murder, and then led to a cell. It was a rather large concrete room, almost luxurious by my recent standards, with a bed, a table, a shower, a toilet, and a sink. The guard who locked the metal door behind me returned a short time later with some prison clothes. When she opened the door I could hear muffled voices in the hall. I was surprised. The jail appeared to have only five cells or so. Why were there so many guards around? The deputy said the guards in the hall were attending to another prisoner. Good, I thought. At least I'd have a little company. I asked who it was.

"John Sidote," the guard said.

I went berserk. I'd never even thought that I might be in the same jail with him! I started screaming that I couldn't stay there, that he was going to come and get me. I was so terrified of him, and so convinced by now of his power to hurt me, that I was sure he'd find a way to get to me and kill me during the night. My hysterics finally subsided and the guards who'd come in to try to calm me down left. But neither they nor I got any sleep that night. Every time I heard a sound I was on my feet again, screaming, pounding on the metal door, begging to be let out. I guess they believed I could keep it up indefinitely. The next morning I was driven to Carson City, about ten miles away, and jailed there.

chapter 22

Back in 1977 I knew almost nothing of what had happened to Jack
Sidote in the seven years we'd been apart—I didn't want to know.
I hadn't seen him in all that time and I'd talked to him only twice:
once when we discussed divorce over the phone shortly after I left
California for New York, and again when I telephoned his mother
in 1974 after learning from my parents that Mrs. Sidote had suffered
a recurrence of a cancer that had first been diagnosed some years
earlier. I called out of respect for her, but Jack answered the phone.
We had a short, cold, desultory conversation. I believe I asked him
how things were going, not wanting any details and not getting any.
But in 1983 I'd have occasion to learn all about how things had gone
with Jack between 1970 and 1977.

After he got out of jail in the summer of 1970 Jack had his
parole transferred from California to New York and moved in with
his parents in Wappingers Falls. Almost from the first he had trouble finding and keeping steady work. He worked intermittently at
odd jobs, a few months as a house painter, a few more installing floor
tile. It was the kind of blue-collar, menial labor he despised. He
began drinking as soon as he got out of jail and developed quickly
from a heavy binge drinker into a full-blown alcoholic. By 1974, by

his own account, he often drank as much as a quart of hard liquor a day, with beer on the side. Between 1974 and the beginning of 1977 he was in and out of alcohol rehabilitation programs seven times, never with any lasting success. He'd go into a hospital program for as long as five months at a time, only to begin drinking as soon as he was discharged. By 1975 he was having alcoholic blackouts, as well as delirium tremens with hallucinations, both auditory and visual. His liver was damaged and he was beginning to bleed internally from alcoholic gastritis.

The Jack Sidote I'd known had been a Jekyll-and-Hyde personality, charming one minute and sadistic the next, a chronic failure terrified of failing, a man who couldn't analyze his own difficulties or take responsibility for his own life, who rationalized his own inadequacies by blaming them on other people, usually on me. The charm evidently had withered under the onslaught of his constant drinking, while his negative side had flourished. His difficulties at the time included more problems with the law, as well as trouble controlling his old pattern of taking out his anger and frustration in violence against women. In 1973, drunk and jobless, Jack went to the home of his old patron John Lipani. While burglarizing the house he was confronted by John's wife, Marie, also an old friend. He beat her savagely. He testified later that the incident happened while he was in the grip of an alcoholic blackout.

Jack was charged with assault and first-degree burglary and spent six months in the Ulster County jail before his lawyer bargained to have the charges dropped in return for Jack's plea of guilty to the charge of third-degree burglary. After entering the plea Jack was freed on bail to await sentencing. He remained free while the case dragged on and on, as New York authorities tried to decide whether or not to sentence him as a "predicate felon," that is, a criminal with a record of an earlier felony. There was a question of whether his manslaughter conviction in California would bear on his sentencing in New York. If it did, he could face a long sentence in a state penitentiary in New York.

In May of 1976 Jack was thinking about suicide. The DTs and hallucinations were ongoing, and he was complaining of severe anxiety attacks and of losing touch with reality.

Early in January 1977, Jack was living in Albany, sharing a small apartment with a roommate. Less than four months earlier he'd been discharged from a 120-day stay in an Albany VA hospital, his seventh attempt to dry out. He'd been drinking ever since his discharge. One night when he was alone in the apartment he turned on the gas stove, blew out the pilot light, and stuck his head in the oven. The suicide attempt was thwarted when his roommate came home and dragged him out of the gas-filled apartment.

Did he want to live or die? Did he want to be in jail or out? Maybe nobody knows the answers but Jack, and maybe he doesn't even know himself. He seemed to believe he had nothing to live for, but he lived. When he was in jail he worked hard to get out, and when he was facing jail he worked hard to stay out. He was con-wise and clever and he knew all the angles—all about plea bargaining, and trading information for freedom, and doing "good time," and snowing a parole board. Yet prison was an answer of sorts for Jack. In jail he was all the things he couldn't be on the outside. He was a big man, a leader, a success. He knew how to get along with the other inmates and the prison staff. He knew how to follow the big rules and bend the little ones, how to survive with a little style. And in jail he was sober. He couldn't drink. Freedom for Jack meant alcohol and alcohol was killing him. In jail at least he could live.

Maybe those thoughts were running through his mind in the cold hours before dawn on January 22, 1977. I have no way of knowing. I was a continent away from him at the time, living a life as sunny as his was dark. In California I was happy, productive, optimistic, safe. And in New York he was drunk, sick, suicidal, defeated, facing a possible long stretch in a bad jail. I can't know all that was in his mind, but there's one thought I'm sure was there: I'm convinced that he blamed me for every disaster in his life. It was my fault that he left the good life as a flashy bartender in 1965 and that he abandoned his wife and daughter. It was my fault that he served time in Chino and was in trouble with the law again. It was my fault that he found himself back in New York a drunk, a failure, with no job and no money and no crowd to cheer while he sang like Sammy Davis, Jr. I'd lured him away from everything good in his life and then I'd left him. He loved me and I'd left him, slut that I was—not only left him, but gone off and married another man. I was living and he was dying and it was all my fault.

I believe he was determined that if he had to go under, he was going to take me with him. I believe that was his guiding thought that night when he picked up the phone and called the Albany police and told them he wanted to talk about some murders.

After Jack's phone call two uniformed policemen picked him up at his apartment and drove him to the Albany police station, where they turned him over to two detectives. Drunk but reasonably coherent, he gave them the first of his several accounts of the murders that he and I allegedly committed together during the trip from New York to California in 1965. There are police records indicating that he originally mentioned at least three murders, not two, along with a number of robberies that he committed alone in the course of the trip. However, there are no surviving details of the possible third murder or other crimes. His first confession was not recorded on tape or by a stenographer, and all that remains of it are the written recollections of the two detectives who heard it.

By their account, Jack told them that in November of 1965 I enticed a "Spanish or Venezuelan" businessman out of a Bourbon Street bar in New Orleans so Jack and I could drive him to some remote place and rob him. Later, Jack said, I beat the man and robbed him, dumped his body behind a warehouse, and left him for dead. After that murder, he said, we drove to Nevada and killed a second victim, a San Francisco man that I picked up in a Lake Tahoe casino and later shot to death in our car.

The two Albany detectives either didn't believe Jack or had no real evidence to hold him on in their jurisdiction, so they sent him home. At the same time, they put accounts of the murders on a nationwide law enforcement teletype hookup, flagging one for Nevada and one for New Orleans. The next day they went to Jack's apartment and asked for more details of the alleged killings, which he provided. Still, they didn't arrest him.

Within a week or so, however, the Albany police got word from both Nevada and Louisiana of unsolved murders in those jurisdictions that seemed to fit Jack's descriptions. He was arrested and turned over to the New York State Police, who took him to their headquarters in the town of Highland. There he told his story again, but not until he'd been given a lot of vodka by his interrogators. The officers said later that they had to get him something to drink because he was suffering badly from DTs during his confession.

By February 9 Jack apparently had shaped up enough to give his first formal, on-the-record confession, this time to representatives of the Ulster County district attorney's office in Kingston, New York. And, though he's always maintained that he confessed only to clear his conscience, he was also vitally concerned that day with clearing up the matter of his predicate felon rap. Before he started talking about any murders, he wanted to talk about that.

"I have a slight reservation as to my being sentenced as a predicate felon under this current problem I have here in Ulster County," he told his interviewers. "I'm going to cooperate, but it remains in the back of my mind that if I get sentenced as a predicate felon, I could get four years in a state prison here."

(In 1983, prosecutors trying me in Louisiana would make much of the fact that Jack confessed to two murders "against his own interest," putting himself in jeopardy of two life sentences in jail for no other reason than to cleanse his soul. It's possible, though, that he believed he might fare better with courts in Nevada or Louisiana, where he had clean slates legally, than he would in New York with a possible predicate felony sentence. In fact, with my life to bargain with, he might do very well indeed. He might even get immunity from all charges in exchange for testimony against me. That way he'd not only get his long-threatened revenge against me—that was the main thing—but at the same time he might be able to squirm out of the jam in New York. Of course, there's no way to prove that he was thinking along those lines. It is a fact, however, that his original confession to the Albany police was made precisely four days before he was due to be sentenced in the Lipani burglary. It's also a fact that by the time he finished confessing in New York, the authorities did decide he would not be sentenced as a predicate felon. He was sentenced in the Lipani case to the six months he'd already served in the county jail and the matter was dropped.)

After talking about his local legal problems, Jack got on with a long, detailed account of the Nevada murder. I don't know how much of what he said about his own role in the killing was true. I do know that everything he said about me was a lie.

We were running short of money during our stay in Carson City, so we decided to rob somebody, he said. "We figured that was the only way to get money." Our plan was to go to a Lake Tahoe casino and pretend to be brother and sister, tourists on our way from the East to California. We'd pick out a victim and I'd come on to him, luring him out to our car. Then we'd drive him somewhere out of town and rob him. With this in mind, he said, we went to Harrah's Casino on the night of December 18, 1965.

"She sat next to this man and we introduced ourselves," Jack told the police. "I was drinking and she was carrying on a conversation, getting friendly with the guy, whatnot, and I guess after about an hour I got pretty well drunked up and it didn't seem like things were moving fast. I don't know, maybe I was nervous. I was drinking heavily and finally I said to myself, 'The hell with it, I'm loaded and I'm going out in the car and go to sleep.' I went and I went to sleep in the back seat of the car, kind of conked out, you know, and when

I kind of rolled out of it or came to we were—I know we had left. It was like, you know, being half awake and half asleep."

I was driving and the man I'd picked up was in the front seat with me, Jack said. He stayed in the back seat in his semiconscious state while I drove for some indeterminate period of time.

"And suddenly I was jolted awake," Jack said. "I heard, like, noises, whatnot, and as I was getting up I heard some noises like bangings, shots, cracks. I was stunned, like, you know, and then I had seen them close together like in a haze, whatnot, and when I looked up the guy was slumped over the right-hand side of the car, just slumped over there. She had a gun in her hand . . ."

The gun, Jack said, was a .22-caliber revolver. I allegedly used it by wrapping my arms around the man in an embrace and shooting him in the head. After the shooting, Jack said, we dragged the man to the side of the road. I supposedly grabbed his wallet and told Jack to take a diamond ring off the dead man's finger. Headlights were coming, Jack said, so we jumped back into the car and I drove us back to Carson City. He went to our room and drank while I went out again to get rid of the gun and clean the victim's blood out of our car. I came back two hours later, he said, and told him we had to leave town because the oncoming truck whose headlights we'd seen might have seen our license plates. With that, we decamped for California.

On March 16, 1977, Jack gave his first formal account of the Louisiana murder. This confession, like the Nevada story, read like a nightmarish piece of fiction to me.

With money running low in New Orleans, he said, we decided for the first time to solve our financial problems with a robbery. I was supposed to find a victim in some French Quarter bar ("Bourbon Street is a pretty good hustling area," Jack informed the state police) and entice him out to our car.

"We decided I was going to stay in the trunk of the car, and she was going to drive this subject to a remote area and we were going to roll him," Jack said. "So we proceeded to do that."

While the victim and I were riding out of town, Jack said, he lay in the trunk and held a piece of cloth between the lid and the trunk lock so the lid would stay ajar and he could breathe.

"Anyway, it seemed we were driving quite a while, and apparently she hit a chuck hole and the trunk lid slammed shut," Jack recounted. "Finally the car stopped, and there was some mumbling; they were standing by the back of the car and I heard her say something. Virginia said that she felt ill or nauseous; she had some pills in the trunk of the car, medicine. She needed some reason to get the trunk open. When she opened the trunk door I came out and grabbed this guy, and that's the first time I had seen him. He was, oh, I'd say about fifty years old. He was maybe a little shorter than I am, say five foot seven, very portly, very heavily built.

"A struggle ensued, and I just tried to knock the guy down," Jack went on. "I had a tire iron." (In the original confession to the Albany police *I* had the tire iron; Jack was unarmed.) "I wanted to get his money and leave. During the struggle Virginia was standing by the side of the car and she yelled, 'He saw my driver's license. He knows my name. We got to kill him.'

"I guess when the guy heard that he started fighting, like, desperately," Jack said. "He was a lot—I'd say he went about 210 or so, very stout, and I couldn't get my leverage. He was pushing me towards the back of the car. There were two lug wrenches in the car." (There was no mention of lug wrenches in the Albany confession, nor would they ever appear again in Jack's later versions of the story.) "I said to her, 'You got to help me.' At that time she grabbed a lug wrench and struck him on the side of the temple. He let go of me and he fell and then she struck him again, and at this time the guy was, like, passed out. I don't know what he was. Anyway, she grabbed his wallet and jumped back in the car and we left."

Asked to describe where the killing took place, Jack said it was a rough, stony, flat area, "strictly rural." (The warehouse he described in the Albany version was gone now.)

After the murder we drove back to our hotel in New Orleans, he said. His clothes were "pretty well battered up," so I went to our room and got him some fresh ones while he stayed in the car. Then we drove "some place on a dark street," where Jack changed clothes and we threw away his soiled clothes and the lug wrenches. We went back to the hotel and retrieved $1,400 from our victim's wallet, along with some "Spanish or Venezuelan" currency. After pocketing the money we tore up the wallet and flushed it down a toilet.

"That night Virginia flew to Dallas, Texas, from New Orleans, and I stayed there and I flew out the next day to Dallas," Jack said. (In his original version nobody flew; we drove from New Orleans together.)

In my years with Jack I never once saw any sign that he had a conscience, much less a troubled one. That being so, I found the end of his March 16 confession revoltingly cynical in its hand-wringing piety and phony remorse. The twelve years since the killings had been "like a nightmare" for him, he said, and he had to drink to escape his guilt.

"The reason I was drinking like that was because I was so disgusted with myself," he said. "This was my way of trying to escape or trying to kill myself, man, because I couldn't stand what I had become or what I had done. I guess through these statements maybe, or through this revelation maybe, you know, that in the future because of this, these statements, I will spend the rest of my life in prison. But I couldn't live on the streets anymore the way I was, knowing what I had done, having to live with that.

"At first I thought it was for vengeance, to get back at Virginia for what happened when I was in prison, but the more I think about it, the more I realize I had to do it, not because of vengeance but for higher—you know, I had to bare myself."

Shortly after the March 16 confession he was extradited to Nevada and jailed in Minden. It was the same jail where, some five months later, I would spend one night just a few feet away from him, separated only by a concrete wall and by the distance between the two paths our lives had taken in the seven years we'd been apart.

chapter 23

Because of Jack, and for no other reason, I found myself in Nevada facing possible trial for the murder of a man named Donald Fitting, a hotel employee from San Francisco, killed in 1965 while vacationing in Lake Tahoe, left dead beside a deserted road somewhere between Lake Tahoe and Carson City. Donald Fitting. Not even his name was familiar to me. He was a man I'd never seen, never met or spoken to. Certainly, I'd never robbed or killed him. I'd never robbed or killed anybody. But the longer I stayed in jail, the more convinced I was of Jack's power to make people believe otherwise. His lies had brought me this far; they could do worse. He could see to it that I stayed in jail the rest of my life.

Theoretically, I should have been able at least to go free on bail once I'd been extradited to Nevada, but the bail question got tied up in an interstate snarl of red tape. Louisiana had deferred to Nevada to take first crack at prosecuting both Jack and me. At the same time, however, Louisiana had issued detainers against us pending the outcome of the Nevada case. Because of the Louisiana hold I was denied bail, and my hope for at least a taste of freedom vanished. The Carson City jail became my home for the next three weeks.

Though there was nothing especially horrible in my treatment or surroundings in Carson City, I found jail there even more oppressive in some respects than Sybil Brand had been. I was in an unfamiliar place, miles away from most of my friends, and I felt more disoriented and alone than ever. I still had visitors—Ray and Danny and Clara, among others, made regular trips to see me—but nobody could do much to lift my spirits. Every day the prospect of going on trial for murder seemed more real.

Bob Tuller kept assuring me that Nevada had no case and, rationally, I knew he was right. I had plenty of time in jail to think it through. Under Nevada law, a person could not be convicted of a crime solely on the word of a co-principal in that crime—that is, another person who'd participated in it. There had to be corroborating evidence. In this case there was none. What little physical evidence there was didn't support Jack's story; it contradicted it. As Jack told it, while facing Donald Fitting I was able somehow to wrap my arm around him and shoot him from the back and a little to one side. But the victim had been shot directly in the center of the back of his head. For me to have done it the way Jack described it, I'd have to have been double-jointed and had an arm five or six feet long.

Nor was there any evidence to put me at the scene of the crime. The New York police had questioned Wasyl Bozydaj, the young guy we'd been traveling with. He could confirm only that he and Jack and I had been staying in Carson City around the time of the murder and that Jack and I sometimes went out alone together at night—hardly incriminating testimony. There were no other witnesses against me and there was no other evidence. There was only Jack's word, the uncorroborated word of a co-principal, an alcoholic, suicidal, self-confessed thief and murderer. Sometimes I could muster the optimism to assure myself that it wasn't nearly enough to convict me, or even bring me to trial. On the other hand, it had been enough to keep me in jail for more than three and a half months already.

In mid-September Louisiana, clearly unready to proceed with its own case, dropped its detainer against me, although it left standing its arrest warrant for murder. The result was that I was finally allowed to make bail. The bail was set at $75,000 and Ray and some of my friends came up with the collateral and the ten-percent surety. I was, for the moment, free—within limits. I had to remain within the jurisdiction of the Nevada courts, so I couldn't go home to Los Angeles. A friend with a house in Lake Tahoe was kind enough to put me up while the legalities ran their course. I stayed with her and waited.

What luxury it is just to be able to decide for yourself when you'll eat, when you'll bathe, when you'll get up in the morning and go to bed at night. In the days before I went to jail I took those privileges for granted. Now I cherished them, reveled in them. Such small things, but they restored to me some measure of self-assurance and peace. For one whole week I had the time and freedom to regroup for whatever was coming. I had time to get ready for the preliminary hearing on my murder charge, which was set for September 22. On that day I'd be face to face with Jack Sidote for the first time in seven years.

On August 4, while I was still in Sybil Brand fighting extradition, Jack and the Nevada authorities had come to terms on a plea bargain. Charged with murder, which carried a life sentence, Jack agreed to plead guilty instead to voluntary manslaughter and robbery in the death of Donald Fitting. In return for the reduced charges, he also agreed to testify against me. He must have believed, or at least hoped, that his deal would get him off with a light sentence. He was in for a rude shock.

According to a Nevada law, an accomplice in a crime is not allowed to testify against an alleged co-perpetrator until the accomplice receives all the benefits of any plea bargain. Consequently, on September 20, two days before my preliminary hearing, Jack was brought before a Nevada District Court judge in Minden to be sentenced under his plea bargain. The maximum sentence for manslaughter was ten years, the maximum for robbery fifteen years. On both charges, the maximum is what Jack got. The judge ruled that he would serve ten years and fifteen years, the sentences to run not concurrently but consecutively. Twenty-five years! That meant that even if everything broke exactly right, Jack might have to serve more than four years before he'd be eligible to get out on parole. Jail-wise as he was, he'd miscalculated badly. And knowing him as I had, I could well imagine his reaction. The bastards had screwed him. The fucking DA had let him down by not putting the word in with the judge, who could have gone easy instead of throwing the book. Now there was nothing to look forward to but a long stretch in jail, not because Jack had killed and robbed—that was beside the point—but because the fucking bastards wouldn't give him a break. It was all their fault.

I could see his rage at my preliminary hearing two days later.

Maybe it was that too-familiar look that made me feel he hadn't changed much over the years, at least not physically. The rage was holding him together and bearing him up, and the old cockiness was still there.

My reaction to him hadn't changed much either since last we met. He was sitting only a few feet away from me, waiting to testify, and I found that I couldn't keep my eyes off his face. He never once looked at me, but I kept staring at him, much the same way I might have stared at a deadly snake. I felt a gut-deep fury at what he was doing to me, along with a crawling revulsion at ever having known him, lived with him, let him touch me. But squeezing aside those emotions was the old fear. It hadn't diminished at all in seven years; it was still as strong as on the day he'd tried to kill me. I shook with it. I couldn't stop shaking. On that day I was more afraid of him than of anything the courts might do to me.

He was called to testify, and I watched him saunter to the witness chair. Now he'll do it, I thought. He'll tell the lies. He may rot in jail, but so will I. He'll see to that.

Jack sat down, took the oath, and announced that he had a statement to make. "Due to the severity of the sentence I received last Tuesday in this case, I feel like justice in this matter has been duly served," he said, "and therefore I choose to remain silent at this hearing."

It took me a minute to realize what he was saying, but at last it sank in. He was not going to testify against me! He might be just toying with me; he might have plans for me later. But for the moment, at least, his anger at the authorities who were sending him to jail was stronger than his need to hurt me.

I almost collapsed with relief, but it was mixed with anger and frustration and a growing horror. Jack was the one who had brought me here, and now he was the one letting me go. My fate depended on his whim, and I wasn't even going to have a chance to answer "not guilty." For the first time since I'd left him, I began to understand the extent of his power. I'd thought I was free of him years ago, but it was beginning to dawn on me that I might never be free. Jack Sidote could reel me in anytime he felt like it.

Despite Jack's failure to testify, despite the lack of any corroborating evidence, the man presiding over my hearing relied on the police's *hearsay* testimony about Jack's confession to find probable cause to charge me with murder.

In Nevada a preliminary hearing need not be held before a

judge. Mine wasn't. It was before a justice of the peace. And the justice of the peace, who was not even a lawyer, decided on the basis of Jack's lies that I should be tried for murder. I would wait almost two more months, still free on bond but with the threat of an upcoming trial, before that outrageous abortion of justice would be reversed.

After the justice of the peace's decision my attorneys filed for a writ of habeas corpus, demanding that Nevada either try me or free me. A hearing on the writ was held in Minden on November 14 before District Judge Michael E. Fondi. Judge Fondi said that Jack's story, as recounted at my hearing, was nothing but hearsay and should never have been treated as evidence in the first place.

More important, the judge said that Jack's story, hearsay or otherwise, wasn't sufficient reason to hold me for trial. Judge Fondi had, he said, "examined the record as closely as I can" and found nothing "sufficient to corroborate anything with respect to [Jack's] confession or to the fact that Mrs. Foat was an accomplice to the crime he confessed to." The writ of habeas corpus was granted.

My long-awaited freedom lasted for something under five minutes. While I was leaving the courtroom a Nevada deputy arrested me on behalf of Louisiana authorities, who had issued a new detainer against me. Once again, I was led off to the Carson City jail.

The rearrest was less a blow than it might have been because I'd expected it. Nevada authorities had advised their counterparts in Louisiana of Jack's refusal to testify at my preliminary hearing. The Nevada prosecutors also informed Louisiana that they believed Jack *would* testify sooner or later, but that his testimony wouldn't be enough to bring me to trial. The fact remained, they said, that *there was no corroborating evidence.* The upshot of these interstate communications was that if Louisiana wanted me tried for murder, it had better get its own case ready. Nevada didn't have one.

Inexplicably, though, Louisiana couldn't seem to decide what to do with me. During the six months following my initial imprisonment in Sybil Brand, my lawyers had tried repeatedly to get some kind of decision from the district attorney's office in Jefferson Parish, the suburban New Orleans jurisdiction in charge of the case. Bob Tuller had even traveled to Gretna, the parish (county) seat, to ask the prosecutors face to face what their plans were. He couldn't get a firm answer. The Louisiana authorities said at first that they'd wait and see what Nevada did. Once they did see, however, they still wouldn't commit themselves to a definite course of action. They did not seem willing either to drop the case or to assert it. They ordered me held when I was freed on the habeas corpus writ, but when Nevada police asked them to teletype a formal arrest warrant, none was sent.

As it turned out, my last jail term in 1977 was only an overnight stay. As soon as I was rearrested my attorneys filed for a supplemental writ of habeas corpus. On November 15 Judge Fondi granted it, apparently convinced that Louisiana wasn't seriously pursuing a case against me.

I was free, and yet I wasn't. Technically, the Louisiana charge was still hanging over my head. On the day of my rearrest my attorneys had tried one last time to clear it up, only to be met with Louisiana's usual ambivalence. They telephoned Assistant District Attorney Shirley Wimberly, who was handling the case, and asked him again what Jefferson Parish planned to do about me. Wimberly told Bob Tuller he didn't plan to prosecute. As far as he was concerned, the case was closed. However, the conversation was never confirmed in writing. In 1983 a lot of time and money would be spent trying to prove that it never took place. In any case, the arrest warrant that had been issued by the sheriff's office was not dropped. Wimberly's office was given my address and telephone number in Los Angeles—if Louisiana wanted me, it knew where to find me— and there the matter stood. The only other thing I could have done to resolve it was go to Louisiana and demand to be arrested, a grim option that I was not prepared to take. Otherwise, I could just wait.

It seemed that the chances were that the Louisiana case would just molder away, another random bit of unfinished paperwork to be shifted over the years from filing cabinet to microfilm to computer, stored and harmless. But I knew there was also a chance that on any given day of my life the police could show up at my door and the nightmare could crank up all over again, the old horrors against a new backdrop. I knew that, yet I had no real choice but to live with it.

Bob Tuller suggested that I try to put it out of my mind. I should go home and start picking up the pieces of my life, he said. I should get on with things. There was no real case in Louisiana, just as there had been none in Nevada. The Louisiana matter was the flimsiest of ghosts, locked away in a dark closet. Only the remotest happenstance, the most bizarre scenario, could ever open that closet door.

.   .   .

Ray drove me home from Nevada, neither of us saying much. I felt oddly detached, as though I hadn't yet salvaged myself from the wreckage of the last six months. I examined my emotions and found them as arid, flat, and featureless as the desert outside the car. The worst was behind me and I was going home, but there was no relief or happiness in it, not even the comfort of feeling that the nightmare was finished, disposed of and explained away. I felt depressed, spent, drained, and exhausted, tired to the bone. I'd been through almost four months of jail followed by another two months of grinding, relentless anxiety, and for what? I still didn't understand how it could have happened in the first place. And now the whole meaningless, merciless farce had trailed off to an anticlimax of legal limbo. I was free but living under a cloud. I hadn't been convicted of anything, but I hadn't been exonerated of anything either.

Picking up the pieces of my life sounded like a fine idea, but which pieces was I supposed to pick up and where was I supposed to put them? Were Ray and I going to try to patch up our marriage? Could I pick up where I left off with my business? The story of my arrest and the subsequent situation in Nevada hadn't made a big splash, but it had been in the papers. Word got around. What did I tell my clients, or, for that matter, business acquaintances who'd accepted at face value my good reputation in the community? "Sorry about that business of being an accused murderer, folks, but that's all over now. What do you say we just forget it?" I couldn't kid myself. There would be questions in a lot of minds now. It remained to be seen just how bad the damage actually was. Then there was my standing as a feminist and the respect I'd enjoyed among my fellow feminists. I could only hope they'd see what happened in Nevada for what it really was: another form of battering.

Back in Los Angeles, Ray and I agreed to give our marriage another try. I think he felt particularly protective of me at the time, and I was grateful to him for standing by me during the ordeal. It seemed to be enough for a new start, but that was an illusion, based on his support and protectiveness, my dependence and gratitude. The crisis had thrown us back into the pattern of our early relationship, but only temporarily. I think Ray hoped, and even believed, that my experience with jail would revive some of the old vulnerability he'd once loved in me, would shock me back into being the soft and deferential woman he'd met back in San Pedro all those years ago. But I could no more go back to being that woman permanently than I could go back to being a high-school girl in New Paltz. That's not who I was anymore.

We spent Christmas at home together and early in 1978 we went to Hawaii for two weeks to rest and to work on cementing the marriage. By the time we got home we were bickering again. All the old difficulties that had been put aside during my troubles were now back on the table, and along with them, new financial worries stemming from my legal bills and other financial setbacks. In the spring of 1978 Ray moved out of the house again, this time for good. The marriage was over.

My catering business was on the rocks, too. It hadn't been a good year at the Warner Racquet Club, and for a time I went from month to month paying off debts that had accumulated there while I was in jail. Eventually I had to concede that the business couldn't be saved. I left the club in the fall of 1978, salvaging only my cooking equipment, which went back into my own kitchen. I began operating in a small way out of my house again, just as I had when Affairs Unlimited was first starting out.

My husband was gone and my business was decimated, but I hadn't lost everything. The part of my life that had mattered most before the disaster had survived it. NOW welcomed me home, and I realized more than ever that the women's movement *was* my home.

chapter 24

After the Majority Caucus's national takeover of NOW in 1975, the internal power in California NOW rested with a group of women who called themselves the California Caucus. Although they didn't necessarily hold the high offices in the state organization or its big chapters, these women considered themselves the revolutionaries, the theorists, the political strategists, and the queenmakers of the women's movement in California. They were powerful regionally and closely allied with the national NOW leadership. Because of my willingness to work, as well as my philosophical kinship with this group, I was part of it even before my arrest, and I returned to it once I was free. Almost from my earliest involvement with NOW I was a member of the cadre, the favored inner circle, and as such I was marked for leadership.

My potential as a leader must have been hard to spot in my first few meetings with the California Caucus, however, because I seldom opened my mouth. I was associating with women who were among the most influential shapers of NOW policy, and I was grateful just to be included by them. If I ever disagreed with any of their policies or tactics I was far too awed to say so, which may have been just as well for my career in the movement. It was a time when disagreement was not tolerated and dissent was grounds for ostracism, a time of strict, almost cultist, orthodoxy. It's easy now to see how unhealthy such an atmosphere was, but at the time I wasn't interested in the problem. I just wanted to get back to work.

I knew firsthand how jails dehumanize women, and almost as soon as I returned to California, I was named co-chair of NOW's statewide Women in Prison Task Force. Working to better the lives of women in all state and federal jails, we concentrated a lot of our effort on the California Rehabilitation Center, a facility mainly for women convicted of drug-related crimes. We got state funds to bring art and writing programs into CRC, and still more state money to set up a law library there. We brought in sports programs and set up specially modified consciousness-raising sessions. We started an ongoing study of how women are discriminated against by the criminal justice system, and from what we learned, we prepared testimony for state legislative committees and proposed model legislation aimed at equalizing the treatment of women under the law.

Along with the prison work, I plunged into the fight to ratify the Equal Rights Amendment. California had been among the early states to ratify, so in 1978 our state-based efforts focused on neighboring Nevada. Several times I traveled with co-workers to Las Vegas, where we stood outside casinos, handing out pro-ERA leaflets. We walked city streets distributing ERA information door to door, and when state elections came around, we worked to elect pro-ERA candidates to the legislature.

The ERA had been submitted to the states in March of 1972 and the time limit for ratification was to expire in 1979. As the deadline neared it was obvious that we were going to fall short of the thirty-eight states we needed. But early in 1978 two young law students in California came up with what they thought was a way to buy more time. The U.S. Constitution didn't mandate a time limit for ratification, they said, and therefore the deadline could be extended. Many ERA supporters doubted the idea could work. But in Washington NOW leaders got a bill introduced in Congress to extend the deadline, and back in the states the membership got to work pushing for the bill's passage.

In California I helped put together a strategy called the California Plan, which was so effective that it was soon adopted by other states. It featured car caravans of NOW members traveling throughout the state and holding town meetings. We'd show a film about the suffragists and then urge people to continue what our foremothers started by raising money and organizing in support of the extension. When we weren't on the road we were home writing letters and sending telegrams to Congress, and encouraging other people to do so. We were soon on a first-name basis with Western Union operators. That fall there was hardly a NOW member in California who wasn't busy every night of the week working for the extension.

The final vote on the bill was scheduled for October of 1978, and NOW was mobilizing a march on Washington as part of its final lobbying push. I went to Washington for the national board meeting where the march was planned, then flew home to help assemble a large delegation from California.

More than a hundred thousand of us from all over the country marched on July 9. Dressed as a suffragist I walked down Constitution Avenue carrying one end of a long banner that bore the text of the Equal Rights Amendment. It was a proud moment for me, and a nostalgic one. I thought back to the civil rights March on Washington fifteen years before, and I thought of all the strange twists and turns my life had taken since then. At that moment I believed that the best of my life had outlived the worst, and I was reunited somehow with that young woman who stood in the sun in 1963 and listened to Martin Luther King and cried, sure that she was doing what she was born to do. I was sure again. I was doing what I could to make the world a place where women had choices that I hadn't had, and so were less likely to make the mistakes I'd made and suffer the consequences. I was sure, and all the wrong turnings seemed almost trivial.

In 1978 I was elected vice president of California NOW. At the top of my agenda was the 1979 NOW National Conference, which was to be held in Los Angeles. Some four thousand feminists would be in town for three days of meetings, workshops, strategy sessions, elections—activities that would go a long way toward determining the future of the organization. The conference was going to be a major event, and the state leadership recommended to the national board that I coordinate it.

The assignment meant constant meetings with committee chairs, city officials, and hotel personnel. It meant overseeing details like housing, entertainment, exhibitions, and child care. It meant rounding up volunteers to work phones, type, provide transportation for visitors. It meant frequent trips to Washington to report to the NOW national board. It was a mammoth job, lasting from the fall of 1978 through October of 1979, when the conference was held. It was so big, in fact, that by the summer before the conference I found myself in a suite of offices with a paid staff member to help handle it. Fortunately, I was an experienced organizer and my knowledge of hotel management and catering was invaluable.

October finally came, and there were all the usual disasters that are bound to crop up in an event of that size: a foul-up in hotel reservations for the huge New York delegation, fights with a nutrition-mad child-care expert who was convinced the hotel was trying to poison her charges with complimentary sugar cookies, a long-winded and unsolicited welcoming speech from the California governor. But, blessedly, most of the catastrophes were behind the scenes. On the surface the conference was a streamlined triumph, widely praised as the best in NOW's history. The workshops, meetings, banquets, and concerts all ran smoothly. Ellie Smeal, the venerated commander in chief of the ERA battle, was elected to her second term as national president with only nominal opposition. Exhibitors poured money into the NOW treasury. And the national leadership, which had to put far less of its time than usual into the nuts and bolts of producing the conference, was very pleased.

My frenzied pace of 1978 and 1979 carried over into 1980. That was the year that NOW was making an all-out push to concentrate ratification work in states where the ERA had a reasonable chance of passage. I went to Illinois as a field organizer, shuttling from Chicago to Bloomington to Springfield. In Bloomington my friends and I rallied the overworked, exhausted local NOW members behind a strategy to find pressure points where area legislators might be vulnerable to force applied by pro-ERA constituents. With that effort going well we went to Chicago to help organize a pro-ERA march. The event brought out about a hundred thousand partisans in Chicago.

In Springfield we kept an all-night vigil in the state capitol's rotunda on the night before the senate vote. The voting was called off midway through the roll call, when it was clear that we were going to lose by three votes. Worse yet, there were those of us who could see in the loss in Illinois the handwriting on the wall for the ERA nationally. Yet, incredibly, after the vote the strained silence of the vigil erupted into a long, noisy party. We gathered in a senate meeting room, where we cried and laughed and toasted each other and damned the opposition. We were releasing tension from weeks and months of work that seemed to have come to nothing, but it was also a celebration. We were celebrating ourselves. People whose lives once centered on maneuvering shopping carts through supermarkets now knew what it was to maneuver legislators through votes.

We'd felt the stirring of our personal power and the solidarity of our collective power, and we would never be the same. In the long run, we weren't going to accept defeat. We'd lost that night, but we weren't losers. Things would be different someday because something had happened to all of us that was going to make things different.

One thing we were learning from the ERA fight was that we had to move out into electoral politics if we were to influence national policy. With that lesson in mind, I ran in 1980 as a Kennedy delegate to the Democratic National Convention. I'd met Ted Kennedy several times at political events and I was impressed with him. His voting record on women's issues was impeccable, and his staff was one of the most effective in Washington. Besides, I was disillusioned with Jimmy Carter. He'd been soft in his support of the ERA, I thought, and he'd given only lip service to other women's issues. Campaigning hard, I was elected as a convention alternate, and then appointed as an at-large delegate and later as a floor whip by Kennedy's California organization.

The VIP treatment given the large and powerful California delegation was heady stuff. We flew to New York in a chartered jet and stayed at the Waldorf. We were courted by the candidates and sought out by the national press. But aside from the prestige and glitter, an issue of real substance was at stake. The convention was a chance for feminists to prove that we were canny and effective politicians—not just window dressing for the Democrats.

Our main goal was to get strong pro-ERA and pro-choice planks into the party platform. We put together a feminist network that was so large and complex that it amounted almost to a convention within the convention. Several reporters called it the most effective operation on the floor, outshining both the Kennedy and Carter forces in strategy and tactics. Rallying behind such leaders as Gloria Steinem, Bella Abzug, and Shirley Chisholm, we set up offices and opened communications lines and canvassed delegates to lobby for our planks. The payoff was that both planks, worded the way we wanted, were voted into the platform. One committed the party to withhold money and strategic support from state and local Democratic candidates who opposed the ERA. The other was on the abortion issue: It condemned government interference with a woman's right to choose when and whether to have children, and it committed the party to protecting that right, regardless of a woman's economic status.

We had won the platform fight but Kennedy's losing the nomination was a blow. Without him, it would be harder to implement our program. However, we felt we'd won the big fight, and we were able to go back home and campaign energetically, if not especially for the candidate, then at least for the platform. I worked for Carter throughout the fall, doing everything from organizing fund-raisers to driving sound trucks. It was a losing effort, but a learning experience.

I was busy and happy and fulfilled in the years following my 1977 arrest, though I had financial problems. I was still marginally in business at the Warner Racquet Club, however, when, in 1978, I got a call at the club from a man named Jack Meyer, who said he was looking for a caterer for his daughter's wedding and had found Affairs Unlimited toward the top of the Yellow Page listings. I met with him and his daughter, liked them, catered the wedding, and started seeing Jack socially.

He was a television producer, some sixteen years older than I, divorced, with two grown children. A kind, caring person, Jack had a strong social conscience and was proud of my work as a feminist. At the same time, he was a traditionalist whose abiding love of family came before everything else in his life. I think it was that sense of family, more than anything else, that drew me to him. Watching him with his children and his brother and cousins and nephews and nieces gathered for a Jewish holiday dinner, I realized how much I missed my own family. I'd come so far from those noisy, wonderful family dinners at Grandma Ida's farmhouse back in New Paltz— come so far and lost so much. I missed my parents, and I missed the sense of continuity and tradition that comes with belonging to an ethnic household. I missed the love, the fond bickering, the unquestioning support. I needed all that, and with Jack I found a readymade family that seemed to fill the need.

Our relationship was no grand passion but there was a lot of warmth and affection in it, and in August of 1979 I moved in with Jack. Unfortunately, it took only a few months for the arrangement to get uncomfortable. Preparations for the NOW National Conference were in high gear when I moved in, and while Jack was understanding about the demands on my time then, he couldn't see why there was no letup afterward. I couldn't give him the time he needed and he couldn't give me the freedom I needed, so soon after the conference we parted amicably and I moved out.

It was more than a year before we saw each other again, but when we did we realized that we'd missed each other. We started dating again and decided to get married. There was a lavish wedding and a wonderful honeymoon in Europe, but we came home to the stark reality that the marriage just wasn't going to work. We married at a time when I was exhausted, depleted, and looking for a safe haven. I'd been through the trauma of 1977 and then the final breakup with Ray and the incessant work that followed. And as so many women do when they're at low ebb, I fell back into the old pattern of my girlhood. For all my hard-won strength and independence, I wanted somebody else to carry the load for a while. I wanted to be taken care of.

I should have realized that I'd come too far for that. The fatigue was temporary, but my commitment to the life I'd built was not. I had my way of doing things and Jack had his, and fond as we were of each other, neither of us had the will to put the other first or even the flexibility to fit the other in. I saw that and I left Jack less than two months after the wedding. The marriage was annulled within a year.

Aside from my political and feminist work, neither of which produced income, my main concern in 1980 was getting back on my feet financially. By the end of 1979, my worldly capital amounted to a couple of thousand dollars that I'd cleared from the sale of my house. I'd scrapped my catering business altogether, since I had no time for it, and I was, ironically, overworked but unemployed. By the spring of 1980, however, I would have not one job, but two.

After I moved out of Jack's house the first time, I moved in with Jan Holden, a close friend from NOW. That event was important in my life because for the first time I was not reaching out to a man for companionship and emotional support, as I'd always done before. I was beginning to value more and more the friendship between women and the strength they could give each other.

Jan and I together started a company called Anodos Productions. Anodos produced fund-raising events for nonprofit organizations. I organized the events and catered those that required food. Jan, who had produced plays and concerts, had a wealth of contacts in the entertainment industry, and through her I met many Hollywood luminaries. Anodos's biggest achievement came in 1981 when we produced a play called *Women of Courage,* co-written by Jan and Debbie Jones. We had a cast that any movie producer might envy: Patty Duke Astin, Jayne Meadows, Patty McCormack, Jean Stapleton, Olivia Cole, Karen Grassle, and Tovah Feldshuh, all generous women and good feminists.

While coordinating projects for Anodos, I also went to work for the Amalgamated Clothing and Textile Workers Union. Michael Linfield, the union's strike coordinator for the West Coast, hired me as his assistant for the boycott supporting the strike against the J. P. Stevens textile company, the strike remembered by most people as the basis for the movie *Norma Rae*. With a basic question of union-busting at issue, the strike had a lot of the fervor of the early days of American unionism, a fervor that I came to share. But along with old-fashioned zeal, the union brought some brand-new techniques to the fight. In addition to a consumer boycott of J. P. Stevens products, the ACTWU pioneered the technique of "corporate isolation," under which financial pressure was brought to bear on other companies on whose boards J. P. Stevens board members also served.

I stayed with the union for a little more than a year. It was satisfying work, and the pay was good enough to push financial worries off my priority list for the time being. Best of all, though, I learned how effective corporate isolation could be, and I believed it could be adapted from labor disputes to legislative fights. Some antifeminist California legislators would soon learn to their sorrow just how adaptable the technique was. In 1981 I used what I'd learned in the strike to organize NOW's opposition to twenty-two antiabortion bills in the state legislature. We defeated all twenty-two.

Maybe it was the approach of my fortieth birthday in 1981 that got me thinking about long-term personal goals. I was happy and busy, but my life existed only in the present tense. I'd laid no groundwork for permanent financial security, and I was worried about the future. What I did was to resurrect one of my oldest, fondest ambitions: to become a lawyer. I wanted to stay active in NOW, of course, but not necessarily as an officer.

I talked over my plans with some friends and political supporters, who pointed out that I'd been, in effect, running California NOW for several months, because of the illness of the state president. It was time, they said, for me to have the title as well as the job. Elections were coming up, and I should run for the state presidency. The ERA fight was coming to an end and, win or lose, the outcome would bring changes in NOW and a greater need than ever for creative leadership. We were moving more and more into party politics and intra-organizational alliances, and my help was needed there.

I argued that I had neither the time nor the money to take on the state presidency as a full-time job. It was then that Ellie Smeal suggested that money shouldn't be a problem. Several states were giving their NOW presidents a salary, and California, with the largest membership of any state, could certainly afford to do the same. So it was that in 1981 California NOW changed its by-laws to permit a salaried leader, and I was elected to a two-year term as the organization's first paid president.

Law school would have to wait, along with any other personal plans I might have. I was swept back into constant activity. I traveled all over the state, pushing for more grass-roots participation and more input from local chapters as California NOW's membership almost doubled, from 20,000 to nearly 40,000. There was so much going on: An ERA mobilization kit, soon adopted as a national model, gave chapters a step-by-step program for rallying support in local communities; a fund-raising office was set up in San Francisco and our lobbying office in Sacramento was strengthened; I prepared and presented testimony before local, state, and national legislative committees on such issues as reproductive rights, gay and lesbian rights, education, reapportionment, comparable-worth employment, and joint parental custody; an ongoing statewide network of women's organizations and political action committees was established; marches and rallies were organized; I spoke on radio and television and to conferences and conventions. I belonged to local and state Democratic committees and was on the board of the Americans for Democratic Action, the Democratic Women's Caucus, and the Governor's Women's Council. As part of this political activity I supported Los Angeles mayor Tom Bradley's campaign for governor, Jerry Brown's candidacy for the Senate, and Leo McCarthy's race for lieutenant governor.

By now I was living alone in an apartment in Los Angeles, but I saw very little of it. On a typical week, if no political campaigns were in progress, I might spend three days in Los Angeles, three more in San Francisco, and one in Sacramento. There was no time to think deeply anymore about where I was going. Certainly, I didn't think much about where I'd been.

There were times, of course, when I'd be lobbying some U.S. senator, or sitting on the speakers' platform at a political rally, or chatting at a cocktail party with people whose faces I knew from movie screens, and I'd think about how far I'd come and how fast. I'd be dressing carefully for some special event when a high-speed unreeling of memory would overtake me, and I'd see a little Italian Catholic girl in her Confirmation dress, waiting for her prince to come; or a young woman, pregnant and terrified, wearing somebody else's cast-off maternity clothes; or a battered wife with torn clothes and bruised flesh. I'd see a ragged blue pinafore and white knee socks, and I'd hear a grating voice drawling "Locker check, ladies. Line up." But for the most part I put it all out of my mind—my past, my journey, jail, Jack Sidote, Nevada, Louisiana. I'd become an expert at repression and denial over the years.

Even my work with women in prison was part of the denial process. Being able to help them meant I was separate. I was free. Just as when I first learned that battering had a name and a pattern to it, and I thought in terms of "those poor women" and never "poor me," I now went into prisons and looked at the inmates and thought "those poor women." Them. Not me. I denied unless I was forced to confront. That didn't happen often, but it happened.

There was the time when my co-chair on the Women in Prison Task Force came to me, full of enthusiasm for a new project she'd conceived. She belonged to the Los Angeles Women's Chorus and she'd gotten her fellow singers to agree to bring women's concerts into the prisons. It was, I agreed, a wonderful idea. The task force had worked mainly in state prisons, not county ones. We went to places that looked more like schools with dormitories than jails with cages. This time, however, it was going to be different. The Women's Chorus had decided to start the program close to home. They wanted to go to Sybil Brand.

I called the jail and made the arrangements, ignoring my dread, pushing it away. I went to a meeting in the office of the captain, the woman in charge of the jail, to discuss the program. Even there I managed to be aloof, detached. I'd never been in her office before, never even been on that side of the jail. How curious, I thought, that I stayed there for three months and saw so little of the place. It was an idle thought, nothing more.

The night of the concert I went with the chorus to the visitors' gate at the prison. The guard there told us we'd be entering a different way, through the gate the buses used in transporting their prisoners. Did we need directions? No, I said. I knew where it was.

Then we were in the auditorium. I knew it well. I'd been to weekly movies there. The singers started setting up for the performance, and I sat on a table in the back of the room, trying to hold on to the detachment, the aloofness, feeling it slip away, feeling the anger begin to well up, and the fear. Then it was time to start, and the women prisoners began to file in, section by color-coded section. I saw the red pinafores come in, and the pink ones, and then the blue ones. My color. The one I'd worn here.

I knew I had to get out because if I didn't I was going to scream and scream and not be able to stop. But I couldn't scream and I couldn't move. I was riveted there. Tears were pouring down my face, though I made no sound. The music was soaring, but I couldn't make out the words. I could only stare at the women in their pinafores, feeling both watcher and watched. I was terrified. I didn't know who I was.

Then, slowly, the world righted itself, and I began to hear the music. The women were completely caught up in it, bonded together through it. They were laughing and clapping and moving to the music. At the same time, anxiety crept into the faces of the guards. Women in prison are kept in line through intimidation and isolation, but the prisoners in that room, at that moment, were strong and united. It was the guards who were afraid. I saw their fear and felt absolutely exalted by it, but only for a moment. I knew that after this hour or two of pleasure and power, the inmates of Sybil Brand would spend hundreds of hours of loneliness and cowering dread, not necessarily because the system was stronger than they were, but because they believed it was.

chapter 25

Revolutions are about power. They're started either by or on behalf of people who lack power and who want it, if only enough to control their own lives. The feminist revolution was no different. Women were powerless, and we began to unite and work to change that. In some measure, we succeeded.

One problem with revolutions is that they can bring power to people new to it, who don't know how to handle it. For some of them, the power becomes a drug and they become addicts, greedy for it and amoral in their pursuit of it. At first there's only the power within the revolution itself: who will make the decisions, devise the strategies, direct the energies. Small as it is, that power is important to people who've had none at all, and they fight and haggle over it.

Then, if the revolution expands, power in the larger society beyond the revolution is at stake. At that point the revolution rolls over the revolutionaries. It often cannibalizes its own. That was true of the French Revolution, the Russian Revolution, the revolution of American blacks in the 1960s, and dozens of smaller revolutions. The cannibalism always comes in the name of the revolution itself, the good of the movement, the expendability of any one person in the face of the greater good. But that noble reason is not the real one. Like the revolution itself, this struggle is about power. The addicts who want more power refuse to see that when you betray your own, you betray the revolution. This usually happens about the time the movement ceases being revolutionary and is either co-opted by or joins the social mainstream. The feminist revolution was no better or worse than others. It was the same.

The women's movement I saw always had intricate internal politics and shifting alliances. There was niggling over offices and titles and talk of who'd been in the fight first or worked hardest and what they'd done or failed to do lately. There was always speculation about who was rising and who was falling. There were power plays and coups and countercoups. But the internal differences didn't seem very big or visible in the early days, partly because the movement itself wasn't very big or visible. Besides, the outside hostility directed against us acted as a cohesive force. There was no nasty epithet we hadn't heard used against us and few social pressures we hadn't experienced. In the heat we tended to cling together.

Sometime in the late 1970s things began to change. When we won the fight for the ERA extension in 1978, politicians who'd once thought of us as a lunatic fringe started taking another look. After our display of skill and savvy at the 1980 Democratic Convention, the whole country was taking another look. We didn't hear so much about "dykes" and "bra burners" and "radical trash." We'd proved that we were rational, astute politicians who could work effectively within the system. We couldn't be dismissed with a joke or a sneer anymore. We were a force that had to be reckoned with, one way or another.

Around 1975 or so, if somebody from a NOW chapter went to a candidate and said, "The chapter would like to lend its support to your campaign," the politician would say, "That's nice, but come and work as individuals. Your endorsement might hurt." By 1980 the candidates were seeking us out and asking for endorsements. Old, established political organizations wanted alliance with us, and those alliances were working and making us all stronger.

We had arrived. We were winning respectability—and losing the revolution. For some feminist leaders, invitations to the right cocktail party became more important than helping women in jail. A spot on a talk show was more important than women starving in slums or on the streets or forced to have babies that they didn't want and couldn't afford to feed. New power was to be had and they didn't want to jeopardize it with all those controversial, ugly issues.

I had learned a lot about power in revolutions, and I was about to find out about the cannibalism. I had been, in my time, as powerless as a woman can be. When I first tasted my own power, and the power of women who were united in a cause, I liked it very much indeed. I was ambitious for it, worked for it, and got it. I loved the political ins and outs and I thrived on the internal intrigues as much as anyone. But I've had a lot of time and reason to think about it, and I honestly believe that for me the power was never more than an interesting game, and finally only a means. It was a tool to be used for and shared with other women, for their betterment as well as my own. It was not an end in itself. I don't think I ever misplaced the ideals amid the power. I think I kept faith with the vision. I think most feminists have kept faith with the vision.

I don't remember exactly when I first met Shelly Mandell, although I knew her by reputation long before we became friends. She joined NOW about the same time I did and also belonged to the California Caucus. She rose to prominence in the organization quickly, just as I did. She served two terms as president of the large and influential Los Angeles chapter and was then elected to NOW's national board. She was one of the leaders of the ERA campaign in California, and we saw each other at innumerable meetings. It was 1979 before I got to know her well. I was coordinating the NOW National Conference, and Shelly, as president of the Los Angeles chapter and one of my committee coordinators, was deeply involved in conference planning.

Feminist politics was the basis of our relationship, but in time Shelly and I got to be personal friends as well. She was a bright, energetic, forceful woman who seemed willing to do anything for you if you were her friend. I liked her for all that, and I suppose I liked her, too, because she reminded me of myself in a lot of ways. We were about the same age and had the same interests, and we had rather similar backgrounds. Shelly was a native Angeleno from a working-class Jewish family. Like me, she wasn't college-educated, though she was taking some college courses and planning to go to law school. Shelly had come up the hard way and she was extremely shrewd and street-smart. She'd acquired a certain social poise because she'd worked hard to acquire it, just as I had. She was ambitious. She wanted to better herself, and that was something I could certainly understand.

We shared a love of political maneuvering and we were both good at it. Shelly was probably more instrumental than anyone else in talking me into running for state president of NOW in 1981 and in seeing that I could afford to take the job. I was unopposed when I ran, but there was serious opposition to changing the state by-laws to make the presidency a paid position. It was Shelly who led the floor fight at the state convention to change the by-laws.

She moved as well in local Democratic politics as she did in feminist circles. She knew everybody, and it was she who introduced me to a number of politically influential people when I first got involved. In those days Shelly and I were inseparable pals. We turned up at the same parties, worked on the same projects, shared many of the same friends. I think now that Shelly may have considered herself my mentor, whereas I considered us equals and allies. I also believe that she came to see me as a competitor and to resent my power in NOW.

At about this time, another woman, Elaine Lafferty, joined our circle of friends. Elaine was some years younger than Shelly and me, and her main interest in the women's movement seemed to be party politics. When Shelly and I went to the Democratic National Convention as delegates in 1980, Elaine, an alternate delegate, came along. It was there that she and Shelly became close friends. Though it did not seem to me that Elaine and I were compatible, she was Shelly's friend, and I accepted her.

Early in 1981 we even talked of going into business together. Shelly and Elaine and Jan Holden and I wanted to open a feminist restaurant in Los Angeles. The idea eventually fizzled out, but before it did, we decided to run background checks on ourselves to make sure there'd be no barrier to our getting a liquor license for a restaurant. Shelly had a contact in the city courts with access to a computer that had information about criminal records, so she ran the check. I remember her telling me that something had turned up about a murder warrant against me, but my impression was that she was talking about the case that had been dropped in Nevada. That didn't disturb me particularly. Jan and Shelly and Elaine already knew about it. Most people who knew me knew about the case. There had been stories about it in the NOW newspaper in 1977. It was old news. Nothing to worry about. If she'd learned anything more, surely Shelly would have told me.

There had been a time when Shelly was perhaps the most promising prospect for national leadership in all of California NOW. Everyone expected that after she finished her term on the national board she'd be elected to national office and perhaps even become president one day. But in 1981 her star began to fade. She had begun to miss meetings of the board, and of NOW's powerful national Political Action Committee (PAC), which she also served on. On several occasions, because she wasn't available, I had to go over her head on certain state matters that required input from the national office in Washington. She told me she bitterly resented that. I, in turn, resented the times she went over my head in some things involving the national board and PAC. We managed to maintain a shaky friendship, but we had some vicious arguments.

Despite all the dissension, Shelly and Elaine came to me in 1982 with a proposition: I should run for national president of NOW, and they would manage my campaign. In fact, I'd already been thinking about running. I felt that NOW's national leadership was losing touch with the chapters and the rank-and-file members. I thought the power should be decentralized. I also thought the organization needed to rediscover its roots and recommit itself to some tough and controversial feminist issues, among them reproductive rights, lesbian rights, prostitution, racism, and violence against women.

I thought my chances of being elected were pretty good. Ellie Smeal's second term would end with NOW's national conference in the fall of 1982, and she couldn't succeed herself. The field was wide open. I was president of NOW's largest state organization, and ever since I'd coordinated the national conference in 1979 I'd had considerable national visibility. My potential base of support was very wide. I'd gotten letters and phone calls from all over the country urging me to run.

When I held a meeting with some friends in the California NOW leadership to discuss running, the reaction was mostly positive. However, the question of my legal situation came up. I said I could see no problem in the future. As for my past difficulties, I didn't plan to make them a campaign issue. If questions about Nevada did arise, I'd simply tell the truth. Surely if anybody could understand, other feminists could.

Still, I decided eventually not to go after the presidency. In July I went to a national board meeting and talked to several other women who were thinking about running, including two I respected very much. One was Jean Conger, a good friend who'd been NOW national secretary and later Ellie Smeal's executive assistant and a key figure in the national ERA campaign. The other was Jane Wells-Schooley of Pennsylvania, NOW's national action vice president. (There were three vice presidencies. Action was responsible for implementing NOW policy. The job included overseeing proposed legislation, for instance, and shepherding it through Congress.) Jean decided not to run, but Jane was in the race to stay and I didn't want to run against her. She had more experience on the national level than I did, and I thought she'd be better for the job. At the same time, I thought that I might be very good for her job. The action vice president was the officer closest to the issues, and the issues were what interested me most. I left Washington having decided to run for that office and to back Jane for the presidency. Jean Conger and Jan Holden would manage my campaign.

My regard for Jane was not the only reason for stepping back from the top post. Despite all my brave talk, Louisiana stuck like a thorn in the back of my mind. The national president had tremendous visibility. Her name was known all over the country. What if some ambitious official in Jefferson Parish decided to make some headlines by indicting the national president of NOW for murder? What if he opened that long-shut file drawer?

In any case, the decision was made, and I went home and told Shelly and Elaine what I planned to do. They were furious. Not only had I scuttled their plans, and done it without consulting them, but I was also backing a candidate for president whom Shelly opposed. It seemed to me from Shelly's attitude that whatever fragile truce had existed between us was broken, and so was our friendship.

I campaigned throughout the country that fall and went to the convention in Indianapolis in October with high hopes. The feedback we'd been getting suggested that I was very likely a winner for action vice president, despite competition from three other candidates, one of them on a slate backed by Ellie Smeal.

Nobody could have worked harder than my campaign team did for me. Dressed in blue T-shirts bearing my "Go Foat" campaign slogan, Jean and Jan and their co-workers scoured the convention drumming up support. They canvassed delegates, defused trouble spots, collected and analyzed information, and distributed an impressive campaign brochure they'd put together. The team included a large contingent of friends and backers from Southern California, and also Kay Tsenin of San Francisco. Kay had become my best friend over the previous year and was the one person in the world I trusted most. A brilliant lawyer, she was my action vice president for California NOW. I'd learned while working with her how heavily I could rely on her sensitivity and stability, her loyalty, her sense of humor, her hardheaded common sense.

It was the day before the election when we first heard about the rumor campaign. One of my workers had gone to Jean and Jan and asked what all this talk was about some outstanding murder warrant against me in Louisiana. She'd heard about it, she said, from somebody in the Los Angeles chapter. Within a couple of hours we confirmed that the rumor was circulating throughout virtually every state delegation. "Well, we've got to do something about this," I told my friends. I tried to appear calm and unruffled, but it was more to bolster their spirits than mine. I knew better. My team made a valiant effort to explain the whole complicated legal rigamarole to every delegate who would listen, but it was far too late. The election was only hours away, and the damage was done.

When I confronted Shelly and Elaine with my suspicion that they'd started the rumor, they denied it. Yes, they said, they were backing the Smeal slate, but they would never stoop to anything so low. Nevertheless, it seemed to me that other people in the NOW administration were also involved in what had happened and that the decision to stop my candicacy had been made.

However the campaign against me started, I was angry and hurt, but more than anything else, I was bitterly sad. I was no stranger to cruelty, but not at the hands of women.

I lost the election, and that was a disappointment but not an especially big one. When I learned the election results after a long night of waiting, I showered, changed clothes, and went to a plenary session to take part in a debate on issues. I congratulated my successful opponent, as well as her fellow candidate on the Smeal slate, Judy Goldsmith, who'd been elected president.

When the conference was over, I went back to California feeling almost relieved. At least I had my own life back. I would go ahead and finish up my term as state president, which ended in July of 1983. Then I'd proceed with my original plan to finish college and go on to law school. Meanwhile, there was still so much to do. There was a need to regroup and find new directions after the defeat of the ERA. There were political races in California that NOW was interested in. I'd keep busy. And, I knew, I'd be happy.

Despite Indianapolis, I was happier in 1982 than I'd ever been in my life. The future was falling into place. The present was filled with all the activities I loved—the feminist work, the politics, the time I spent with my friends. I took pride in the fact that California NOW under my presidency had grown larger and stronger than it had ever been before. And as for power, I still had all that I wanted or could use. With my ties to the women's movement, the Democratic Party, and organized labor, I was uniquely situated to get things done, and that fact was widely recognized and respected. If I had some cause for bitterness, I had no room and no time for it. My life was too rich and too full.

In California, a complicated fight had been brewing over the makeup of a slate of candidates to run as delegates to the 1983 California Democratic Convention. The slate would represent a coalition, which I'd helped put together, of NOW and several other like-minded political groups.

I was taking part in a board meeting in Washington when I was called out of the room for a long-distance phone call from a harried politician in Los Angeles. It seemed that Toni Carabello, editor of the NOW national newspaper, as well as Shelly and Elaine, had approached him with complaints about the slate. All the bickering was weakening the coalition, he said. To keep the peace he'd worked out an intricate compromise to put Elaine's name on the slate. He'd go ahead with it if I gave my okay. I gave it, but only because I didn't want to make things worse than they already were. I felt, that our internal dispute only served to confirm every tired cliché about women not being able to get along or work together.

I went back to the board room and walked over to where Shelly was sitting. "You can tell Elaine and Toni," I said coldly, "that I've given *my permission* for Elaine to be on the slate." I walked on toward the back of the room and Shelly followed, clearly as angry as I was. Who did I think I was, she wanted to know. She had more political power than I could ever hope to have. I'd find out who had the power.

That all happened in December of 1982. It was the ugliest kind of scene, and I tried to forget it. I went home to California in time to sit on a podium with Leo McCarthy's family and a group of state dignitaries in Sacramento as McCarthy was sworn in as lieutenant governor of California.

As the record later showed, Shelly Mandell went home and put in a phone call to Jefferson Parish, Louisiana.

chapter 26

It was a Tuesday morning, January 11, 1983, and I was rushing to get Kay Tsenin to her plane. She'd been in Los Angeles for a meeting and was taking an early flight back to San Francisco, provided she could catch it. I had a well-deserved reputation for last-minute arrivals at airports, and this morning I was running true to form. We were late, as usual, and I was speeding.

We left the freeway and barreled down a shabby street leading to the Burbank airport, the tiny commuter airport I knew so well from my constant trips around the state. As we turned into its long, U-shaped driveway, I sensed something strange. Something was wrong here. It was only a little after eight o'clock on a weekday morning, and the airport ought to be bristling with traffic. Yet my car was the only one in the driveway.

We looked up and saw a helicopter, flying low and still lower, almost as though it were going to land on top of my car. It hovered there and I drove on, inching along at about five miles an hour now, looking around with real curiosity. I nudged Kay and pointed to the right, toward the Pacific Southwest Airlines terminal. The steps leading up to it were lined with uniformed policemen carrying rifles and wearing what looked like riot gear.

"What do you think's going on?" I asked Kay. "It looks like they're waiting to arrest some terrorist or something. Maybe some big-time criminal is coming into the airport."

"I don't know," Kay said. "Whatever it is, it must be really big."

I glanced into my rearview mirror and saw that my car wasn't alone anymore. There was a line of police cars behind it, stretching back nearly to the driveway entrance. Suddenly, the one directly in back of me started flashing its red light. I pulled to the curb and stopped, puzzled and exasperated. Maybe they'd seen me speeding or noticed that my license tag was expired. I was always careless about that kind of thing, but good God, here they were about to nab John Dillinger or somebody, and they were taking time out to give me a traffic ticket? Well, who could figure cops? I started rummaging through my purse for my driver's license.

"Kay, you can still make your plane," I said. "Go on and run for it. This must just be some traffic thing and I can take care of it."

I looked up and was surprised to see some men in street clothes walking toward the car. One of them looked familiar, but I couldn't quite place him. Medium height. Sandy hair. Where had I met this guy? Then I remembered. Warren Eggar. Warren Eggar of the Fugitive Division of the Los Angeles Police Department, whom I'd met in 1977 when he walked into my home and arrested me for murder. So then I knew.

I felt fear so icy it made me calm, and when Eggar got to the car and told me to get out I obeyed woodenly, saying nothing, asking nothing. We stood together beside the car. It was then that I noticed for the first time the cameras clicking all around me, the television crews that had materialized from nowhere.

"This can't be happening again," I informed him quietly. "This has all been taken care of."

He said something like, "Oh no, it hasn't."

"I'd like to leave my jewelry with my friend," I said. "I don't want to take it to Sybil Brand."

He nodded.

I bent down to the car window and stripped off three rings, a bracelet, a watch, and put them in Kay's hands. I felt sorry, so sorry, for the frantic, stricken look on her face.

"Call Bob Tuller," I said.

"What's happening?" she yelled. "What the hell's going on here?"

"It's 1977," I explained. "It's happening all over again."

— 212 —

Then Kay was out of the car, shouting at the police, saying that she was my attorney and they couldn't do this, it was all a mistake. Nobody was listening. I held out my wrists for the handcuffs.

The ride to the police station seemed very long. Someone was talking, telling me about my rights, but I didn't listen. I was examining an odd thought that had popped into my head. Maybe you should just say yes, I told myself. Yes, I did whatever you say. Say yes, and then maybe they'll just take you off to some quiet place and leave you alone, and you won't have to go through this humiliation and pain anymore. Maybe they won't take you to that place and strip search you and spray you with disinfectant like some animal and put you on a mattress on a cold floor and make you be alone and afraid again.

But I couldn't say yes. Yes wasn't true and yes was no escape. There *was* no escape. The filth had reached out again, a well of slime that rose and flooded and lapped at my heels no matter where I went or what I did or who I was. I'd struggled and clawed and crawled to get from where I'd been to who I was now, but I hadn't climbed high enough to get free of the slime. I'd told myself and everybody else that women were powerful, women had choices, they could do whatever they wanted. And now I was hearing, "Sure, lady. Just see how powerful you are. Just see how free. You just can't seem to learn who's boss, can you?" I'd stepped out of line again and I was being slapped down again. In a way, I accepted the inevitability of it.

If I'd stayed in some house in the suburbs and kept quiet this wouldn't have happened. Nobody would ever have heard about Ginny Foat or bothered with her. The file drawer would have stayed closed. There were no television cameras and helicopters and armed troops in 1977 when I was just a housewife in Canoga Park. So why now? Were the rifles and riot gear necessary because I was a public menace? Maybe so. I'd made waves. I'd angered some politicians. I'd done my damnedest to threaten the status quo. I'd dared to believe and behave in my own way, not the "proper" way, and to that extent I was dangerous. I'd never intentionally hurt anybody in my life, but I was dangerous, and this is what had come of it. These cops, and the courts and prisons behind them, and the whole social system that disapproved of women like me, were going to show me who was boss. The murder charge was a farce. I knew it, and as I would find out, *even the people who brought it against me knew it.* I was in for a public stoning, but it wasn't because I'd killed anybody. It was because of who I was.

— 213 —

But this time I knew there was a choice—maybe not about what they were going to do to me, but about how I would face it. They had the power to take away my freedom, but it wasn't my freedom they were really after. It was what I believed and my dignity and self-respect. Well, they weren't going to get them. I'd fought too long and hard for them, and I'd fight to keep them. There'd be no whining or whimpering this time. I wouldn't give them the satisfaction of seeing my fear.

Scared as I was, I could feel the anger welling up and crowding the fear aside. They had no right to do this to me. So many times in the past I'd accepted the judgment of others and doubted my own, thinking that the majority must be right, the system must be right, and I must be wrong. I must be guilty and worthless and bad. No more. Not this time. They could condemn me, but they couldn't make me doubt myself. They could humiliate me, but they couldn't make me ashamed.

We got to the police station and I was led to a room with a table and a tape recorder. Déjà vu. Eggar was there, along with two officers from Louisiana. It was time for the questioning. This time, of course, I knew better. I had nothing to say, I told them. I'd wait for my lawyer. They said fine, and then proceeded with the questions. They were going to Nevada to make a deal with Jack Sidote for his testimony. Did I want them to deal with him or with me? Did I want to testify against him? Maybe we could work something out. I had nothing to testify to, I said. I had nothing to say. That was too bad, they said, because they had clear evidence of my involvement in the murder of Moises Chayo. They'd found the Pontiac Jack was driving in 1965. Chayo's blood was in it. My fingerprints were all over it.

The story was no more absurd than the rest of the situation, so it was several days before I sorted out in my own mind what the "clear evidence" amounted to. Blood in the car? Blood I'd never seen? Blood that came from a man who supposedly was murdered not in the car but outside it, his body left where it fell? And the fingerprints. Of course my fingerprints would be on a car that belonged to the man I lived with, a car I'd ridden in hundreds of times. The car had been traded in 1966. How many fingerprints had joined mine in the past seventeen years? Did they all belong to murderers? The story was ridiculous, an obvious scare tactic. In the coming months, all the "evidence" I would hear would be just about that "clear." In time, I'd almost get acclimated to a world where nothing made sense.

After a while, the police seemed to be convinced that I really wasn't going to answer them. The questioning turned into conversation. How was the women's movement doing in California, they wanted to know. What did I do for NOW? The Louisiana officers started telling me about some program for battered women in Jefferson Parish. These two men, who'd come a couple of thousand miles to arrest me, were sitting and chatting with me, being companionable, even trying to impress me with how enlightened they were about feminism. I'd once thought that nothing could be crazier than the things that happened to me in 1977. I was wrong.

The chitchat eventually trailed off and everybody stood up. It was time to cart me off to jail. I was entering my new quarters at Sybil Brand about the time the noon news was coming on the communal television set in the cell block. There were pictures of me, including the footage taken that morning. Some of the early reports said I'd been apprehended while trying to escape at the Burbank airport.

chapter 27

There was another press gauntlet to run when I got to Sybil Brand, but once inside the gates I expected I'd be treated much the same way I had been in 1977—just another prisoner, another number. I'd go through the booking procedure and be sent to a general population cell block, probably to sleep on the floor until I could get a place in the working dorm. But that wasn't the case. About midway through booking I was pulled out of a crowded holding tank by a guard, who said I wouldn't be going with the rest of the women in the group. I was going to Cell Block Five Thousand. That was the first indication that this stay in Sybil Brand was going to be very different from the last one.

I remembered vaguely what Five Thousand was, and it occurred to me on my way there that I should have known that's where I'd be sent. It was the cell block for women awaiting trial who, for various reasons, couldn't be integrated with the other prisoners. Some of them were high-publicity cases like me, women who were personally prominent or who were accused of crimes that had gotten a lot of public attention. Others were jailhouse snitches, or material witnesses, or women accused of crimes against children. The prison administration's thinking was that none of us would be safe in the general population. I was led down some stairs—Five Thousand was below ground—and put into a cell by myself. Before long I settled into the routine of my new home.

The population of Five Thousand varied during the time I was there, but there were usually about twenty of us. Each of us had her own cell, a little cubicle with bars for a door. The bars looked onto a corridor, where lights burned day and night. From a central desk in the cell block a guard could see most of us and hear all of us.

What kind of day it was in Five Thousand depended a lot on which guard was in charge. The guards were all sheriff's deputies, not trained corrections officers, and they fell into three categories. There were some compassionate women, who tried their best to make life more bearable for the inmates. There were others, the majority, who were little more than babysitters, indifferently doing their jobs. And there were a few who really enjoyed their work. They liked to taunt and belittle the inmates. They liked the arbitrary strip searches and cell shakedowns. They were petty and spiteful, taking full advantage of the small-time tyranny their jobs allowed.

Most mornings we got up around six o'clock. The lights in the cells would come on and a radio would start blaring music of the guard's choice over the PA system. Usually it was hard rock. It went on all day and ended only when the lights were turned out at night. We'd have a few minutes to make our beds and put on our pinafores —we wore pink pinafores in Five Thousand. The cell doors would open automatically and we'd be allowed into the dayroom for break- fast. The dayroom was a large, glass-enclosed cage where we had all our meals and where, on some days, we were allowed to sit and talk or watch television. Aside from the television set, the main furnish- ings were two long metal tables, each lined with metal stools. The tables and stools were bolted to the floor. Access to the dayroom was controlled by the guard in charge on any given day. On good days we could spend most of the time there. On other days we might be locked in our cells all day except for meals. Each prisoner had the option of staying in her cell, even if the dayroom was open. We were also allowed to skip meals if we wanted to, which was tempting. The food was plentiful, starchy, and bad.

After breakfast we could shower. There were four shower stalls for the cell block. In a few hours there'd be lunch, and then, around four-thirty in the afternoon, dinner. Once a week we had what was called "double scrub." We'd be given clean sheets, clean towels, and a clean cotton nightgown, along with a mop and some detergent. We'd scrub our cells from ceiling to floor. Another routine was "exercise." Twice a week, if we were lucky, we were allowed out into a small courtyard that had a tattered volleyball net in it. We could play volleyball or just jog around. If it rained, or if a visit made you miss the exercise session, you were out of luck. It was possible to go for weeks on end with no fresh air and no physical exercise beyond what you could do in your cell.

At seven-thirty every evening we all had to be back in our cells, unless an exception had been made. If there was something special we wanted to watch on television, we could apply for late-night television privileges; if we'd been good girls, permission was granted. Usually, though, the lights went out at eight-thirty, just after the final degradation of the day. "Wristbands, ladies," a guard would call. We'd stand at our cell doors and stick our arms through the bars. On our wrists were plastic bands, color-coded with our pinafores, bearing our names and prison numbers. For prison purposes they confirmed our existence, who we were and what—names and numbers. Talking was not allowed after lights-out, though some guards were pretty lenient about that rule. Reading wasn't allowed either. Crying was permitted.

Most Sybil Brand inmates considered Five Thousand the "real class" of accommodations at the institution. I suppose, comparatively, it was, at least in regard to the physical facilities. But the privileges were superficial, and they went along with a special set of restrictions. For instance, we couldn't go outside the cell block, even to the visiting room or the infirmary, without being handcuffed and escorted by at least one guard. It was "for our own protection." General population prisoners, even those convicted of murder, could come and go in most parts of the prison without handcuffs. Not one woman in my cell block had been convicted of a crime, but in many ways we had less freedom than anyone else in the institution.

What truly made Five Thousand different was not the "privileges" but the attitude that prevailed among the women who lived there. I remembered, from 1977, what life was like in general population. You didn't dare put down a candy bar or a piece of dirty underwear because it would be stolen instantly by some woman who'd been degraded to the level of an animal scrabbling for survival. I remembered the work dorm, which wasn't much better. But in Five Thousand the inmates were like a family, each member protective of the others, each doing her best to keep the others' spirits up.

I met women there I'll never forget: Melinda, who was always so cheerful; Carol, a nurse with a keen intelligence; a sweet middle-aged woman who allegedly belonged to the so-called Grandma Mafia —they'd supposedly been running a cocaine ring; and Carlitha. Carlitha was a bright, beautiful young black woman who, at the age of seventeen, had given some information to a man who used it to commit robbery and murder. Wise, brave, funny Carlitha, now nineteen going on forty, who would soon be sentenced to twenty-five years in jail. It was she who befriended me and comforted me the day I got to Five Thousand and who remained a loyal friend. She always had a kind word or a joke for somebody who was down, and she had strength enough to share with me and anybody else who needed it. There were nights when I'd find myself giving in to the fear and depression and crying into my pillow, trying to muffle the sound but not able to stop the tears. And Carlitha would call gently from her cell, "Don't be sad, Ginny. You're gonna beat 'em." Carlitha, who was black and poor and had no chance of beating them herself.

Emotions tended to be extreme in Five Thousand because there was so little distraction to pull you out of a mood once you were in it. If the day started off badly, the depression accumulated and compounded and by nightfall you were crying. I cried many nights. Worse, I heard other people crying, and there was little I could do about it. Among punishable infractions at Sybil Brand, "physical contact" was right at the top of the list. A woman might come back from court having had her children taken away from her and put up for adoption because she was in jail and therefore had "abandoned" them. She'd be in agony, but it was forbidden even to put an arm around her or squeeze her hand in sympathy. To do that was "deviant behavior" and could mean a stretch in isolation or even a transfer to Cell Block Four Thousand, the mental ward. It was after my second stay in Sybil Brand that I developed the habit of hugging my friends when I saw them instead of just shaking hands or saying hello. The lack of physical contact in prison, the absence of simple human warmth, was a terrible deprivation. It made loneliness a sickness.

I tried to keep a diary, but I couldn't find the words to describe the world I was in, or the way my senses were deprived and at the same time assaulted. When I woke every morning I'd try to keep my eyes closed as long as I could, delaying the moment when I'd have to look at steel bars and confront the reality that I was still in jail. But after a while, it didn't work. Sounds told me where I was, and in some ways sounds were the worst reminders of all. One day, though I'd never done such a thing in my life, I found myself writing a poem about the sounds.

Sounds . . .

I remember
Trying to mimic sounds of life
In silence,
Moving hands and arms and face muscles,

Laughing
As we played charades,
Laughing at myself,
Laughing at each other.

Sounds . . .

Do you remember
The sounds of your mother's womb?
The steady nurturing
Of her heartbeat, synchronized gurgling sound with yours?

Sounds . . .

The scream
I knew was mine
As I entered the world of common sounds.
People laughing,
Dogs barking, horns honking, kids crying, buses moving,
People laughing,
Sounds of life.

Sounds . . .

An echo world now,
Surrounded by steel and concrete
Voices ricocheting off the silence of cinder blocks
Grays,
And blacks,
And greens,
All silent colors.

Sounds . . .

An echo world now.
The rapid clicking of shackles tightening,
          biting,

Biting,
At my wrists,
   My waist,
         My ankles.
The sound still there
Even after the sound has stopped
The loud whine
As the hydraulic pulley opens the bars to my cell.
Teasing with freedom,
But only opening to another set of bars.
The roar of them closing again,
Locking into place, like a Fourth of July firecracker,
Bringing me back to the reality
There is no freedom.
I am a woman.

   Sounds . . .

Get up, ladies!
Shut up, ladies!
Wristbands, ladies!
Shut up, ladies!
Line up in two's, ladies!
What are you hiding, ladies!
Bend over and spread them,
                lady!

They have what's outside
They have always had what's outside,
Now they want what's inside.

   Sounds . . .

Sobs muffled
In a plastic pillow
On a plastic cot,
            in a steel cage.
Creaking of springs
As nightmares unfold
As dreams of freedom die.
The low gospel song
Hummed by a woman
Condemned from birth.

Sounds . . .

The birds,
The sunset, the sunrise,
The waves,
               kissing the sand
All sounds now foreign
to my echo world.

Oh!
To just hear the sounds
Of my mother's womb
The voice of a sister
                    not in pain
The word
Woman.

Words on paper expressed grief, but they also helped hold it at bay. I began trying to share words with the other women in Five Thousand, to touch and comfort them with words for lack of any other way. Sometimes after lights-out I'd read to them. There was no light in the cells, but if I stood and leaned against my barred door and turned the book outward, the light from the corridor was enough to read by. I'd read quietly, and the guards usually wouldn't interfere. I'd read feminist poetry from books like Pat Parker's *Womanslaughter,* or books on feminist theory, or biographical books about women who'd been strong and brave in the face of trouble. I hope it helped them. It helped me.

My circumstances were different in Sybil Brand the second time around, and I was different, too. In 1977 I'd been so dazed and confused, and so thoroughly afraid, that all my thoughts turned inward. Each new day seemed to bring a new horror that was worse for being unexpected, and I could focus on nothing but myself and my terror. This time I was a little less afraid. The strip searches were no less awful, for instance, but neither did they come as a surprise. I'd been in jail before. I knew the drill. There was a certain sad confidence in that.

In 1977 I'd been too scared to be angry, but I was angry now —at what was happening to me and at what I saw around me. I was looking outward, seeing and hearing things that hadn't fully registered the first time. In 1977 the street language intimidated me by its strangeness. Now I listened to the words and thought about what they meant. I heard women in holding tanks saying to each other, "How many holes yo' man got?" "Mine got fifteen holes. He sumthin'." They were prostitutes talking about their pimps and about themselves. My God, I thought, on the outside we're trying to get women to stop calling themselves "girls," and these women are calling themselves "holes," thinking of themselves as "holes"—not just pieces of meat but worse, as so many bits of anatomical emptiness.

I started conducting my own impromptu consciousness-raising. We could get newspapers in Five Thousand and I read them every day. At mealtimes I might say something like, "Did anybody see that article on surrogate parenting?" Somebody else would say, "What's that?" and pretty soon we'd be deep in a discussion of children and parenthood. We covered a lot of ground that way—battering, prostitution, the child abuse and incest so many of the women had suffered themselves. These women, strong enough to survive in a world uglier than I would ever know, were realizing how strong they were.

At Kay's suggestion, I asked the women to help write testimony in support of a state bill to limit strip searches. By the time I left the prison they were writing about "the *women* of Sybil Brand," and they underlined "women." Of all the things I've done or will ever do as a feminist, I think I'll always be proudest of that.

I was also proud of what few changes I helped bring to the prison in 1983. They were possible partly because of a woman named Carol Painter, who was an administrator there at the time. An enlightened and sympathetic person, Lieutenant Painter genuinely wanted to make prison life more humane, and I believe she did her best to push a cumbersome bureaucracy toward reform. I never knew her to be callous or unreasonable about legitimate inmate requests.

There was the matter of eating utensils, for example. In Five Thousand all meals were served with plastic spoons only, despite a court decision ordering that we were to have regular tableware. We wrote a petition, signed by everyone in the unit, and Kay presented it to Lieutenant Painter. As a result, we were allowed to eat like adults instead of spooning up food like infants.

We used to call Five Thousand the Zoo because we were on display so often. Because it was the least overcrowded part of the prison, our unit was the main attraction for politicians or law students or other groups touring Sybil Brand. There was one guard who took particular delight in conducting the tours and in stopping at every cell to give a long, loud, detailed account of the case the inmate was accused in. She sounded exactly like a zookeeper reeling off the habits and habitats of so many skunks, rats, and weasels. We wrote a petition to keep her out of Five Thousand, and she was restricted from the unit. There were petty reprisals from guards who were her friends, of course, but we didn't care. We'd asserted our basic claim to be treated as human beings, and somebody had listened.

In 1983 I looked around and saw that the childish pinafores we wore, so shoddy to begin with, were now so worn that they threatened to fall into rags. They came back from the laundry each time with new rips and tears, and even with constant mending they were always tattered. If we had to look like ragged little girls, how long would it be before we thought of ourselves that way?

Although I turned down hundreds of requests for interviews while I was at Sybil Brand, I did agree to talk to *Life* magazine reporter Rinker Buck. He came to the prison several times, and Lieutenant Painter let us use her office for the interviews. To go with his story Rinker wanted some pictures of me in my prison uniform. On the day when photographer Enrico Ferorelli came, I chose my rattiest pinafore and a worn-out prison sweater. I stood at the end of a corridor, while Enrico positioned himself a short distance away. Lieutenant Painter and Kay were standing with him, and I could see the lieutenant eying my tattered dress, perhaps seeing it as it would look through the camera lens.

That evening during dinner a deputy called me to the door of the dayroom. She was holding two new dresses and sweaters that Lieutenant Painter had sent down. The whole room fell quiet. I stood and looked at the new clothes without touching them, angry at being singled out this way, angry that anyone would think I'd consider taking them. "I'm only one of twenty people here," I said finally, "and each one of us has rips in her dress and each one of us has a sweater that's in rags." Then I walked away and left the deputy standing there. The next time the unit went to dress exchange (we turned in two dirty ones for two clean ones twice a week) every one of us was given a new dress. Around the same time, twenty-five new sweaters were delivered to Five Thousand.

Knives and forks, a few cheap sweaters and dresses, a little relief from a woman who treated us like animals. They don't sound like big victories, but they were. In jail there aren't any small ones.

But any victories in those first three months of 1983 were within the confines of my cage. Beyond the walls and bars of Five Thousand there was a steady stream of setbacks, disappointments, losses, and bitter betrayals.

In the first few days after my arrest I'd speculate with Kay and other friends in the visitors' room about how it could have happened. Why, after so long, was Louisiana suddenly interested in me? Maybe politics was behind it, we thought. Maybe some powerful state official I'd opposed politically was getting even. It took only about a week for the truth to come out, or at least the essence of it. Some details we'd learn only months later, and many we'd never learn at all, but the basics were on the front pages of the newspapers that January for anybody to read. It was Shelly Mandell who had opened that musty file drawer in Jefferson Parish.

Only days after our argument in Washington, Shelly had telephoned the parish sheriff's office requesting information about any outstanding warrants against Virginia Galluzzo, also known as Ginny Foat, who was now living in Los Angeles. I don't know what, if anything, she found out on the phone, but early in January she put her request in writing. She included in her letter a birth date:

June 21, 1941. That was not my correct birth date, as Shelly well knew. I was born on June 2. *Yet, the incorrect date she gave matched the incorrect birth date on the 1977 Louisiana warrant—the birth date that the computer evidently needed to find what Shelly was looking for.*

How she knew she should give that date I don't know. Nor do I know how she knew to contact Jefferson Parish. I'd told her only that there had been a warrant in a case in New Orleans, an entirely different jurisdiction.

The first stories in the paper were soon followed by others with Shelly's explanation. Actually, she said, she was trying to do me a favor. She was working as administrative assistant to Los Angeles City Councilman Marvin Braude. Braude was thinking of appointing me to a vacancy that was coming up on the city's Human Relations Commission, she said, and she was only trying to make sure that nothing would stand in the way of the appointment. The story just didn't hold together. I didn't live in Braude's district, and even if I had, the vacancy was earmarked for a minority appointee. Besides, as city officials were quick to tell the papers, background inquiries for such jobs were usually run by the mayor's office and went no farther than the local police department. Shelly had written the letter on Braude's official city stationery. She lost her job about two weeks after the newspaper stories first came out.

I don't think there's any way to describe the devastation I felt when I found out about Shelly, or that I still feel today. I remember many nights I spent lying on the cot in my jail cell with the same thought chasing itself through my head: The person who put me here wasn't some impersonal outsider. Whatever our differences, Shelly was one of my own. She was once one of my best friends.

The news of Shelly's involvement only added fuel to what was already a conflagration in California NOW, a fire that was spreading to feminist circles all over the country. Within hours of my arrest the state organization was polarized. There were women who backed me and there were those who wanted to forget I existed. Who fell into which camp seemed to have nothing to do with who liked me and who didn't, or who'd supported me or opposed me on issues. I found some people who'd been political adversaries rallying around me immediately, offering any kind of help they could give. These people saw that mine was another case of blaming the victim. But at the same time, women who'd been my friends, women I'd known for years and walked picket lines with and worked phone banks with, were saying things like "How do we know who she was or what she

— 226 —

did before we knew her? How do we know she's innocent? She's hurting the organization. Why should we be expected to stand by her?" Some were more polite than that. There were those who said, "Ginny would be the first to say that the movement is more important than any individual." (Not true. I would have said the movement *is* the individuals.) And there were those who said, "Our support can only hurt Ginny. In conservative Louisiana her standing as a feminist will work against her." It all meant the same thing.

There were nationally respected feminists who saw the issue for exactly what it was and came to my support. With her usual no-nonsense clarity, Gloria Steinem said that I was a woman in trouble and my sisters should stand by me. Former White House aide Midge Costanza said that I'd been jailed because I was president of California NOW and for no other reason. But the fact remained that to certain segments of NOW's leadership I'd become an embarrassment. Headlines about a NOW leader being arrested didn't play well in Peoria. Jails weren't nice. Murder charges weren't nice at all. In my view, the bottom line was this: The women who were truly in touch with what feminism means stood behind me. The ones who followed the power did not.

In California the power grab was on. With me in jail, Kay became acting state president, and she was the target of the new anti-Foat faction. When she refused a directive from the national office to urge me to resign, she was hounded with petty grievances and false accusations by women trying to force her out of her job, or at the very least trying to make her choose between her loyalty to NOW and her loyalty to me. Many of my other friends in NOW were being harassed and ostracized, told, of all things, that they weren't good feminists if they supported me. Sister was fighting sister, privately and in the press. The organization was in chaos; and I could only sit in jail and watch, saddened beyond words not only at the betrayals, but at seeing the movement that had been my whole life tearing itself apart in a public controversy, and one that centered on me.

I'd been in jail less than two weeks when I had a visit from the national president of NOW, Judy Goldsmith. I'd been told beforehand that she was bringing NOW's lawyer with her, and I'd asked Bob Tuller to be there for me. When Judy walked into the room the jail provided for conferences with attorneys she found me highly emotional, almost in tears. I was very moved. I assumed she was coming to offer support and encouragement, probably not from the organization officially, but on her own, and on behalf of individual members. She hugged me and we sat down to talk. After a few sympathetic comments she got down to business.

We had to stop the turmoil in NOW, she said, and the best way to do it was with a joint statement from the two of us. She had one ready. She put it in front of me and I read it over. The gist of it was that I was disassociating myself from NOW. I couldn't quite take it in. Was it possible that the only reason she'd come was to bail out the organization by cutting me loose? I said something about its not being acceptable to me, and she and I and the lawyers started trying to work out one that was. We finally came up with one in which NOW expressed sympathy and granted my request for a paid leave of absence from my office.

The next day Judy held a press conference. She said that "the best thing all of us can do for Ginny at this point is to allow her the freedom to pursue her own case . . . What we have here is an individual's personal tragedy, for which we have great compassion." And, later, "The bottom line is this: We won't waste any more precious feminist energies on internal fights."

There was nothing in her statement throwing me directly to the wolves, I suppose, but some reporters who heard it apparently read nuances between the lines. The headline in the New York *Daily News* the next day said: "NOW: Won't vow aid in official's slay case."

My despair was nearly total at that point, but there were people who wouldn't let me give in to it. If I had enemies, I also had a lot of friends. I had three or four visitors every day during the twenty-minute visiting period. Many more saw me in the attorneys' room, where time was less restricted and you could talk face to face instead of over a telephone and through a pane of glass. I saw Kay there, along with other friends who were lawyers. They cheered me up, made me laugh, let me cry, goaded me into new strength when mine threatened to fail.

They gave more than moral support. Right after my arrest, friends started the Ginny Foat Defense Fund (GFDF) to raise money for me. I had very little of my own, and it was becoming clear that I was going to need thousands of dollars, maybe hundreds of thousands, before the case was over. Dozens of friends volunteered time to work for the fund, and a distinguished board of directors was assembled. Letters were sent to women's groups all over the country and ads were placed in newspapers and magazines asking for support.

The response was staggering. Whatever the official position of NOW's leadership, support from the grass roots was overwhelming.

Individual chapters took it on themselves to raise money for me. It came from New York, Georgia, Florida, Illinois, Texas, Mississippi —from all over the country—and with the checks came letters, essentially with a single message. They wanted me to know that I wasn't alone.

Support came from NOW chapters and from other women's groups, but it came mostly from individuals. The mail poured in. Most of it was from people I'd never met, who knew me only from stories they'd seen on television or read in the press. However sensationalized or skewed those stories were, it was obvious that many people, especially women, could see through to the truth of what had happened between Jack Sidote and me. A woman who was living on Social Security and had just had a lung removed sent a check for two dollars and fifty cents with a note attached. "I wish I could send more," she said, "but I hope you get the S.O.B."

Not all the letters contained money, but almost all offered hope and prayers and encouragement. And many—hundreds—shared stories of their own. So often I'd open a letter that began, "I understand what you're going through because I lived with a man like that . . ." and then went to tell about the writer's own suffering. I'd known the statistics for years, but I'd never understood in such a personal way what they meant in terms of lives scarred by battering. I spent hours in jail trying to answer all the letters. They made me realize I wasn't alone and I wanted those women to know they weren't alone either.

At a time when my whole world was disintegrating, those letters were a lifeline. They helped give me back my faith. For them, and for the dozens of friends and thousands of strangers who were there for me, there are no adequate thanks.

On my first day in Sybil Brand, Kay called me to the attorneys' room. "Just hold on," she said, "we'll get this straightened out in a matter of hours." I knew better. "No, you won't," I said. "I'm going to be here for ninety days." In fact, I stayed in jail for more than three months while legal battles were fought on my behalf in both California and Louisiana. Most of them we lost.

I hadn't even been indicted in Louisiana at the time of my arrest, but it took only a week for prosecutors there to take care of that. They trotted Jack Sidote out before a Jefferson Parish grand jury to tell his tired old story, and as of January 18, 1983, I stood officially accused of the 1965 murder of Moises Chayo. Jack was given immunity from all charges in return for his agreement to testify against me. The admitted killer of Chayo, he would not be punished for the crime. I, if convicted, could face life in prison.

Kay and Tuller had gone to Louisiana to try to head off the grand jury indictment, but it was no use. They turned their attention to finding the best available defense lawyers. Kay had made a number of contacts in the state and asked for recommendations of local attorneys, just as Tuller had done in 1977. Both times, the same two names kept coming up: John Reed and Bob Glass. Both were in their late thirties; John was a graduate of Harvard and Bob of the University of Pennsylvania. Both had come south in the late 1960s to work for New Orleans's Community Legal Services program, doing poverty law and civil rights cases. They'd liked the city, stayed, and gone into private practice together, building an impressive record in criminal law. Kay retained them the day the grand jury indictment was handed down.

Back in California, my legal team was fighting extradition and at the same time fighting to get me bail. I was denied it under a Louisiana death penalty statute that was in force at the time of Chayo's murder but had since been struck down by the U.S. Supreme Court. Despite the fact that Louisiana had notified California it had no objection to bail, the California courts refused to grant it. As far as bail was concerned, they said, the defunct statute was still in effect.

Briefs in my case kept running up and down the hierarchy of the California court system. They represented hours of work by my attorneys, Richard Hirsch and Michael Nasatir, as well as other lawyers who volunteered their time out of friendship. Some of the arguments were brilliant, but after a time I just wanted them to stop. They were only delaying the inevitable, and I couldn't stand it anymore—the waiting, the tension, the life in jail. I couldn't stand being dragged into court day after day to hear another "Writ denied." I hated the time spent chained inside a cage on the bus on the way to and from court. I hated the crowds of reporters and photographers who showed up for every hearing. I hated seeing the face of Warren Eggar, the Fugitive Division detective, who, for some reason, made it his business to come to every hearing. Eggar, who kept the file on my case long after it was supposed to have been turned over to the sheriff's office, apparently had some special interest in what happened to me. He once told Bob Tuller that he'd have me pulled into court every day until I agreed to extradition. And, in fact, there were days when I made that long, dismal court run for no reason at all.

I wanted the circus to stop. I wanted to agree to extradition and go to Louisiana and get on with whatever was waiting for me there. I begged John Reed on the phone to let the extradition fight drop, but he wouldn't hear of it. He and Bob Glass needed time to prepare their case. They had two investigators working to find people in New York, Louisiana, California, who might have known Jack and me when we were living together and might be able to testify about what our life was like. Potential witnesses in a case eighteen years old! Some had moved or just vanished. Some had died. Bobbie was dead. Dick Masters was dead. The investigation was difficult. It was going to take time. Meanwhile, John and Bob were working on pretrial motions. They thought they had a good chance of having the case dismissed on the grounds that Louisiana had denied me my constitutional right to a speedy trial. They needed time to work on that, too. I'd just have to hang on.

I was trying to hang on, but it was hard. And it was made no easier by the fact that day after day I had to watch the disintegration of my reputation at the hands of the press. It seemed that I was very hot news. Along with the usual news stories, column after column, sometimes page after page of features appeared. They laid out almost every conceivable detail of my personal life. Reporters had interviewed practically everybody I'd ever known—friends, enemies, the men in my life, going all the way back to Fred Schindler in New Paltz. I didn't see why how I looked in a bathing suit or what my high-school yearbook said about me or where I'd worked as a waitress were relevant. Many of the stories were filled with inaccuracies, and even those that got most of the facts right sneered up from the page with sleazy speculation and pat conclusions that were as wrong as they were facile. There were two favorite angles. One went something like "Shady past catches up with prominent feminist." The other was "Who is the real Ginny Foat? Activist or murderer?"

I got to read Jack Sidote's account of our sex life, always rendered for the benefit of women reporters. I read his description of my career in New Orleans as a go-go dancer wearing a skimpy costume with toy guns on my hips—one of his more colorful fantasies. I'd never been a go-go dancer, and the most lurid costume I'd ever worn in bars where I worked was a blouse and slacks. Nevertheless, the press had a new fun catchphrase to use in writing about the "go-go dancer turned feminist." I was treated to the sight (as were my friends and, worst of all, my parents) of Jack Sidote in a CBS interview calling me a "no-good bitch" and a "whore" on national television.

In jail I read the stories and watched the television accounts with a mixture of shame, outrage, and bewilderment. Who was this woman they were writing and talking about? I didn't recognize her. She wasn't me. And why were they doing this to her? She wasn't a public official or even a national leader of a movement. About a handful of people outside California and the women's movement had ever heard of her. And even if I was accused of murder, what did my high-school yearbook or when I lost my virginity have to do with the case?

I examined my right to privacy and concluded very quickly that I had none. Yes, there were things in my life I was ashamed of, Jack Sidote chief among them. But few people are blameless; few would relish having the whole tapestry of their past spread out for all the world to look at. Almost everybody has the right to decide what about his or her life to withhold and what to share, and when, and with whom. I didn't. The public, including a pool of potential jurors down in Louisiana, obviously had the inalienable right to know precisely everything about me.

Whatever the outcome of the case, I was already convicted of playing hookey in high school, of being a barmaid (as though that honest work were shameful), of living with Jack Sidote, of being married four times, of being some kind of rabid radical. And I began to understand that even if I was cleared of murder, I would never again have sole title to my own life. All the people I would ever meet for the rest of my life could bring to that meeting information they had no right to and misinformation they probably believed. However much they might wish me well, they would also judge me. I would always be on trial.

I could do nothing but watch it all in silence because I was forbidden by my lawyers to talk to the press myself. Anything said for the record, however bland or innocent, was potential ammunition for the prosecutors. The interviews I did give, to *Life,* came only after the California attorneys decided we had to try something to counteract all the negative publicity. I turned down everything else, though, from Barbara Walters to reporters for suburban weeklies. It wasn't that I didn't want to talk; I did. I wanted to scream.

On the one hundred and first day of my incarceration I went to court and agreed to be extradited to Louisiana. There were a few more appeals we could have exhausted, but John and Bob were finished with their preliminary work and ready for me.

The extradition hearing was not allowed to pass without drama. It was, after all, my farewell performance in Los Angeles, and the courtroom was packed with the press and with my friends. After the legalities were disposed of, the judge—the same one who'd refused me bail—gave a little speech praising me for my "exemplary behavior" in court over the past three months and wishing me luck. I suppose he meant well, but I found it hard not to laugh, or maybe cry. What had he expected me to do? Raise a clenched fist and shout feminist slogans? Or maybe whip off my bra and burn it—not a bad trick when you're handcuffed. In essence, he was patting me on the head for being a good girl. I'd cooperated with the Inquisition nicely, and maybe if I kept on being nice, sooner or later the torture would stop. At that moment I wondered why I didn't shout some slogan or mount some kind of protest against this insanity. But I didn't. I mumbled a polite thank-you, still trying, as I'd tried all my life, to be nice. Then all my friends started cheering, wishing me well as I walked out of the courtroom. It was a standing ovation.

I was taken back to Sybil Brand to await whatever arrangements had to be made to take me to Louisiana. The extradition hearing had been on a Friday. The following Monday, as soon as I woke up, a guard told me to pack my things and get ready to go. It seemed I was going to get some more special treatment. A helicopter was coming to the prison to pick me up and take me to the Los Angeles airport. Nobody had ever heard of such an arrangement at Sybil Brand before and I was by no means grateful for it. Helicopters scare me. But, of course, there was no choice but to follow orders. I started cleaning out my cell, packing the few personal items I wanted to take with me. Everything else I gave away—a little money, some warm socks, my books, my new pinafore. A guard brought me my own clothes and I got dressed. I was exchanging emotional good-byes with my friends in Five Thousand when the guards came to take me upstairs.

Warren Eggar met me there. We were taking the helicopter, he explained courteously, to avoid the press that might be waiting right outside the prison. I suppose it was his idea of a joke. The helicopter had landed just outside the prison gates, and the area was swarming with reporters and photographers and cameramen. They got some excellent footage of me climbing into the helicopter, handcuffs and all, followed by a smiling Warren Eggar.

chapter **29**

Eggar and I did avoid reporters in the airline terminal because we didn't go through the building. The helicopter landed on the opposite side of the airport and an LAPD car picked us up there and drove us directly to the plane. Before I was turned over to my new keepers, one of the Los Angeles officers unlocked my handcuffs. I looked at my wrists and saw that I was still wearing my prison wristband, the one I'd worn now for one hundred and three days. Only a small scrap of plastic, it was heavier to me than the steel handcuffs had been. I asked the officer to cut it off and he did. Then I was loaded onto the plane.

It was a commercial flight—a full one, thanks mostly to my entourage. I sat next to a woman deputy from Louisiana. Two male officers sat nearby, as did Tom Porteous, an assistant district attorney from Jefferson Parish. Bob Tuller and his wife sat right behind me. Most of the other seats were filled with representatives of the television networks and national magazines and newspapers. The circus was going on the road.

Local radio stations were broadcasting minute-by-minute reports of my plane's progress toward New Orleans. "Ginny Foat is forty-five minutes away." "Ginny Foat is a half hour away."

My arrival at the airport was a nightmare. The mob of reporters and photographers was so thick I could barely move through it, a sea of jostling, shouting people who crowded around me throughout the endless walk from the plane to the airport's main terminal. They screamed out questions. One of the more relentless reporters kept jabbing a microphone at me and yelling, "Ms. Foat! Ms. Foat! Are you guilty?" When I tried just to keep walking and ignore him he shrieked into his microphone, "She's not answering! She's not answering!"—as though my failure to stop then and there and present my case was a clear indication of my murderous nature.

Kay Tsenin and Jan Holden had flown to New Orleans the night before and were there to meet me, moving along on either side of the crowd, acting as ground wires to keep reality from fading out altogether. Each time I felt I couldn't take another step I'd look at one of them and get a wink or a thumbs-up signal and I'd keep going. We were inside the terminal when my legs finally gave out under me. I grabbed the arms of the police escorts on either side of me and hung on, stumbling the last few feet to the door of the terminal like a marathon runner who can't make it to the finish line unaided.

Then there was the blessed quiet of the police car that was taking me to Gretna, across the Mississippi River from New Orleans. I'd never been in Jefferson Parish before, and my first impression was that it looked as dejected as I felt. There was none of the charm and romance of New Orleans here. We drove along highways lined with service stations and fast-food joints and then through ramshackle residential neighborhoods. Finally I got my first glimpse of the ugliest scenery of all. The Jefferson Parish courts and jail were housed in two squat, square, modern buildings set one behind the other and connected by a breezeway. We pulled up to the front building and went inside, brushing past another group of reporters.

My reception at the jail was at least as bizarre as anything I'd been through yet. It was easy to see that my arrival was expected, and the staff and facilities were ready for the occasion. I was ushered into a holding cell near the booking area—a clean holding cell with a clean mattress in it where no mattress ordinarily would have been. There was also a clean toilet. I couldn't recall ever seeing a clean toilet in a holding cell before. After I was shown the accommodations the booking procedure began. The officers were going through my personal belongings when I heard somebody yell, "Here come the gypsies!"

I turned around in time to see the entrance of some twenty dark and handsome people dressed in brightly colored clothes. Most of them were women and most of the women appeared to be pregnant. They were all talking at once and they were all angry. They'd been accused of robbing a supermarket. It occurred to me that the press outside the jail was missing the boat. Surely this colorful group was more interesting than one bedraggled feminist.

All the gypsy women were jammed into a cell about the same size as my private one, and my booking continued. A matron took me into a bathroom for the strip search. But when I started to undress, the woman held up her hand as if to stop me. "No," she said, "I just can't do this to you, Miz Foat." So we simply sat in the bathroom and chatted for about five minutes, her kind voice rising and falling in that strange accent I'd learn was peculiar to certain natives of the New Orleans area, an indescribable mixture of Brooklyn and Deep South. I'd be staying in my cell downstairs tonight, she said, and it was much nicer than the regular jail upstairs. Most of the people she worked with were good people, she went on. They wouldn't give me any trouble. I was grateful that she didn't search me. Of all the contraband to smuggle into jail, I'd hidden some makeup and an eyebrow pencil in my bra.

As soon as I was back in my cell, a guard came to ask me if I had enough cigarettes and matches. A little later one of the gypsies asked for some matches, to which my guard replied, "You think you're in the fuckin' Hilton, or what?" Then he told me sweetly that he'd just made a fresh pot of coffee and asked if I'd like some. I was dying for some but I declined. I was worried about the gypsies, who by this time were screaming for water. They were also demanding their right to a phone call. I had a pay phone in my cell.

The matron brought me my jail uniform, which looked like an orange version of a hospital scrub suit. I climbed into it while she carefully collected my own clothes. "You're gonna have to wear these clothes to court tomorra, Miz Foat," she said. "You don't wanna get 'em all wrinkled." Women guards from the jail upstairs started dropping by my cell and asking for autographs. When the watch commander for the night came on duty, he stopped in for a chat. His daughter had seen me on television, he said, and she was a big fan of mine. I wrote an autograph for the daughter. Late that night the early edition of the local paper, the New Orleans *Times-Picayune*, came out and my picture was on the front page. There was a round of requests for me to autograph the picture. The next morning I was taken upstairs for a shower. I was provided with a blow dryer and cosmetics (no need to bother with the stash in my bra), and my clothes were brought to me hung neatly on a hanger.

They looked as though somebody had pressed them during the night.

I couldn't get over the irony of it, the simple craziness. These people didn't know if I was innocent or guilty, and they didn't seem to care. I was a celebrity! I must have been the most celebrated accused murderess they'd had on the premises for years. I had an interesting thought: I wonder if Mary Queen of Scots felt the same sense of absurdity when she was in jail for treason. I bet her guards at the Tower of London were real nice to her, too, right up until the time they took her out and chopped off her head.

I'd been in the Jefferson Parish jail about two hours when Kay arrived with Bob and John. It was my first face-to-face meeting with my Louisiana attorneys, although I felt I knew them pretty well already from Kay's descriptions and my many phone conversations with John. Both were tall, slender, and soft-spoken. Seeing them in person, I was a little disconcerted at how young, almost boyish, they looked. But it was obvious that both of them were brilliant, and they seemed to have the situation well in hand. I liked them, and I'd come to like them more as I got to know them better. We talked about what was going to happen the next day at my arraignment. I'd plead innocent, of course, and a trial date would be set. Then, we hoped, the judge would set bail.

As soon as they'd taken my case, John and Bob had started filing briefs aimed at making sure I'd get bail, but the Louisiana courts decided that the issue wasn't "timely" until I was in custody in the state. Now that I was, we were optimistic about my getting out—optimistic, but not certain. Then, too, there was the question of how much the bail might be and where the money would come from. Kay and Jan had been busy contacting women's groups in Louisiana, as well as individuals who might be sympathetic to my case. The idea was to form a support network that we could tie into for as long as I was in the state—assuming that was months and not years. People had responded warmly, offering places to stay, legal help, whatever they could. But with all our attention focused just on getting bail, the problem of raising the money had yet to be solved. Certainly I didn't have it, and the Ginny Foat Defense Fund was doing all it could just to keep current with my legal bills.

Kay assured me that everybody was working on the problem, and I knew that was true. We all knew how important it was for me to be free to help work on my defense, free to do it and strong enough to do it. I'd been in jail for some three and a half months now, and the strain was beginning to tell. Besides, I already suspected that however well I was being treated in my holding cell, the jail upstairs would be something else again, something that might make Sybil Brand look like a palace.

The next day I was taken through the breezeway to the building behind the jail for my arraignment. It was then that I got my first look at the Honorable Robert J. Burns of the Twenty-fourth Judicial District Court, the judge who, for a time, would be an important fixture in my life. He, too, was younger than I'd expected, with dark, receding hair and heavy, black-rimmed glasses that gave him a rather scholarly look. On April 26 he set bail at $125,000.

I was taken back to jail to wait for the bond to be arranged. This time, however, I wasn't ushered back to my cushy holding cell on the first floor. I was taken upstairs and booked into the main jail, and it was just as bad as I'd feared. The women were unkempt and ragged, as though all spirit and self-respect had been worn away from them. The jail itself, a circular arrangement of cells divided in the middle by a glass cage where the guards stood, was filthy. Plaster was falling off the ceiling and off what little I could see of the walls. Most of the wall space inside the cells was obscured by graffiti and carelessly tacked-up pictures.

As soon as I got there I asked for materials to clean my cell, which was full of dust and plaster chips. As I scrubbed I looked around at the unmade beds. I found myself thinking, They would never put up with this sort of thing at Sybil Brand. These inmates would never get away with . . . Suddenly I stopped scrubbing, horrified at myself, at what I was thinking. Was this what my life had come to? Rating jails? Feeling loyalty to the last one as if it were some kind of alma mater? I looked again at the women in the cells. If I had to stay here, how many weeks or months or years would it be before I became just like them—dirty, ragged, not caring anymore about myself or anybody else, content to let my life slip away in daily measures of tedium, inching toward death and grateful at the prospect of it . . . ? What if I had to grow old in a place like this? I stopped cleaning and went to bed, escaping into sleep.

I was awakened for lunch, some kind of gruelly mess that I couldn't bring myself to eat, and then I went back and sat on my cot and waited some more. Finally, late in the afternoon, a guard took me downstairs, where Kay, Jan, Bob, and John were waiting. I was free! A New Orleans physician named Norma Kearby, a total stranger to me, had put up several properties she owned to guarantee my bail. I had dinner with Dr. Kearby that night. She was an attractive blond woman, witty, gracious, and self-assured. She told me she was a longtime member of NOW. She also told me her friends called her Nikki. So did I. She was to me a very good friend indeed.

When I first got out on bail I went directly to Bob and John's office. The trial date had been set: October 11. We had more than five months to prepare—if it came to that. Both lawyers were still hopeful that my speedy-trial assertion would be successful. In the meantime, though, there were some immediate problems that needed attention. One pressing issue was whether to call a press conference.

If the national press had been tough, the New Orleans press was brutal. *Times-Picayune* reporters seemed to have a good working relationship with the Jefferson Parish district attorney's office, which was leaking information like a rotten bucket, misinformation that turned into headlines in the local press. In addition, there had been some highly prejudicial stories that were prompted unintentionally by my own friends in California. Some of them had talked too much and too publicly about their fear that I wouldn't get a fair trial in Louisiana because the state was too conservative and would hold my politics against me. My friends were acting in a crisis, thinking only about trying to prevent my extradition. Unfortunately, they were not thinking about how their remarks would play two thousand miles away to potential jurors whose fairness and intelligence were being questioned.

Bob and John were worried about trying to pick a jury in the bad climate the press was creating. After much debate, they decided I should hold a short press conference to try to undo some of the damage. I met with the press the day after my release. John told the reporters at the outset that I couldn't answer questions about the case. I didn't, except to say that I had not killed Moises Chayo or anybody else. I also said that I had faith in the jury system, that I was sure I'd get a fair trial and sure I'd be acquitted. I hoped I sounded more confident than I felt.

Apparently, I didn't win anybody over. About a week after the press conference the *Times-Picayune* carried one of its "informed sources" stories saying that Wasyl Bozydaj was going to testify to seeing me with bloody clothes on the night of the murder. The informed source evidently made that one up from whole cloth.

There was never any record of Wasyl's saying anything remotely like that to investigators either in New York or Louisiana. At the trial the question would never even come up.

After the press conference I spent another week or so in New Orleans, trying to give Bob and John an overview of my side of the case and working with them on their speedy-trial motion. I don't know how much help I was. I was tired and distracted, with things weighing on my mind that had nothing to do with the case. I knew I had to get back to California, at least briefly, to straighten out some of the chaos I'd left there. I'd given up my apartment while I was in jail, and my friends had moved my furniture and personal belongings into storage. They'd also cleaned out my office at NOW headquarters. All that had to be sorted out. I had to decide where to move my things—where I was going to live, in the event, of course, that I was able to return to California permanently. There had been inquiries about a book and a movie about me, and those had to be dealt with. It seemed that I still owned enough of my life to sell it, and I was going to have to. The defense fund had raised more than one hundred thousand dollars, but by now the best estimates were that my defense was going to cost in the neighborhood of a quarter of a million dollars.

But beyond all that, far more important than all that, I had to get home—home, to New Paltz. I had to see my father.

Over the years I found myself growing closer to my parents despite the geographical distance between us. We'd talk on the phone at least once a week and visit back and forth whenever we could.

Daddy would always start our phone conversations with, "Well, I see you're still out there saving the world," but time had turned what was once a criticism into a gentle joke between us. I don't know if he understood everything I was trying to do in the movement, but I do know he was proud of me, in a way that neither of us could have anticipated in the days when we both believed the only possible success for a woman was as a wife and mother. When my name was in the newspapers in connection with my feminist or political work, I'd send him clippings, and he kept them and cherished them. His daughter was somebody special. I know he felt that, and the pride he took in me was probably my own greatest source of pride. I'd waited for it so long.

When I was arrested in 1977 my parents were frantic, but I

wouldn't let them come to California or Nevada. I kept in touch by phone, but I told them that if they came I wouldn't see them. I couldn't bear to have them see me in jail. I felt the same way after my second arrest. I talked to them often from Sybil Brand, and the worry in their voices grieved me more than all the other wreckage in my life, but I begged them to stay in New Paltz. I told them I'd see them as soon as I could.

I'd been visiting them for Christmas in 1981 when Daddy had his first heart attack. The doctors diagnosed coronary artery disease, and in June of 1982 he had open-heart bypass surgery. The operation went well but he couldn't seem to recover from it emotionally. He had a new awareness of his physical vulnerability, maybe his mortality, and it frightened and depressed him. The cheerfulness that was always so much a part of his nature was fading from his voice. I worried, but I knew he was a fighter. I believed he would pull out of it and get better.

Then I was arrested for the second time, and he gave up. I'd call him from prison and say, "You've got to get better; I need you," and he'd say, "I can't. I'm not strong enough to help you." And I knew that for him that was the worst of it, not his physical weakness or his fear, but the awful frustration of knowing that I was in trouble and there was so little he could do to help.

As soon as I was freed on bail in Louisiana I called my parents. I told Daddy that I had to go to Los Angeles to straighten out some things, but I'd hurry. I'd get to New Paltz as soon as I could. We cried together on the phone and he told me how happy he was that I was out and how much he loved me. That was the last time he ever talked to me.

I went from New Orleans to Los Angeles and I did hurry. Daddy hadn't said anything about his health being worse, but I felt a terrible urgency to get home. I rushed around trying to create just enough order to last a little while, to hold together until the ordeal in Louisiana was over, one way or another. But I wasn't fast enough. I'd only been back in California a few days when my mother called and told me Daddy was in a coma.

By that night I was in St. Francis Hospital in Poughkeepsie, trying to understand what I was seeing. My father was lying in a bed with his eyes closed. He looked peaceful, as though he might be sleeping, except that all around him were the machines that were keeping him alive. I tried to take that in, but I couldn't. This was my strong father who'd tried all his life to protect my mother and

— 241 —

sister and me, the gentle man who could cry, who felt things, who loved me without reservation. I couldn't believe he was so weak now and so near death.

I sat by his bed and held his hand. I'd heard that people in comas sometimes can hear and understand, even if they can't respond, so I talked to him. I begged him to fight. I told him he couldn't go. He couldn't leave me. Awful things were happening to me and I needed him. I asked him to squeeze my hand if he heard me, and I thought I felt him do it.

I went back the next day and the next. I begged him over and over to open his eyes. Then one day he did, but it had nothing to do with me. Something new had gone wrong, the doctors said, and he couldn't control his eyes anymore. They didn't even blink, just stayed open. A brain scan and other tests showed that there had been brain damage. The doctors didn't know how bad it was or what condition he would be in if he came out of the coma. Meanwhile, he could go on in the coma for months, years.

One day my mother and Emilia and I were on our way to the intensive care unit to see him when we were stopped by a nun who worked with the hospital's hospice program. She'd been visiting Daddy every day and she wanted to talk to us about him. He was hanging on, she said, because we wouldn't give him permission to go. We needed to tell him that it was all right for him to die. It sounded so cruel and final, but I knew she was right. Because we couldn't bear to lose him, we'd been selfish. One at a time, we each went in to be with him and to let him go.

This time I didn't beg him to stay. I told him about all the things in my life that I could never bring myself to tell him before, some good things and some of the terrible things that I hadn't been able to share. I told him I knew he'd always done his best for me, never deserted me, no matter what had happened. I promised that I'd help take care of my mother and sister and that we'd all be all right. I told him how much I loved him and how glad I was that he'd been my father. I said I knew he would help me from wherever he was going. And I told him that he should go, that it was time to go.

He died a couple of weeks later.

chapter 30

We buried my father at the end of May and I stayed on in New Paltz for a while to help my mother with his estate. Then I went back to California to finish straightening out my own affairs. By midsummer I was back in Louisiana, as depleted and depressed as I'd ever been in my life, to resume preparations for the trial that I now felt was inevitable.

The speedy-trial motion was to be heard on July 22, and though Bob and John were still optimistic about its chances, my own feelings were mixed. I'd developed the fatalistic conviction that this time, one way or another, the drama would be played out to the end. I almost wanted the motion to fail. If the case was thrown out I'd still be under the cloud that had followed me ever since the Nevada case in 1977, the legal limbo in which nothing was finally judged or decided. I wouldn't have to go to jail, but neither would I be cleared. Many people would be convinced that I'd beaten a murder rap on a technicality. I wanted a jury to say, "Not guilty."

Of course, there was a part of me that hoped the motion would prevail. Anything to end the nightmare. Anything to allow me to go off somewhere and hide and try to heal. Anything to avoid my having to get on a witness stand and bare every part of my life to the world.

John's performance at the two-day speedy-trial hearing was brilliant. His main argument was simple and compelling: If Louisiana wanted to prosecute me for the murder of Moises Chayo, why didn't it do it in 1977? Not a single circumstance had altered since then to change the prosecution's prospective case. Jack Sidote's testimony, the sum and essence of that case, had been available six years before. Louisiana, for its part, contended the testimony had been "unavailable" in 1977, since Jack wouldn't testify against me in Nevada. The claim was ridiculous. Sidote could have faced a long prison sentence in Louisiana's horrific state prison after he finished his time in Nevada. He had, after all, confessed to Chayo's murder. Louisiana had plenty of leverage against him but chose not to use it. When he petitioned the state to drop its case against him in light of the Nevada conviction, Louisiana obliged immediately. There was no dickering for his testimony against me, no threatened prosecution if he failed to comply. Even Sidote, in an affadavit we submitted at the hearing, said that if Louisiana had sought his testimony in 1977, he would have given it.

Louisiana contended that *I* had done nothing in 1977 to resolve my case—as though it were up to me, not the state, to get myself prosecuted. The contention was not only absurd but untrue. Bob Tuller tried on three different occasions to get some kind of resolution in Louisiana and the state wouldn't provide it. Assistant District Attorney Shirley Wimberly told him that his office had no case and would not pursue one, but he would not put that assurance in writing. By 1983 Wimberly was no longer in the office, and the men who were simply denied that any such assurance had ever been given.

Another of the state's arguments was not only preposterous but self-contradictory. The prosecutors said on the one hand that they couldn't go after me following the Nevada case because they didn't know where to find me. On the other, they said they thought I was in jail in Nevada. In fact, Jefferson Parish had been informed of the outcome of the Nevada matter immediately. Furthermore, the sheriff's office was given my address at the time, an address at which I continued to live for two more years. After that, when I became prominent in NOW, I "hid out" in the newspapers and on television like any other sensible fugitive from justice. No wonder I was so hard to find.

John and Bob had other arguments about what the state's failure to prosecute the case in a timely fashion had done to my life, not to mention my ability to defend myself. There was no possibility, for instance, of an alibi defense. The six-year delay came on top of a twelve-year gap between the time the murder was committed and the time Sidote confessed to it. How many people can remember exactly what they were doing on a particular day or night eighteen years before? How many can provide witnesses to corroborate them? And what of the witnesses who had died while Louisiana sat on its case? That list now included my father, who could have testified to receiving a letter in which Sidote threatened revenge against me after I left him.

I thought John's arguments were overwhelmingly persuasive. Judge Burns did not. On July 22 he denied our motion. An appellate court upheld him, saying that the "delicate balance" between the rights of the defendant and the rights of the state could be maintained only by a full airing of the facts of the case. In other words, I would have to go to trial before anyone could say for sure whether I should go to trial or not.

Bob and John expected at least a hearing before the Louisiana Supreme Court. But on September 30 the high court upheld the appellate court without granting a hearing. The October 11 trial date now appeared firm. And as the trial moved closer, the dread of testifying preyed more and more on my mind.

As it turned out, I was given a last chance to avoid testifying. Shortly before the trial was scheduled to start, Bob and John met with Judge Burns and with Gordon Konrad and Tom Porteous, the two top aides to Jefferson Parish District Attorney John Mamoulides. Konrad and Porteous were in charge of prosecuting me. At the meeting, Porteous suggested that his office might be willing to drop the murder charge against me in return for a guilty plea to a charge of accessory to murder after the fact. The plea would have meant there would be no trial and no testimony. Nevertheless, Bob and John laughed off the suggestion and said there would be no deals. They didn't believe the prosecution had a case, they said, and they were confident I'd be acquitted. I hadn't been an accessory and I wouldn't say I had been. We were ready to go to trial.

When Bob and John and I discussed the proposal, we agreed not to follow it up. Afraid as I was of testifying, I wasn't willing to bargain away my self-respect and whatever future I might have left in order to avoid it. Besides, I was puzzled by the offer. If the prosecution thought it had a strong murder case, why was it making this proposal? And if it didn't, why was I going through this ordeal in the first place?

· · ·

At the time, it didn't seem possible to my attorneys and me that the prosecution had nothing more than the testimony of Jack Sidote. We spent hours speculating about what else there might be. Maybe a political enemy of mine was planning to give perjured testimony about some imaginary confession on my part. Or maybe Wasyl Bozydaj had come up with some incriminating twist in his story that we weren't expecting. There had to be something more than Jack Sidote. Even in Louisiana, where, unlike Nevada, the unsubstantiated word of a co-principal in a crime is enough to indict, there had to be more.

In fact, there wasn't anything more. And the prosecutors of Jefferson Parish went to trial *knowing* there wasn't. It would be more than a year after my trial before I'd be able to piece together the story of what really happened behind the scenes in my case.

Louisiana, unlike most other states, allows a sheriff's office to issue an arrest warrant without any assurance that the district attorney's office will extradite or indict or prosecute. It can issue a warrant without even *informing* the district attorney's office. In my case that's what happened. Shelly Mandell's letter arrived in the office of Jefferson Parish sheriff Harry Lee. Deputies who in all likelihood had never heard of Ginny Foat ran a routine check and found a six-year-old warrant that was still outstanding. They teletyped the warrant to the Los Angeles Police Department, where it found its way to the Fugitive Division, to Warren Eggar and his colleagues.

There are two versions of what happened next. According to the sheriff's office police report, on January 7, Sergeant Vincent Lamia got a message to call Eggar and Detective Tom Gorey at the LAPD. The Los Angeles police told Lamia that the Virginia Galluzzo named in the warrant was now calling herself Ginny Foat and living in Los Angeles. She was, they added, currently serving as the president of California NOW. They wanted to know if they should go ahead and arrest me on the Louisiana warrant. Lamia asked Eggar and Gorey to hold off on the arrest, the police report says, until he could talk to somebody in the district attorney's office. Lamia allegedly then called an assistant DA named Bill Hall, who "concurred with the decision" (*whose* decision is not specified) to have me arrested.

Another version of the story surfaced, however. According to this account, *nobody* in the district attorney's office was informed of what was happening until the day of my arrest—*after* the elaborately orchestrated scene at the Burbank airport, *after* the arrest was national news. The prosecutors suddenly had a red-hot case on their hands, and one they knew virtually nothing about, since at that point they couldn't even locate my file.

Apparently District Attorney John Mamoulides was furious. He went to Sheriff Lee's office and demanded to know what was going on. Did Lee at least know the whereabouts of John J. Sidote, the crucial witness in the case? At the time, the sheriff did not. But by an odd coincidence, Sidote turned out to be easy to find.

He had been paroled from his twenty-five-year sentence in the Donald Fitting murder in October of 1981. Apparently he started drinking almost immediately and found it hard to get work or keep it. Once again, Jack Sidote was down and out. On January 4, 1983, one week before my arrest, he walked out of a bar, got into a car, and ran over a stop sign. He was picked up by the police for driving under the influence, a parole violation. When Jefferson Parish started looking for him, Sidote was conveniently back in jail in Nevada, his parole revoked, serving an indeterminate part of what remained of his sentence. Theoretically, he could be in jail another twenty years or so.

Right after my arrest Tom Porteous was dispatched to Nevada to talk to Sidote. In their first interview, for whatever reason, Jack said he wouldn't testify. Porteous then told him that if he refused, he could be prosecuted himself for Chayo's murder. The threat was probably hollow. Sidote had in writing Louisiana's 1977 agreement to drop the case against him, and he therefore had an excellent chance of avoiding prosecution of the grounds that he failed to get a speedy trial.

In any case, apparently Porteous wasn't very impressed with his prospective star witness; he telephoned his office to say, in effect, that even if Sidote testified he would never convince a jury of anything. He wasn't likeable or sympathetic, and he certainly wasn't credible. But, back in Jefferson Parish, the calls were coming in from CBS and *The New York Times* and *Newsweek.* Porteous was told to go back to Sidote and offer him anything he wanted, within reason, but to get his testimony. Porteous went back to the jail and Jack was given immunity. He agreed to testify, but shortly after that he seemed to change his mind again. He filed papers in Nevada accusing Porteous of forcing him to agree to testify by threatening him with an invalid murder warrant. This time not only Porteous but Konrad and Mamoulides himself flew to Nevada to see him, and a codicil was added to the immunity agreement: Whatever the outcome of the trial, Louisiana would put in a good word for Jack with the Nevada Parole Board.

In New York, Louisiana detectives talked to Wasyl Bazydaj. According to the police report, Wasyl had nothing more incriminating to say than he'd said in 1977; that is, he had no knowledge of any crimes or of any participation in them either by Jack or me. Nevertheless, Wasyl came to be billed as the chief corroborating witness for Sidote's story.

In the month before the trial both Porteous and Konrad spent time in California, talking mostly to women who'd known me through NOW. Rumors were flying. The most persistent one was that I'd confessed to both the Nevada and Louisiana murders in front of Shelly Mandell and Elaine Lafferty while having dinner at a restaurant in Los Angeles. The prosecutors could not find Shelly, either to interview her or subpoena her testimony, but her lawyer told the press that she "knew nothing that would help their case." Elaine flew to Louisiana on her own, saying that she was writing a book about me and wanted to cover the trial. She was subpoenaed the minute she got off the plane, but the prosecution never put her on the stand.

Until the end of September the prosecutors, like Bob and John, apparently doubted that the case would ever go to trial. They, too, thought that our speedy-trial assertion was persuasive. When it lost, they apparently were surprised—surprised and none too happy with their victory. Perhaps they started talking about a plea bargain after our motion failed because, ironically, they wanted to be let off the hook almost as badly as I did. They'd gotten hold of something that was no case at all but at the same time was very visible. The fact that their case was weak, that the expense to the taxpayers was considerable, and that my life and my family's would be ruined seemed to be less important than the potential publicity they might enjoy.

My own recurring nightmare was that though Jack Sidote's word was all the prosecution had, it might be enough. Rationally, it didn't seem possible. Sometimes to reassure myself I tried to put his story in perspective by seeing how it would sound if the sexes were reversed: Suppose that some man who came from fairly humble beginnings and made some mistakes early in his life managed to work his way up to a position of some respect in his community. He became, say, the president of a state chamber of commerce, as well as a political activist, a man whose support was courted by well-known public figures. And suppose that out of the blue, this man's ex-wife, now a derelict, a mentally disturbed, suicidal ex-convict, a chronic alcoholic and confessed multiple murderer, telephoned the police one night with a story about how this prominent man had helped her commit murders years before. Would the man be locked up and indicted and brought to trial? Would there be the remotest chance that he'd be convicted and sentenced? I didn't believe there would be. A far more likely outcome would be that his ex-wife would be put away in some institution and never heard from again. Surely a jury would see that. Surely twelve ordinary, sensible people would see how sexist and how absurd this case was.

And yet, on nothing more substantial than Jack Sidote's story, I had already been arrested twice in the course of six years and had spent almost eight months in jail. I'd lost my father, many friends, the position of leadership and respect I'd worked so hard for. My life had been turned into a garish public spectacle. There was that power of a man's word—any man's word, it seemed—against a woman. A man's word in a system dominated by men had been enough to get us this far. It might go all the way.

We were leaving nothing to chance. Bob and John's investigator, Gary Eldridge, had been working for months, interviewing everyone he could find who might be able to testify to Jack's character, or mine, or his abuse and domination of me. He talked to people in Louisiana, Florida, Nevada, California, while a colleague of his did the same thing in New York. Gary and I pored over maps together, trying to reconstruct the exact route of that 1965 trip from New York to California. We tried to find people who'd worked for the Ponderosa Bar, which had long since burned down. We often failed. Again and again, I couldn't remember things. Sometimes Gary would come up with a potential witness who might have proved useful, someone who could help show the jury the kind of woman Ginny Galluzzo had been, a woman so different from the one I was now. But I could hardly ever place the person. It had all happened so long ago, and I'd tried so hard to forget. The potential witness would be discarded.

The investigators had volunteer help from my friends. Debbie Jones, for instance, found herself touring hard-hat bars in California, looking for former patrons of the No Regrets. Jan Holden spent hours going through old high-school yearbooks in Carson City, trying to get a lead on the identity of the hitchhiker who'd traveled from New Orleans to Nevada with Jack and Wasyl and me. At one point we even thought we'd found him, but the boy, now a man, wanted no part of the case and refused to confirm that he'd been with us.

Early in the summer we decided we needed help in Nevada, someone to form a bridge with Sidote and monitor his dealings with the prosecutors. We hired Annabelle Hall, a well-known criminal attorney in Reno, who became a dear friend and an invaluable part of the defense team. She was very helpful in bringing to light some of the details of Jack's decline in the years after I left him. Around midsummer we hired the National Jury Project, which, among its other services, set up panels representative of potential juries in Jefferson Parish and presented the outlines of our case and the anticipated case of the prosecution. The panels' reactions helped shape our strategy in preparing for trial. We lined up testimony from experts on battering and on the mentality of alcoholics.

But with all the help, all the thousands of hours of work by so many people, all the money we were spending, it became clear that, finally, the trial's outcome would hinge on only one issue: Would a jury believe Jack Sidote or would it believe me?

With his dismal past, Jack would be an easy witness to impeach in many ways. But the prosecution would argue that he had to be telling the truth. In implicating me, he had implicated himself in two murders. He had, by their analysis, acted against his own interest in confessing. He had risked spending the rest of his life in jail. No man, they would argue, could be so warped or so bent on revenge that he would do such a thing to himself.

We had to prove that the prosecution was wrong. To do that, we had to destroy Sidote's credibility completely: We had to show the full scope of his malice against me and the lengths he would go to for revenge. We had to show how he might even have expected to gain, not lose, by confessing to murder. The second thing we had to do was up to me. I had not only to tell my story, but to relive it and make the jurors relive it with me. I had to make them feel the pain of it. If I was to make them believe me, I would have to feel the pain again myself. And that, it appeared, was the biggest problem we had.

chapter 31

Too much work was involved in my case for both my lawyers to give full attention to all aspects of it, so over the months a pattern developed for dividing the labor. Bob concentrated on things having to do with Jack Sidote. He would cross-examine Jack and present the defense's main closing argument. John would give the opening argument and focus on my testimony.

From his earliest connection with the case, John had sensed that the issue of battering would be crucial to my defense. According to Sidote, I was the dominant one in our relationship, the strong and conniving woman who'd lured him away from his family and then taken the lead in murdering two men, all but forcing him to be my accomplice. But if the jury could be made to see things the way they really were between us—his brutality and dominance, my passivity and fear—then Jack's story would be shown up for the ridiculous invention that it was. With that in mind, John started trying to get me to re-create the years from 1965 to 1970.

"What did he do to you?" he'd ask.

"He'd hit me."

"What do you mean, 'He'd hit me'?"

"My nose would bleed. I'd get bruises."

"What else?"

"He'd tell me awful stories."

"What kind of stories?"

"Like he killed somebody."

Our sessions would end with John throwing up his hands in defeat and disgust. He'd say something like, "There's no emotion in what you're saying. No affect at all. You might as well be talking about something you saw on the late show, something that happened to some other person."

I'd try again, but it would be no better. I kept giving him little swatches of sentences with no feeling in them, the same little swatches I'd lived with and hidden behind for thirteen years, the ones I'd pull out and display every time I had to talk about Jack Sidote. John needed the whole story, the feeling and texture of what my life had been like, and all I could give him were these sanitized and condensed snippets of reality. I tried to do better but I couldn't, and I couldn't even understand why I couldn't.

The Jury Project's panels were hearing our case based on what John knew so far, and the reaction was horribly negative. "So he slapped her around, so what?" was the kind of feedback we were getting. "What does that have to do with whether she killed a guy?" There was more contempt than sympathy: "If he treated her that way, why didn't she get out? What was wrong with her?" And worse: "She knew what kind of bastard he was and she still stayed with him. She must have known what was going on. And if she was so afraid of him, he probably could have gotten her to do anything. Murder somebody? Sure, why not." Murder wasn't the only charge the jury would consider. There was also manslaughter. From what the Jury Project was telling us, manslaughter looked like a distinct possibility.

That terrified me, but it didn't open me up. I had to have some professional help, John decided. On September 30, the day we lost the final speedy-trial appeal, he called a therapist named Anne Teachworth, who was the founder and director of the New Orleans Gestalt Institute. I had my first session with Anne that same night.

I think she knew from the first the truth that John had intuitively sensed, the truth that I was still blind to: I *was* talking about something that happened to somebody else. I was talking about bad things that had happened to a woman I didn't know very well and didn't like at all. To defend myself against a past I hated I'd set up a partition in my mind, with a woman on either side. On one side was Ginny Galluzzo, on the other Ginny Foat.

All the bad things had happened to Ginny Galluzzo, not me,

and she probably deserved them. She was stupid and weak and gutless. She was tacky and cheap. It was Ginny Galluzzo who wore tight, flashy clothes and gaudy jewelry and a mountain of hairpieces. Ginny Foat had taste; she'd never be seen looking like that. It was Ginny Galluzzo who'd take up with any kind of lowlife, pal around with all sorts of scuzzy characters. She'd hang around the pits at racetracks and work on cars, getting filthy, having a few belts afterward with men who had tattooed arms and dirty fingernails. Ginny Foat could never do that. Ginny Foat didn't like to get her hands dirty. She didn't like to be seen with scruffy-looking people. She'd learned to handle herself. Smart, sophisticated Ginny Foat didn't spout bad grammar in a Brooklyn accent. She had polish, style. She was at home with movie stars and famous politicians. Ginny Foat's friends were accomplished people, professional people. She wouldn't even know an ignorant bimbo like Ginny Galluzzo— Ginny Galluzzo, who was so awestruck by a sleazy singing bartender that she let him brutalize her for years and almost kill her before she had sense enough to get out. Never would Ginny Foat give a man like Jack Sidote so much as an hour of her time. Of course Ginny Foat couldn't testify about living with Jack Sidote. What did she know about it?

For thirteen years I had managed to live with myself by making Ginny Galluzzo the repository for all my agonies and all my failings. I'd dumped them on her, hobbled her in place in the past, and then disowned her and tried to outrun her. For Ginny Foat to be happy and secure, Ginny Galluzzo had to stay in the past, forgotten and out of sight. But somehow she'd caught up with me. And now, prepared or not, strong enough or not, I was going to have to face her. Now I needed her. This time it was Ginny Foat who didn't have the guts, who couldn't endure the shame of getting up on a witness stand and telling the degrading story that had to be told. Ginny Galluzzo had to testify for me.

Anne and I would meet in quiet places with low lights. After the first session she bought records, songs that had been popular when Jack and I were together, like Dean Martin's "Houston," which had been a great favorite of Jack's. She wanted me not only to remember my life but to re-experience it. She would play the records and tell me to listen to the music, to go back through it, to imagine that it was years ago and I was living with Jack. "What are you seeing now, Ginny?" she'd ask. "What is he doing? What is he saying? Now you're on the bed and he's on top of you. He has the belt in his hand. What is he doing? What are you feeling? Stay with the feelings, Ginny. Feel the pain." We went back to the time before Jack. We talked about my first marriage and the pain of that failure, about my baby and the pain of that.

Her methods were all too effective. In slow, agonizing steps I was walking back through the maze of my past, seeing all the ugliness, opening the door to the room where the bad things were locked away. At the end of every session I'd be crying, shaking with pain and fear and fury, angry at Anne for what she was making me see, angry at Sidote, at myself. Then the anger would pass and I'd just feel numb and drained, exhausted, sure that I couldn't go through any more of this torture. And there was no rest from it. As soon as I left Anne I'd have to go to John and go over all of it again, showing him whatever I'd gouged out of myself in the session that just ended. Finally, the process was too much for me. Anne and I decided to have John sit with us and hear it all firsthand.

At first I doubted that I would be able to tell my awful story in front of another person, but realistically, I knew that my squeamishness was laughable. Here I was nervous about talking in front of John, who by now was like a brother to me, when all too soon I was going to have to tell everything to a world of strangers.

I saw Anne every day for more than a week. Toward the end of our time together we talked a lot about Ginny Galluzzo and my feelings toward her. One day we set up a chair for her to sit in. Anne told me to see her sitting there and to talk to her and tell her how I felt. I did. I told her how stupid and weak she was. I told her she made a lie out of everything I believed women could be and wanted them to be. I cursed her for all the mistakes she'd made. Why did she go off with that bastard, that maniac? Why did she hurt her family like that? Why did she stay with him? Why did she let him do what he did to her? I was sobbing, screaming at her. I told her I despised her. She was everything I hated. "I hate you," I shrieked. "I hate you, hate you, hate you . . ."

And as I screamed at her I felt something inside me, some hardness, break and begin to dissolve. I stopped shouting. I felt calm, almost peaceful. It occurred to me that I wouldn't hate some other woman who'd lived the way Ginny Galluzzo had; I'd pity her. Then why was there no compassion for this woman who was me? Anne and I talked about it. What about the good things about Ginny Galluzzo? What about her kindness? What about her loyalty and her capacity to love? Anne asked me if I could see now that Ginny Galluzzo had made it possible for Ginny Foat to exist. Could I see that one was born from the other's pain?

I thought I could see it, or begin to. I couldn't forgive her yet, but maybe I could try to accept her back into my life and, at last, recognize her as part of me. I could, maybe, start to think about forgiving her.

By the weekend before the Tuesday the trial was to start, John had what he needed. We went over the bare facts once, briefly and unemotionally, but we didn't rehearse my testimony. John didn't even tell me exactly what he was going to ask. He said he wanted my story to come out in its entirety on the witness stand and not before. He wanted it to be spontaneous and fresh. For my part, with the trial only hours away I felt that I was as ready for it as I was ever likely to be. Anne had given me some insights that I might never have gained on my own, and they gave me courage. I was still nervous, still terrified, but I felt I had enough strength, just barely enough, to do what had to be done.

Then, the day before the trial, there was a front-page story in the *Times-Picayune* that began, "Prosecutors have failed to find a man they believe heard Ginny Foat and John Sidote talk about how they killed Moises Chayo . . . sources said." The story was bad enough, but the headline above it was disastrous: "Prosecution can't find witness who heard Foat talk of slaying." The "witness" referred to was the hitchhiker we had been searching for ourselves for months, believing he could only help my case. God knows what grounds the prosecutors had for "believing" he heard me talk about a murder, or what grounds the newspaper had for stating flatly in its headline that I *had* talked about one. Seething, John and Bob went to Judge Burns and demanded that the trial be delayed, saying that it was impossible to pick an unbiased jury in the face of such outrageous publicity. Even the prosecutors supported the request for the delay, and Burns granted it. On the day the trial was to have started a new trial date was set: November 7.

I was devastated by the postponement. I'd been ready, and now I was faced with almost a month in which I could do nothing but lose ground emotionally. John and Bob could use the time for some fine-tuning of their case—preparing witnesses, working on their arguments. But my own work was substantially finished. I could only wait and worry and feel my new courage begin to ebb away while the old dread of testifying welled up in its place. I'd been able to prepare myself once. I didn't know if I could do it again.

I spent most of my month of waiting at Kay's house in San Francisco. She nursed me through some terrible lows. On one of the worst nights I told her that I wasn't going to testify. I couldn't. I would rather go to jail for the rest of my life than say some of the things I would have to say. We returned to Louisiana early in November.

My mother and my sister, Emilia, flew to New Orleans the weekend before the trial. They would be testifying for me. It was a great comfort to have them with me, but at the same time it was a new source of pain. I hated their having to be involved in the trial and the circus surrounding it. I grieved for the grief they were feeling, knowing I'd caused it and was about to cause more.

My mother had been very much on my mind. Alone for the first time in her life, she'd hardly begun to recover from the loss of my father. And now this. She was seventy-two years old. I didn't know how much more she could take.

While I was in San Francisco I got a card from the sisters of the Marianite Order who taught at the Holy Cross school in Jefferson Parish, saying that they were praying for me. When I returned to New Orleans I called the school to thank them. I talked to a Sister Clarita, who told me the sisters were having a prayer service for me the night before the trial. They would be happy if my family and I would come.

That Sunday night Mother and Emilia and I and my old friend Clara, who had also come to Louisiana to testify for me, drove to the school. There were perhaps forty nuns at the service. Some played musical instruments while the rest of us sang songs I remembered from many years before. Others read passages from the Bible. Toward the end of the evening there was the ceremony of annointing of the oil. I was given a tray of holy oil to hold. Each sister came to me, dipped a hand in the oil, and made the sign of the cross with it on my own hand. Each one spoke to me, saying a short prayer or some words of encouragement. I cried throughout the ceremony. I was so deeply touched by these good women, who were offering me their love and faith, infusing some of their own strength into me.

I felt very much in touch with Ginny Galluzzo that night. I remembered the child she'd been, the little girl taking her first Holy Communion, sure that one day she'd be a nun. I remembered her growing up, a child of her times and circumstances, feeling so guilty and confused because she wanted things those times and circumstances didn't allow. I remembered the guilt she felt as a young woman failing at marriage, and the greater guilt of failing as a mother. I remembered the guilt that overwhelmed her during the years with Jack Sidote, the guilt she took on herself that should have been his—her fault that he beat her, her fault that he was a drunk and a bum. Her fault that he was a killer. So much was clearer to me now; I was making the connections. Maybe it was guilt that brought me to Jack Sidote in the first place and guilt that kept me with him, and later it was the guilt at ever having been with him that put me at odds with my past and at war with myself. The guilt formed a chain. It stretched all the way back to my childhood, and tomorrow it would lead into a courtroom.

Tomorrow Ginny Foat the defendant would be entitled by law to the presumption of innocence of the crime of murder. And yet Ginny Foat the woman had presumed herself guilty of so many other things for so much of her life. How could I convince twelve strangers I was innocent?

chapter 32

I'd slept only fitfully through the night and I was awake when dawn broke. The earliest light showed that Monday, November 7, was going to be a gray day, damp and chilly. At least it matched my mood. I got up and went to the kitchen of the borrowed house Kay and I were sharing and made coffee. After my first cup I showered, dried my hair, put on my makeup—the ordinary, routine morning things. How odd, I thought, that this morning should start out so much like any other.

I'd pressed my clothes and laid them out the night before—not necessarily an outfit I would have chosen for the occasion, but one that fit the type I'd been instructed to wear. Terry Waller of the Jury Project had been very specific on the subject of dress. Clothes made a certain impression on a jury, she said. The defendant had to have the right look. The look I was striving for was "vulnerable." I was to wear straight skirts, belted at the waist, in solid colors only. Nothing fancy. I was to pick "vulnerable" blouses—soft, full, demure styles with long sleeves and high necks. No suit jackets in the courtroom. Too severe. My customary high heels were all right, but pumps only. No open toes. Too sexy.

I slid into some dark blue pumps while I buttoned my white

blouse up the back. Then I put on a lightweight slate-blue skirt and, because I was cold, threw a matching short jacket around my shoulders. I could take it off later. My hair, for several years now its natural silver-gray, looked okay, but I couldn't seem to stop running a brush through it, trying to get used to the extra inch or so of length it had added in the past two months. Terry had told me to let it grow a little. It would look softer, more vulnerable. Finally, I put down the brush and surveyed myself in a full-length mirror. Yes, I supposed I did look vulnerable. I certainly felt vulnerable.

Kay and I sat in the living room and waited for Bob Tuller and Jan to pick us up and drive us to court. I nursed a second cup of coffee. Neither of us said much. At least, for once, I was ready for something on time, I thought. I wondered if anybody had ever been late for her own hanging.

When we pulled into the driveway that separated the Jefferson Parish Courthouse from the jail in front of it I noticed that the crowd of reporters wasn't as big as I'd expected, nothing like the mob that had met me that day at the New Orleans airport. It puzzled me briefly. Then I figured out that the day wasn't going to offer much in the way of high drama for the press. Today we started selecting a jury—a crucial matter for me, but not one likely to produce any hot copy.

Bob and John met us at the courthouse and we all crowded onto a small elevator. Several reporters managed to squeeze in with us, wedging me against a wall toward the back. A woman in the front kept shouting, "How do you feel, Mrs. Foat?" I stared at the floor and said nothing. It seemed like such a silly question.

I can see the courtroom as though I were still standing in it: off a wide hall on the third floor of the five-story building, just to the right as you get off the elevator. It was a small room, far too small for the scores of people who would try to crowd into it every day once the actual trial started. There were eight wooden pews along its left side and seven on the right across a narrow aisle. Each pew would seat five people comfortably, although on most days many more would jam into each one, while others would sit on the floor between the pews and still others would stand around the walls. The first two pews on the left side were for family members and aides of the prosecutors, the first two on the right side for the defense. The next four on either side were reserved for the press. The walls were a dingy white, although the fluorescent lighting set into the acoustical-tile ceiling made the whole room and everyone in it look faintly green.

The spectator section of the courtroom was separated from the business end by a wooden railing. There the colorless linoleum of the floor under the pews gave way to darkly speckled, utilitarian carpeting. The raised dais where the judge sat was against the back wall, flanked on either side by long windows hung with woven wood blinds. A yellowing ficus drooped in the right window near a Louisiana flag, dark blue, with the picture of a pelican on it. To the left of the judge's bench was an American flag. The wall behind the bench was of dark, cheap paneling and on it hung the state seal, again featuring the pelican. To the left of the bench was the jury box, a double row of green vinyl chairs on a raised platform enclosed by paneling. To the right of the bench and just below it was the witness chair.

The prosecutors' table was on the left side of the courtroom near the jury box, and when we arrived at 10:00 A.M. that Monday it was already occupied. On the far left was John Mamoulides, the district attorney. He had salt-and-pepper hair, dark skin, and a massively square jaw. I knew that he usually left trial work to his subordinates, but apparently he considered my case worthy of his personal attention. To his right was Gordon Konrad, whom I remembered all too well from the speedy-trial hearing. Blond and florid, he had a sharp voice that matched both his gestures and his features, blue eyes so pale they looked like chips of glass, and a large nose and slightly receding chin. Of the three prosecutors, it was Konrad who scared me most. He more than the others seemed to enjoy his job. On his right, wreathed in smoke, sat Tom Porteous. Porteous had gotten special permission from the judge to smoke in the courtroom, which he did often, though less often, you felt, than he would have liked. A fringe of dark, tightly curled hair ringed the back of his nearly bald head. He had a round, open, amiable face. Under other circumstances I think I might have found it likeable. Unlike Konrad, who really seemed to enjoy his work, Porteous would give me the impression throughout the trial that he wished he were on vacation.

We took our places at the defense table to the right of the room. I sat between Bob and John, and, for the time being, Terry Waller sat with us. The Jury Project's job would end only after a jury had been empaneled. A venire of eighty potential jurors had been assembled for the questioning by the prosecution and the defense. A little after ten o'clock Judge Burns called the court to order and the prospective jurors began coming in, three at a time.

We already knew a little about most of them. Working from the list provided to the attorneys, Jan Holden had organized volunteers to drive by the home of each person on the list, see how well-kept it was, and take special note of such things as right-wing bumper stickers on cars or religious statuary on front lawns. The reasoning was that extremely doctrinaire people, especially those with a conservative bent, would not be sympathetic to me. We wanted a solid, middle-class jury, preferably an educated one, and, most important, one that was open-minded.

Konrad, who did most of the questioning for the prosecution, tended to lecture. He prefaced his questions with long explanations of the legal meaning of "murder," of "manslaughter," of the terms "principal" and "co-principal." His questions, once they started, pointed up what the prosecution obviously considered some major weaknesses in its case: As a juror, could you understand how there might be an eighteen-year delay in prosecuting a murder case, providing reasons for it came out during testimony? As a juror, would you have trouble believing a witness who had been convicted of other crimes and was a co-principal in this crime? Several people did express concern over one issue or the other or both. They were rejected by the prosecution.

Bob and John were much more extensive in their questioning, but at the same time more informal and relaxed. John might begin by walking to the jury box, flashing a smile at the three people sitting there, and saying, "You must be nervous. Don't worry. We're nervous too." It worked well. I could see the people settling back in their chairs, letting themselves get comfortable and receptive. After that, Bob or John would escort me from the defense table to the jury box and introduce me. I'd been told to make eye contact with each prospective juror. My lawyers felt that this was an important first step in establishing for the jury that I was a flesh-and-blood person, not just a face in the newspaper or a story on television. It was also a way of impressing on them from the outset that eventually twelve of them would hold my life in their hands. The prosecution attorneys were beside themselves at this tactic.

Our questions were meant to elicit some basic attitudes from the would-be jurors and to ferret out any underlying prejudices: How do you feel about the women's movement? What do you feel about the ERA? Do you know of Ginny's position in NOW? Could you imagine yourself in the defendant's chair? Has anybody ever lied about you to get you in trouble? What kind of a person do you think would do something like that? Do you know anybody who has problems with alcohol? Have you ever heard the expression "mean drunk"? Do you have any knowledge of people involved in domestic violence? Can you understand why a woman might stay in such a relationship?

On the whole, I was a little surprised at the liberality of most of the people on the panel. True, several of them seemed to understand only that I was involved in "some women's league," and one, a woman, said she thought that while the women's movement was okay, "people like Gloria Steinem are too radical." Nevertheless, when the questioning got down to such gut issues as battering and alcoholism, most of the people showed sympathy, or at least the capacity to try to understand.

While each round of questioning was going on, Terry scribbled notes furiously, recording body language, facial expressions, dress—anything that might give us a better feel for the character of each potential juror. Once the questioning was over, the four of us huddled at the defense table to decide whether or not any of the three people we'd just heard from were acceptable. Anybody who seemed too rigid or closed-minded was rejected by the defense.

The process went on throughout the morning and the afternoon, and the next day, and the day after that. By the time court adjourned on Wednesday evening the defense and the prosecution had agreed on twelve jurors and one alternate, and the eighty-person list was exhausted. The next morning Burns called up another ten citizens and the final alternate was picked.

My jury consisted of six women and six men. The women: a secretary, a state worker, a management consultant for women in business, a tutor for the public schools, a clerical worker, a homemaker. Three were married and three divorced. All but one had children. The men: an electrician, the vice president of an electrical engineering company, a railroad employee, a gardener, an accountant, a salesman for an oilfield company. All but one were married. Four were fathers. Ordinary people, good and sensible people. I can't say that I felt safe with them; I'd forgotten how to feel safe. But I was satisfied that they'd be fair.

A little before two o'clock on Thursday, November 10, Gordon Konrad rose to outline the prosecution's case. He began by reminding the jury that I need not have killed Moises Chayo myself to be guilty of the charge against me. If the killing took place during a robbery, and I was participating in the robbery, then I was guilty of murder. Then, essentially, Konrad summarized Sidote's story for the jury: Jack was just an ordinary guy, a good family man, until he met me in 1965. Because of me he deserted his wife and child and set off on a cross-country trip that would mark the beginning of his ruination. When we found ourselves low on money in New Orleans we hatched a plan whereby I'd pick up a man in the French Quarter and Jack and I would take him out and rob him. When the robbery got out of hand, we beat the man to death, robbed him, and fled the city.

Konrad went on to describe Sidote's manslaughter conviction in California, taking pains to make the killing of the Samoan boy sound like an unfortunate accident. He talked about the subsequent jail term, and how Jack and I parted company in 1970 after "a large disagreement and fight." He stressed that Jack and I had virtually no contact with each other for the next seven years, and therefore Jack's confession to Albany police in 1977 was clearly an act of conscience and in no way showed malice against me. It was the act of a man deeply contrite, a man seeking only to atone for his sins. Konrad talked about Jack's plea to robbery and manslaughter in Nevada. (No mention of me here; Judge Burns had ruled before the trial that nothing from the Nevada case could be introduced.) Sidote had implicated me in the Louisiana killing at the time, Konrad said, but Jefferson Parish didn't pursue the matter because it concluded that Jack would not testify against me. Sidote was getting immunity now because he was already being punished in Nevada. It was time for me to be punished, too.

There were no surprises in the opening statement; it was about what we expected. At times I found that I could hardly follow it. I had a feeling of detachment that would come back to me again and again during the trial, a feeling that none of this was real. It was a bizarre play. The audience was sitting behind me in the courtroom and the actors were all in front. I was one of the actors. At some point I'd get my cue and say my lines, but I didn't understand the script. I didn't know what they were talking about. I didn't recognize some of the other characters. Certainly I didn't know this penitent Jack Sidote I was hearing about. The murder Konrad spoke of sounded horrible, but it was no more real to me than a murder in a television mystery. I didn't know the victim. I'd never seen him. What did he have to do with me? I found myself drifting in and out of reality, feeling at times that I could get up and leave during this part of the play and no one would even notice. Then John began his opening statement and reality settled firmly into place again.

"Members of the jury, things are not always the way they seem," he said, "things are not as they seem to be and as the state seems to think that they are. In July of 1970, after five years of living in a cage that John Sidote had fashioned for Virginia Foat, a cage made at first of love, at first of Virginia Foat's extreme insecurity, and a cage later made of fear and terror, Ginny Foat, then Ginny Sidote, made a decision to get out and to leave that man and to leave him forever.

"And when she made that decision, that man beat her as he had never beaten her before. He beat her in the face, he beat her in the breasts, he beat her in the arms, he grabbed her by the hair, he put his hands around her neck, he squeezed as hard as he could, and he almost killed her, and she thought that she was dying. And as he did so, he said, 'I'll kill you. I'll kill you if you ever leave me, and I'll make you pay for my crimes if you ever leave me, and I'll see you behind bars and rotting in jail like me if you ever leave me.' "

Yes, this was real. This was too real.

"Seven years passed and John Sidote, a broken-down, suicidal alcoholic, at the pits of his life, carried out his threat in the early morning hours in the cold of Albany, New York, in January 1977," John said. "Not caring about himself or anyone else, he took out his revenge on Ginny Foat. And he put Ginny Foat, for a while, back in a cage, this time a cage with bars.

"Six more years passed, and in January 1983, someone dusted off John Sidote, the man who had made the accusations when he was drunk and sick, and gave him no choice but to repeat what he had said back in 1977, because if he did not repeat what he said back in 1977, he would have to go to jail himself for the rest of his life. And John Sidote, when he appears before you in this courtroom, will have no choice but to say what he said in 1977, when he made the accusation and carried through the threat he had made in that last fight in 1970.

"But it was not the first time he had made that threat," John said. "And if we are going to understand this case, we are going to have to understand something about Jack Sidote and Ginny Foat and those years long ago."

And so he went on to try to make them understand. He talked about my background, my family, the traditional values I grew up with, my first marriage and its failure, my sense of shame. He was starting to talk about the baby, just leading up to it, when Konrad rose and asked for a conference at the bench.

I was almost relieved. The part that was coming, the story about the baby, was the part I dreaded most. It was my deepest secret. At the same time, I knew that at that moment my whole defense was hanging by a thread. I knew that Konrad was objecting that the baby, and all the other talk about my background, was irrelevant to whether I'd committed murder. We'd expected such an objection. John was countering that it *was* relevant. Unless the jury understood the whole story—who I was, who Jack Sidote was, what the dynamics of our relationship were—there was no way to arrive at the truth. There was no basis for weighing his testimony or mine. Burns considered the arguments and I waited, afraid to breathe. If he ruled against us, it might mean that anything I said about how I came to be with Sidote, how he treated me, and why he was accusing me now, might be inadmissible. I'd be left with virtually no defense. At last Burns made his decision: In light of the gravity of the case, and the crucial importance of motivation, almost everything about my life was relevant. John could continue.

He told about the baby and about my state of mind after I gave it up. He described the Jack Sidote I first met, the classy bartender, the "white Sammy Davis, Jr., the married man who was really a ladies' man separated from his wife." He told about our trip to Florida, the threat outside Washington to leave me on the side of the road. And then the violence and the psychological battering: the beating in Florida, Jack's story about killing a woman. My rationalizations and my growing fear, my dependence, my learning to obey, not to ask questions. The violence in Louisiana, our sudden departure from New Orleans and the reasons Jack gave for it; the violence in Nevada, in California. John outlined the whole story, just as I remembered it, just as I'd unearthed it from the hidden places in my mind. He told about my life after Jack Sidote, and his life after me. He told of Jack's sickness and his need for vengeance.

There were no more interruptions from the prosecution. It was a long statement, and John told it as well as it could be told. The jurors' attention never wavered. But I knew that sooner or later it would still be up to me to convince them it was true.

chapter 33

There was a short recess after John's opening statement. Court reconvened at 3:15 P.M. The state called its first witness: Colonel Roy L. Jacobs of the Jefferson Parish Sheriff's Department. Eighteen years before, he had been Lieutenant Jacobs, the watch commander in charge of the original investigation of Moises Chayo's murder.

Porteous asked Jacobs to describe three photographs of the site where the body was found. It was an undeveloped area at the time, Jacobs said. Its main features were a small road made out of seashells, and a shallow ditch. The last photograph showed a body face down in the ditch. Jacobs said he and two other officers investigated the scene on December 11, 1965. No weapons were found and there were no witnesses. Personnel from the coroner's office removed the body.

We, too, were interested in the pictures of the site. Sidote had told police in 1977 that he and I had left the body near a warehouse. On cross-examination, Bob asked Jacobs if, in 1965, there were any completed buildings in the immediate area where the body was found.

"No, sir," Jacobs said.

"More particularly," Bob went on, "there were no warehouses in that area?"

"No, sir, no warehouses. No, sir."

The state's next witness was Dr. Tom Farris, a pathologist, who performed an autopsy on Chayo shortly after the body was discovered. Matter-of-factly, sometimes in technical terms, Farris gave the grisly details of the condition of the corpse: The body was in an advanced state of decomposition. The face was markedly swollen. There was extensive discoloration of the skin. The hair was completely gone. There were dentures in the upper jaw. There was marked gaseous distension of the abdomen, and the genitalia were also markedly swollen."

This testimony was horribly real to me and ghoulish. I had not known Moises Chayo, dead these eighteen years, but hearing him described this way, like so much spoiled meat, I felt that a ghastly indignity was being done to him. I was glad that all witnesses had been sequestered and that Chayo's son, who would testify soon, was not in the courtroom to hear this.

Now Farris was saying that Chayo had probably been dead for between sixteen and twenty days by the time the autopsy was done. Konrad asked if there were any wounds on the body. Yes, the doctor said. There were five lacerations on the front of the head. "The lacerations extended completely through the skin but the underlying bone was not fractured," he said. "When I removed the calvarium, the brain had completely liquefied, so that it was impossible to determine whether there was any hemorrhage in the brain or not."

"Because of the condition of the body at the time of your examination," Konrad said, "were you able to pinpoint a cause of death, sir?"

"No," the pathologist said, "I could only presume."

"Well, could you reach a medical opinion as to the likely cause of death of Mr. Chayo?"

"I presume that he probably bled to death. . . ."

"And . . ." Konrad prompted.

"I was made aware of where he was found, so I also could presume that he may have drowned."

"Could you tell me if the lacerations about the head would be compatible with the deceased having been struck with a blunt instrument such as a tire tool?" Konrad asked.

"Yes."

— 267 —

"Okay. There was nothing incompatible about those injuries and injury being done by a tire tool?"

"Nothing incompatible," Farris said.

On cross-examination Bob established that the lacerations in the victim's scalp all matched each other and were all linear.

"Now, some tire tools are bent, are they not?" Bob asked.

"Yes," Farris answered.

"Some tire tools have—or old tire tools, do they not have sharpened points in order to get off the hubcap?"

"I'm not that familiar with tire tools," the witness conceded, though only a few minutes before, he'd gone along with the prosecution's tire-tool argument.

Bob was able to establish that any number of weapons could have caused the wounds in question. Then he went on to another point.

"If we assume that Mr. Chayo was standing at the time at least one of those blows was struck, it is your opinion, is it not, that it would most likely have been struck from the front?"

"Yes," Farris said.

"And if Mr. Chayo had been standing the entire time, it would be your opinion that all of those blows were most likely struck from the front?"

"Yes."

Konrad was obviously displeased with that answer. On redirect he wanted to know if some of the cuts on Chayo's head couldn't have been caused by a person standing to the side of him rather than in front.

His witness was dubious: "You'd have to have a pretty strong side-arm to have cut through the scalp," he said.

At 4:20 in the afternoon Raymond Chayo was called to the stand. He was a man about my own age, dark and handsome, with curly black hair just beginning to gray at the temples. Of all the trial testimony, with the possible exception of my own, his was the most painful for me. His words made the death of Moises Chayo real. I was not the only victim here; a man was dead. My heart went out to Raymond Chayo. I wanted to tell him that I knew what it was to lose a father. I wanted desperately for him to believe that his father did not die at my hands.

Raymond Chayo began to cry as soon as he started testifying. His story came out haltingly, at obvious emotional expense. In 1965 he was twenty-three years old, living and working in Panama, when he came down with phlebitis, he said. He decided to seek treatment at the Ochsner Clinic, a well-known New Orleans hospital. He entered the clinic early in October and stayed there about a month and a half. Early in November Moises Chayo flew from Buenos Aires to New Orleans to be with his son. The elder Chayo was a wealthy businessman who had emigrated from his native Syria to Argentina in his youth and made his fortune there. He was married and had a son and a daughter. In New Orleans he checked into a motel near the hospital and spent most of his time with his son.

"He came up to be with me," Raymond Chayo testified. "We were really very close, and he came to be with me, and then he planned to go back to Panama and help me with my business. . . . In fact, he was there [at the hospital] every day. He'd come in every morning, he was there almost all day, all day long with me, and we got even closer then. And then just the day before I was discharged he asked me if I wanted to go to New Orleans, to the city, for dinner with him or something. And I really wasn't up to it. And I was going to leave the next day anyway. We were going to have a lot of time together, so I didn't go." Raymond Chayo never saw his father again. On Sunday, November 21, Raymond was to be discharged. His father was to pick him up and pay the hospital bill, but his father never came.

"He was there every single day," Chayo said tearfully. "And when he wasn't there in the morning, especially that morning, it didn't make any sense because he was always there. He was always there to see me."

As that Sunday wore on, Chayo got so worried that he called the police. Some officers checked his father's motel room and found nothing out of order. His clothes were still there and he hadn't checked out. The next day Chayo called his mother and his uncle, his father's brother, in Argentina. The uncle flew to New Orleans, and he and Raymond waited another week for word of what had happened to Moises Chayo. No word came. There seemed to be nothing more he could do, so the younger Chayo went back to Panama, assured by the police that he'd be notified as soon as there was any news of his father. About two weeks later he was told that a man believed to be his father had been found dead. Chayo returned to New Orleans but was told that it would not be possible for him to identify the body. He never saw it, but he accompanied it back home to Argentina for burial.

Konrad took the envelope that had been brought from the coroner's office and asked Chayo if he could identify its contents. Yes, he said, he believed the things belonged to his father.

Bob was gentle and sympathetic in his cross-examination, but there were several facts he had to establish. In response to questions, Chayo agreed that while his father spent his days at the hospital, his evenings were his own.

"And you knew that he was—he had a soft spot for playing cards, right?" Bob asked.

"Yeah, he was a very good bridge player," Chayo said.

Bob suggested that the elder man might have played blackjack or poker as well.

"He probably—I'm sure he knew the games," Chayo said. "I don't see how relevant this is, but the only game that I was ever aware of him playing was bridge. He was—they were champion bridge players, him and my mother."

Chayo was hostile and defensive. All things considered, I couldn't blame him. He didn't know who killed his father, but he knew I was on trial for that crime and he wanted somebody to pay. Besides, he may have thought that Bob's line of questioning was demeaning his father's memory. Still, Bob bored in.

"Did he like to gamble a little bit as he played cards, Mr. Chayo?"

"Not that I know of," Chayo snapped.

Bob suggested that Moises Chayo had been looking for some card games during his stay in New Orleans.

"He did mention that he was going to look for a bridge game. . . ." Chayo conceded.

"Okay. So you knew before he was—before the disappearance that he had been looking [for], and may have found, some card games over the course of the several weeks that he had been here?"

"Yes, it was a possibility, sure."

Bob's questions were not idle. Jack had told me the night we left New Orleans that he had cheated somebody in a card game. Perhaps, on the night he was killed, Moises Chayo had found the card game he was looking for.

Bob finally turned to other matters. He established the fact that the Chayos were Jewish. I didn't understand at the time why their religion was relevant. I would later. It was also established that Moises Chayo was sixty-two years old when he died, that he was about five feet eight inches tall and weighed one hundred and seventy pounds, that he was light-complected, and that, except for a fringe of gray hair, he was bald. After attesting to all those facts, Raymond Chayo was excused.

Court adjourned at 4:42 P.M. and I thought back over what the prosecution had managed to prove in the first day of its case. It had proved the sad fact that Moises Chayo was dead and had been dead for eighteen years. The exact cause of his death could not be pinpointed, but it was clear that he had been beaten. The weapon that was used could not be described with any certainty. It may or may not have been a tire iron, or, as Jack Sidote's first confession had it, a lug wrench. A man was dead; he left a son who still grieved for him. There was a personal tragedy here. But there had not been one word of testimony, not one bit of evidence, to connect me with it.

When testimony resumed the next morning, Wasyl Bozydaj was the first witness. It was hard to reconcile this man nearing middle age, with his bushy mustache and gold-rimmed glasses, with the boy I'd known so many years before. It was hard to digest the information he was giving for the record: He was thirty-seven years old, had been married for twelve years, was the father of two children. He had served in Vietnam and was now an auto mechanic living in Clinton, New York.

Questioned by Porteous, Wasyl described the Villa Lipani, his job there, his friendship with Sidote, his early acquaintance with me. Intentionally or not, some of his testimony was almost comical. Asked about Jack's marital status back then, he said he thought it was "good, you know. I knew he was seeing other girls on the side, but I knew—as far as I knew he was happily married."

He went on to describe the trip from New York, and as he did I noticed several differences between his recollections and mine. He testified, for instance, that Jack and I together picked him up at his house at the start of the trip. I knew that wasn't true. Wasyl had been in the car when Jack picked me up. He said that all of us had taken turns driving. In fact, I never drove. He said we stayed in Baton Rouge "a couple of days." I knew it was longer. Most of the discrepancies were small; they gave me no cause to believe that Wasyl was lying, only that at a distance of eighteen years some facts were as blurred for him as others were for me. But some of the differences were major. He did not recall, he told Porteous, that Jack had ever beaten me. Jack got "a little upset" when his business deal fell through in Florida, Wasyl said, but he didn't remember any violence. And his description of the circumstances of our leaving New Orleans was utterly strange to me.

I knew that I'd been in our hotel room that night. According to Wasyl, however, Jack and I had gone out together, leaving him there alone. He didn't know what time we left, but we came home around eleven or twelve o'clock. We had been "dressed up to go out, you know, like on Bourbon Street. Jack had a white shirt on and black slacks, I think. And Virginia had a blouse and slacks, you know —pretty." We came home together, he said, and Jack told him that we were all leaving New Orleans. Wasyl was to drive the car to Houston. Jack and I would fly and meet him there. Jack gave him a hundred-dollar bill for expenses. As for the reason we were leaving, Wasyl said, "I don't remember what excuse they gave me at the time, you know, they had a fight at the bar or something, or they were unhappy with their employment, or, I don't know, it sounded good at the time."

Wasyl said he left either that night or the next day—he couldn't remember. Jack and I took separate planes to Houston, he said. I arrived first and he met me at an airport motel. Jack got in about two hours later, Wasyl said, "with another friend of his and mine at the time." Wasyl couldn't say who the person was. He thought maybe Jack and I had met him at the Ponderosa, and maybe the person's brother had gotten Wasyl his job as a soda jerk.

I had no recollection of any flight to Houston. Try as I might, I could not remember how we all left New Orleans, only that Jack had come home one night looking scared and talking about crooked card games and saying we had to go.

Then Porteous led Wasyl on to the grand climax of his testimony.

"During this period of time, the trip from Houston to Carson City to California, were there any unusual incidents or fights?" he asked.

"There was one time where Jack was sick in the car," Wasyl said. "He was sitting in the back and he was—well, he was sick, and he was just rambling, talking, and he did make a statement like— he said, 'You shouldn't have hit him so hard,' and that was it. No more after that."

"Was he speaking to anyone?" Porteous asked.

"He just screamed it out, that's all, you know."

"Who was driving?"

"I was."

"And where was he?"

"In the back."

"And where was Ginny?"

"She was in the front seat."

"And where was this fourth man?"

"He was in the back with Jack."

— 272 —

There were three people in the car besides Jack. Assuming he made the remark at all, he could have been talking to any one of us, or even talking to himself. That was clear from the testimony. But the subsequent headline in the *Times-Picayune* would say that Jack was telling *me* I'd hit somebody too hard. (Later, on an inside page, the paper would print a correction and say that it "regretted the error.") I could only hope that the jury hadn't been left with the same impression that the local reporter had garnered. I could also be grateful that the jury was sequestered and was not reading the papers.

Wasyl's testimony rattled me. I knew I could correct some of his misstatements with my own testimony. But what about the things I couldn't remember? How much damage had he done with that strange story about the night we left New Orleans? How strong a picture had he painted in the jurors' minds of Jack Sidote as an easygoing good old boy?

Bob was able to erase some of the damage with his cross-examination. He established that Wasyl had always looked up to Jack, had admired his style as a bartender at the Villa Lipani, had always considered himself Jack's friend, not mine. When Bob pressed for more details about the night we left New Orleans, he had Wasyl stumbling over his story.

"The only thing I remember is being in the car and they're telling me to go and gave me a hundred dollars and I left. I don't remember the sequence of how I got to the car, or, or what, or if it was the same day, same night, next day."

And later:

"And, of course, you were curious as to why you were being given this instruction, weren't you?" Bob asked.

"At the time they gave me some kind of story that sounded feasible." Wasyl said. "I wasn't suspicious."

"When you say 'they' you mean Jack?"

"Jack, yes, Jack."

And later:

"Now, you told us a little bit that Jack could blow up and get into a rage from time to time; you admit that far, don't you?" Bob asked.

"Yeah, he was . . ."

"Volatile?"

"He'd get mad like anybody would get mad. . . ."

"But a little bit more. He got violent sometimes, didn't he?"

"He never got violent in front of me," Wasyl said, adding that my "swollen eyes from crying" were the only indication he ever saw that Jack and I had violent encounters.

But here Bob had him. He asked Wasyl if he remembered being interviewed by Roger Gardner of the New York State Police in 1977. Wasyl said he remembered.

"Mr. Bozydaj," Bob said, "when you spoke with Senior Investigator Gardner on March 23, 1977, did you not tell him one of your reasons for leaving California was because Jack Sidote was continually beating up Virginia and you did not like the situation and wanted to leave?"

"I said—"

"Did you or did you not say that, first?"

"I might've," Wasyl said.

Porteous chose on redirect to let Wasyl expand on his answer, a decision the prosecutor probably regretted later. Wasyl said he had never seen Jack hit me, "but, you know, it was obvious that he might've hit her, you know."

chapter 34

The lunch break that day stretched for more than two hours. Court reconvened at 2:30 P.M. and Konrad rose to call the state's next witness. "Mr. John Sidote, please," he said.

When Jack entered the courtroom all the old swagger seemed to be intact. There was the same cocky tilt of the head, the same jaunty swing of the shoulders. The parish authorities had spiffed him up nicely for his big moment. He was wearing a dark blue suit with a lighter blue shirt, a striped tie, and brand-new shiny black shoes. All eyes followed him as he made his way through the packed courtroom up to the witness stand, and he seemed to sense the presence of an audience and revel in it. For a minute I had the insane notion that he might grab the microphone in the witness box and burst into "Mack the Knife." He was, at long last, a star.

But as I watched him settle into the chair and begin to talk, I realized that Jack had changed since 1977—or I had. I was afraid of him now, as then. After all, he was the reason I was in this courtroom. He still had that much power, and what he was about to say might send me to jail for life. But in 1977 I'd had the irrational fear that if he felt like it he could step off the witness stand and assault me personally, beat me again. That fear was gone now. How could he? This time the whole world was watching. Besides, somehow he just didn't look big enough to do it. In some way he seemed diminished, defeated. Maybe it was because of all I'd learned about what his life had been like since 1970, but as I listened to him, I realized to my profound shock that he was almost pitiable.

He was giving the usual information for the record. He was forty-five years old, he said, and "currently residing at the Jefferson Parish community jail." Konrad was handling the direct examination, leading him through basic background about his early life, his military service, his first marriage, his work record. Eventually the two of them arrived at 1965, when Jack and I first met.

"You were still living with your wife?" Konrad asked.

"Yes, sir, I was," Jack lied. He went on to give his version of our relationship: "We were—it became more than just casual dating," he said, "and it became quite serious. It—we—I guess we had a tremendous physical attraction to one another and it led to, I believe, a desire on both parts to spend more time together. There were periods of time when we would break up because I was being drawn in different directions, through my relationship with the defendant and—and my wife and family. We did get together on several occasions and I was—I was being drawn more and more to Virginia. . . ."

(Virginia. How strange, I thought. In all the time we knew each other he never once called me Virginia. It was always Ginny. Had he divided me into two people, just as I had? Was there one he loved and one he hated? Was that how he was able to do this to me?)

His "insurmountable" attraction to me was getting in the way of his work, he said, and what with that and his family problems, he decided to leave upstate New York. He managed to make our running away together sound like some kindly act of charity toward his first wife: "I felt that in order not to—to save my family the disgrace of divorce and everything that would bring about, that we would leave the area instead of staying there and—and going through something messy."

Jack said we headed to Florida because he had a friend there with IBM who was going to get him work with computers. (I'd never heard Jack mention computers.) The job didn't pan out, he said, and we headed west. In New Orleans, where he was a bouncer and I was a "barmaid and go-go dancer," we were earning only ten dollars apiece per night. It wasn't enough. So, he said, we decided to roll somebody.

He went on with his now-familiar story of my getting "dressed up" and our going to Bourbon Street, of my locating a victim and Jack hiding in the trunk of the car, of the trunk jarring closed, of his subsequent "fear and exhaustion and panic" because he was running out of air. Finally he came to the murder itself:

"I came out of the trunk," he said, "and the only thing I could think about was—was getting enough air to breathe . . . and I stepped down from the trunk and—and there was a man—a man before me. And I—I started struggling with him and I—I guess I had a—I had a tire iron in my hand and—and I apparently made a motion to strike him, and he grabbed my arm and I grabbed his arm and we were struggling. . . . I remember him yelling 'Madre Dios' or something like that. And—and we were just locked like that and he—he was shorter than I was but—but he was a very strong man, he was—he was very, very powerful. . . ."

To my utter disgust Jack started to cry, sobbing loudly, the tears coursing down his face. I wondered if he had rehearsed this scene or if such hypocrisy could possibly come naturally to him.

"And we struggled," Jack went on, "and I don't know how much time elapsed, but neither one of us could do anything. And then—then I heard like a scream, 'He knows who I am. He knows who I am. You've got to kill him.' And I—I panicked. I didn't— and I said—it didn't register what was being said. And then I—I realized that I couldn't hold him and I said, 'You've got to help me, then do something. Do something.' And the next thing I knew I was facing him . . . and there was a blur, it came from the side . . . from, like, over my right shoulder, or over toward my right, from my right side," Jack said. (The pathologist had testified that the blows had come from the front, not the side.) "And I heard, like, a grunt or something, and I heard 'Uhhh . . .' and— and for that instant the pressure released on my wrist. And then— then I struck the man—I struck the man also." (A new gush of tears at this point.) "And it—there was just a state of confusion. I —I don't recall—the man was struck again. I don't recall how many blows he was being—he was struck. The man fell to the ground and I fell on the ground, too. I was kneeling on my knees and I was—and I was gasping, I recall. I couldn't breathe. And the next thing I knew my shoulder was—my jacket was being pulled and Virginia was there and she said, 'Over here, over here.' And I looked and there was—I went over to where she was going to and there was a ditch there—and [she] stated that, 'We've got to put the man in here.' And we went back and started dragging the man to that area. And we were falling down—kept falling down and she helped me and we dragged the man into this ditch and we placed him in the ditch."

In the confession he signed and swore to in 1977, Jack said that I, and I alone, hit the victim. He said that we left the body where it fell, grabbed the man's wallet, and fled. There was no mention of a ditch or of moving the body.

Jack went on with his testimony. We took the man's wallet and I drove us back to the hotel, he said. When we got there Jack stayed in the car while I went up to our room and got him some fresh clothes. I took them to him and we drove around the corner while he changed. Then we drove back to the front of the hotel, where Wasyl was waiting for us. We gave him some money and told him to take the car and drive to Texas.

"I believe it was Houston—Houston, Texas," Jack said. "I— I don't know exactly if it was Houston or Dallas. . . ."

Konrad showed Jack the pictures the investigators had taken of the murder site in 1965. "Does this appear to be the scene where this occurrence took place?" he asked. "It could be the area, yes," Jack said.

He said that Wasyl left us after being told where to meet us in Texas. Then Jack and I went upstairs to our room. We went through the stolen wallet, extracting fourteen hundred dollars in American bills and "some foreign currency." (Where had the money for Wasyl come from, I wondered. Supposedly Jack and I had been broke, and we went through the wallet only *after* Wasyl left.) Then we tore up the wallet and flushed it down the toilet. It was "still early in the evening," Jack said, "probably nine-thirty or so," so we decided that I would leave by plane that night. Jack would follow the next day. I left. He spent most of the rest of the night drinking. The next morning he took a cab to the airport and flew to Houston. Or Dallas.

Konrad wanted to know about the hitchhiker who'd gone west with us. He was a friend of Wasyl's, Jack said; "either he worked with him or—or he met him through some other way." Wasyl and the hitchhiker had left New Orleans together.

I had worried that Wasyl's testimony contradicted some of what I would have to say, but, clearly, it also contradicted Jack. Wasyl said Jack and I had returned to the hotel room together the night of the murder. Jack said I went to the room alone. Wasyl said we'd come home around eleven o'clock or midnight. Jack said it was much earlier. Wasyl said he'd met the hitchhiker through Jack and me. Jack said it was the other way around. Wasyl said the hitchhiker had traveled to Texas by plane with Jack. Jack said the man had gone by car with Wasyl. I suspected the contradictions were not being lost on the jury, and there were more to come.

Jack went on to describe the rest of the trip, our settling in California, our marriage. He testified at length about the killing of the Samoan boy, larding the story with all sorts of self-serving justifications, and even going so far as detailing the ballistics report in the case, before Bob finally cut him short with an objection. After that, Jack got on with the story of his trial and his time in Chino. Then, at Konrad's request, he described the circumstances under which we parted in July of 1970. We had, Jack said, a "very severe confrontation."

"It had become apparent to me that there was no—no future for us, but no reasons were ever stated why this—why this was happening, you know, and I confronted her on the situation. I confronted her with what was happening, and it—it developed into a terrible, terrible scene, at which time . . ."

"Was there a fight between the two of you?" Konrad prompted.

"Yes, sir."

"Did you strike—"

"At which time I grabbed—I did—I grabbed Virginia in the area of the throat and I started shaking her and we were both screaming at one another. It was a—a chaotic scene, and I was—I was choking her. And suddenly I stopped and she was coherent yet. I stopped and—and I just pushed her and she slumped to the floor and I just thought, after all this, it's not worth it, and I left."

That was our last contact for the next seven years, he said, except for two telephone calls that I'd made to him. He said I called him in California a few days after our separation to complain that he was already living with another woman. The next call was in 1973 when I called his parents' home in New York and asked to talk to him. (How elaborate his fantasies are, I thought. I'd never known that he was living with another woman in 1970, and if I had known I wouldn't have cared. During the years in question he had called me once and we'd discussed our divorce. I'd called his parents' home once to talk to his mother.)

Konrad directed Jack to 1977 and his confession to the Albany police. Why had he done it? Because, Jack said, his life had become "pure hell."

"I had become an alcoholic," he said. "I—I couldn't function normally as a—as—anymore. I—the—the guilt from my participation and—and the fear and the self-hatred that had developed over the years was—had just consumed me. I had to—in some way I had to try to absolve my guilt. I had to."

At that moment I no longer found him pitiable. This dishonesty, this smarmy deceit on top of everything else he'd done, restored my contempt and my utter loathing of him.

He talked about his plea in Nevada and the sentence he got there, his parole violation, his return to jail. Konrad asked why he didn't testify against me then in the Louisiana case. Jack said his decision "was based on the fact that I didn't want to harm her if there was any way possible; that I felt that justice had been served at that time and that I was willing to take my sentence and let the incident be dropped."

I wanted to gag.

There was a short recess and then Bob began his cross-examination. Everything in his manner, his tone of voice, the subtle sarcasm of his questions, told of his contempt for Jack. His technique had Konrad leaping to his feet constantly to make objections, but to little avail. I felt sure the jury was getting the impression that Bob meant to convey.

Bob asked Jack about his immunity agreement. Didn't it require him to testify consistently with all previous statements he'd made about the crime or be prosecuted himself? Jack agreed that it did.

"Well," Bob drawled, "do you think now that you're going to be prosecuted because you stated inconsistent things with those statements?" With that, Bob went on for the next two hours or more to point out the inconsistencies, the differences between Jack's current story and his past ones, between his story and Wasyl's, his story and the physical evidence.

If Jack was confused about which Texas city we were going to, why did he swear three times in 1977 that it was Dallas? Jack couldn't say. If I was supposed to pick up a man on the night of the murder, I must have been decked out in an alluring dress, right? Yes. Not just a blouse and slacks, Bob pressed, but a dress? Yes, Jack said, a dress. And the hitchhiker, he was Wasyl's friend? Yes. And he went with Wasyl in the car? Yes, Jack insisted. Bob bored in:

"You brought him to Houston or Dallas, didn't you, Mr. Sidote?"

"No, sir."

"You and he did something you shouldn't have done and you fled the city with him and you took him to Houston or Dallas, isn't that right?"

"No, sir, that's not true."

"Took him on an airplane?"

"No, sir."

"Got scared and left with him?"

"No, sir."

The judge sustained Konrad's frantic objection, but it was too late. A new thought had been offered to the jury: Maybe Jack *had* committed the murder with an accomplice, but maybe that accomplice was someone other than me.

What about the time? In 1977 Jack had said he first crawled into the trunk of the car about 11:00 P.M. Now he was saying that we picked up the victim, killed him and robbed him, and returned home by 9:30. Which was it? Jack said he must have made a mistake in 1977.

What about the murder site? In 1977 there was a warehouse. Was there any warehouse in the pictures he identified? No. In 1977 he had described the area as rough, stony, and flat. Why did the pictures he identified show it to be grassy, with no stones or rocks? Where was the shell road in 1977? Where was the ditch? Where was the dramatic account of dragging the body? Jack answered that his various statements might "all differ a little to a degree."

What about the victim? In 1977 Jack said the man weighed about two hundred and ten pounds. "Not a hundred seventy pounds," Bob said, recalling for the jury Raymond Chayo's description of his father, "two-ten was your approximation, right?"

"I don't know how much the man weighed," Jack said.

"You said the guy had dark hair, is that right?"

"Yes, sir."

"Dark hair. You didn't say he was bald, almost totally, with just a fringe of gray around the bottom; you said he had dark hair, right?"

"The man was dark, yes."

"You also said he was dark-complected, did you?"

"Yes, sir, it appeared that way."

"Not light-complected, but dark-complected."

Jack had also said that his victim was shorter than he was. In fact, Moises Chayo was some two inches taller. In sum, Jack had described a man who looked nothing like the actual victim. Was it possible that Jack hadn't committed the murder, that he'd only heard about it and worked it into some scheme for revenge against me? Or was it just that, for all his contrition and guilt, he couldn't remember what the man he killed looked like?

"And this fellow, this poor man that you were beating, that you and Virginia were beating, the only thing that you heard him say, you say, was what? 'Madre Dios?' "

"Something to that effect," Jack affirmed.

"This *Jewish* man was saying 'Madre Dios'?" Bob marveled. Jack was obviously trying to say "Madre *de* Dios," Mother of God.

Bob worked on undermining Wasyl's damaging "You shouldn't have hit him so hard" testimony. He asked Jack if he ever talked to himself, ever said things like, "Jack, stop drinking," or "Jack, stop blaming other people for things you've done to yourself." Jack conceded only that he might have lectured himself "subconsciously" about his drinking.

"How about when you're wrecked on alcohol?" Bob said. "Anybody ever tell you . . . that you talk to yourself or about yourself: 'Stop, Jack, stop. Don't do that kind of thing anymore'?"

"No, sir."

"You're really a bad alcoholic, aren't you?" Bob asked.

"At times," Jack sighed.

Again and again, Bob returned to the subject of Jack's alcoholism and dereliction. By 1977 Jack was having DTs, wasn't he? Yes, Jack said, at times. He was having hallucinations? Yes. He had been in and out of alcohol treatment programs at least seven times? Yes. Had he tried to kill himself shortly before making his confessions in 1977? Jack said he couldn't remember ever contemplating suicide. In that event, Bob said, what was he contemplating the night he turned on a gas stove, blew out the pilot light, and stuck his head in the oven? "I don't believe it was a sincere suicide attempt," Jack said.

Bob questioned him for more than an hour on his immunity agreement, slowly erasing the prosecution's picture of a man testifying out of civic duty and desire for atonement. It was established that Jack got even more than immunity and a promise that Louisiana would try to help him with the Nevada Parole Board. It was also reported that he got a commitment from the prosecutors to try to have his parole transferred from Nevada to Louisiana, where he'd be free again, where he may have had prospects for a job connected with offshore oil rigs. I thought the testimony discredited more than just Jack. It showed the jury the lengths to which the prosecutors were willing to go to get Jack's testimony against me. There was the further peculiarity that Jack had told the police in 1977 that before he left New Orleans he heard a radio report about the murder of a "Brazilian or Venezuelan" businessman. Chayo's body wasn't found until weeks after we left New Orleans. After the initial statement, this remark of Jack's did not appear in the prosecution documents.

Jack admitted that he "would hope to get some form of assistance from the district attorney's office," but, he said piously, "there is nothing, nothing that I could get from the district attorney or from anyone else that would make me come up here and lie."

"Now let's talk about that for a minute," Bob said companionably. "Why *do* you lie?"

Throughout the afternoon Bob taunted Jack. When Jack kept stumbling over discrepancies between his 1977 confessions and his present testimony, Bob shouted, "Does the truth change over the course of six years, Mr. Sidote?" Konrad rose with another objection, his normally red face a raddled crimson, and Bob obligingly agreed to rephrase his question. "Does *your* truth change over the course of six years, Mr. Sidote?" he asked.

Bob mocked him. He made fun of Jack's affected language. When Jack talked about our "preordained destination" in Texas, Bob laughed at him. "Preordained?" he sneered. "By whom? By God?" There were chuckles in the courtroom. I knew that Jack couldn't bear ridicule, and I watched closely for some reaction. Aside from a slight flush in his face, there was none.

His calm bothered me. We had hoped to rattle him into losing control, into showing the jury some of the rage that he'd shown me so often. But only occasionally would he rise to the bait. Instead of getting belligerent he tended to act hurt and aggrieved. Once when Bob called him a "drunk," Jack drew himself up with great dignity and corrected him. "Sir," he said, "I am an alcoholic." I understood his composure better when I learned that after his testimony a deputy was overheard asking him if he needed more Valium.

I wondered if he'd be able to hold his act together another day. He had been on the stand some six hours in the session that had just ended, and when court adjourned for the night, Bob still wasn't finished with him. The cross-examination would continue tomorrow, and Bob had hardly touched yet on Jack's treatment of me.

chapter 35

My lawyers and I worked late into the night that Friday, going over all Sidote's testimony so far, making sure we hadn't missed anything, neglected any point. The lawyers were still concerned that the prosecution's point about Jack confessing in 1977 against his own interest would carry weight. More would have to be done about that tomorrow. We'd have to show the jury what he had to gain over the years with his lies. Finally, John and Bob went off by themselves to continue going over the fine points. It was just as well. I was having a lot of trouble concentrating.

I was filled with so much rage that I didn't know what to do with it—rage at the lies I'd had to listen to all day, at my inability to express my rage. Over and over, Bob and John had cautioned me to show no emotion at the defense table. Any sign of "aggressive behavior" would tell against me with the jury. No anger was allowed in the courtroom, just as no anger had been allowed in jail.

I wondered if Sidote had found it as hard to contain his anger that day as I had mine. So many times I'd wanted to stand up and scream: "When is this bullshit going to stop? Why are the eyes of the world on this sniveling little creep? How can he be holding me captive in this courtroom? Why are all of you letting him do it?"

But of course I did nothing of the kind. I sat quietly in my demure little outfit, my hands folded, my face blank. I was the perfect "lady" and I hated it. I hated Bob and John for making me do it. Most of all, I hated myself for going along with it.

Bob had gotten in some good licks for me against Sidote on Friday, and during Saturday's half-day session he got in some more. He started off with some questions about how Jack had gotten along with John and Marie Lipani. Wasn't Lipani good to him? Didn't he treat him almost as a son? Yes, Jack said. Then, suddenly, Bob veered off on another course. In a long series of questions, he showed how Jack was able to escape the predicate felon conviction in New York in 1977 by confessing to the murders in Louisiana and Nevada. It was so complicated and subtle. I could only hope the jury was following it. Once it was over, Bob started bringing out what Jack was getting from his current starring role in the way of ego gratification and money.

"You have given interviews to every woman reporter from the East Coast to the Midwest to the West who has come knocking at your Nevada prison doors, have you not?" Bob asked.

"I gave two stories," Jack said, "one to *California* magazine, one to *Rolling Stone*. I spoke briefly with a lady from the *Chicago Tribune.*"

What about the *Village Voice?* Bob prompted. That was only on the phone, Jack explained. What about the four-hour interview with CBS's Liz Trotta? Yes, Jack said, but that was television. He didn't know that counted.

"When you read in *California* magazine that you were 'a mask of masculinity,' a 'Charles Bronson type,' did that make you feel big?" Bob asked. The courtroom rippled with laughter, and I could see Jack start to squirm. His precious manhood was being attacked and I could see the anger in his eyes. If he's going to lose it, I thought, it's going to be now. Now. But Konrad came up with another objection and the moment passed.

"It's true, isn't it, Mr. Sidote, that you wrote to *Playboy* magazine to sell your story?" Bob asked.

"I wrote to *Playboy* magazine, yes."

"It's true, Mr. Sidote, that you have been in ongoing negotiations with *Penthouse* magazine for your story for the last six months?" Actually, Jack said, the negotiations were over. *Penthouse* was going to buy his story for three thousand dollars.

"Did you ever say," Bob went on, " 'I think the story is explo-

sive enough, deep enough, passionate enough, to be a best-seller'?"
Jack confirmed that he had. "You think that it'll help you do a book
if you succeed in this case in convicting Ginny Foat?" Bob asked.
Then, again, he switched directions.

"Over the five years that you were together with Ginny Foat,
you beat her, didn't you?" Konrad objected that the question was
too vague, so Bob got specific.

"You beat her in Florida and Louisiana?"

"No, sir."

"You beat her when you got to Hermosa Beach . . .?"

"I never beat Virginia Foat," Jack said. "I struck her, but I
never beat her."

His fine distinction drew more laughter from the courtroom,
along with some outright jeers.

"And in 1970, when she left you after that fight, you almost
killed her, didn't you?"

"Yes, at that time."

"You threatened to say that the killings you had committed,
you'd put on her if she left you?"

"I don't recall that, sir."

"She's not the only woman you've beaten, is she?" Bob spat.
"That's your pattern?"

"The only other woman I've ever touched was Marie Lipani,"
Jack said righteously. He was, he said, in an alcoholic blackout at the
time.

"You broke into her house to steal money from this John
Lipani, who was almost like your father? You broke into Mr. Lipani's
house and you attacked Marie Lipani, didn't you? Didn't you?"

"I don't know what you mean by 'attacked,' " Jack waffled. "I
know that later she had a scratch on her face—"

"Scratch on her face?" Bob cried. "I show you a photograph
of her." Bob waved the photograph in the air while Konrad screamed
that it wasn't admissible. The judge agreed, but not before the jury
had clearly seen a picture of Marie Lipani, her face swollen and
bruised, both her eyes blackened.

Bob began to probe Jack's feelings about me.

"You didn't think about Virginia Foat after you left her in 1970
until 1977, is that true?"

"For a period of time. I wouldn't say the whole seven years, but
for a brief period of time, yes."

"It wasn't something that you thought about deeply and at
length in alcoholic reveries, huh?"

"No, sir."

"There were no periods of hate against her alternating with feelings of—of love and—and missing her, huh?"

"If they were alcoholically motivated I don't recall them."

"You don't recall anything? You don't recall feeling vengeful during that period of time, huh?"

"No, sir."

"You wrote a letter to her parents, didn't you, saying that you were going to get her if it was the last thing you ever did?" Jack didn't recall that, either.

"Do you deny that there were periods of time . . . when you thought about how much you missed her and wanted her back—how badly you wanted her back?"

"No, sir. As I stated, in 1970 I knew that we had no future together."

"So that in 1977, on January 22, when you walked into the police station, your motivation had nothing to do with your feelings about Ginny Foat?" No, Jack insisted.

Wasn't it true, Bob said, that Jack felt justified in blaming me for the murder, felt that it truly was my fault, felt that it would never have happened if he hadn't needed money to keep up his "big man" image with me? Again, Jack denied it.

Jack had been on the stand for about three hours now, and at last Bob was nearing the end of his questions. He walked to where I was sitting, stood behind me, and rested his hands on my shoulders.

"John Sidote," he said, "you look at Virginia Foat. You look at Ginny Foat and tell her that she did what you say she did."

The courtroom was hushed. The jurors were leaning forward in their seats. Jack was looking down at his lap. Finally he raised his eyes and looked not at me, but at Bob.

"Mr. Glass, I don't want to be here to testify to begin with," he said. "I feel badly enough that I have to do this. I'm not following your instructions to look at Virginia Foat and tell her that this is the way it has to be. It's not that way. . . ."

"You can't do it, can you?" Bob said. And he was right. Jack could not look at me. A deputy led him out of the courtroom, and he went without looking at me. In two days he had never looked at me once.

There was no court session Sunday, so I had the day free to worry and wait to see Jack Sidote on the witness stand again Monday. I felt sure he'd be back. Bob's cross-examination had all but destroyed whatever credibility he may have had, and I had no doubt the prosecution would try to rehabilitate its star witness. But at 9:03 Monday morning, Gordon Konrad dropped a bombshell. "Your Honor," he said to Judge Burns, "the state is not going to put Mr. Sidote back on the stand for any redirect, and the state will rest its case at this time."

An excited babble broke out in the courtroom. I could hear people whispering to each other somewhere behind me: "Christ, is that it?" "Are they serious?" "Is that all they've got?" Judge Burns called a recess and I walked out into the hall, where the reporters and other spectators usually gathered during the breaks to swap impressions about the trial. I lit a cigarette and eavesdropped on a group of reporters.

"I hear the DA's going to bring out some big guns on rebuttal," one of them was saying.

"You can't do that," another one objected. "On rebuttal you can just rehash the same old stuff."

"Do you think they'll trot Sidote back out?"

"Not if they're smart. What did you think of his testimony?"

"I think he'll get the death penalty."

They all laughed. I put out my cigarette and went back into the courtroom to talk to Bob and John. I knew that technically, at least, we didn't have to put on a case at all. It was up to the prosecution to prove its case against me beyond a reasonable doubt. If it failed, I was presumed innocent. In my view, it had failed. I asked Bob and John if we had to go on. Why couldn't we just stand up and say, "The defense rests"? (Please, I thought, please do it. Please, so I don't have to testify.)

Bob and John wouldn't hear of it. Too risky. We had to consider the strengths of the prosecution's case. Jack Sidote had confessed to two murders that nobody ever would have connected him with otherwise. He did it after he and I had been apart and out of touch for almost seven years. He said he did it for the good of his soul. We had to prove otherwise to show he was lying. Yes, he was a crummy witness. No, the jury probably hadn't believed enough of what he said to bring in a guilty verdict to murder. But there was always manslaughter. We couldn't take that chance. We had to show that he was the kind of man who could hold a grudge for seven years. We had to prove that he called the Albany police not caring if he destroyed himself, blaming me for the human wreck he'd become, wanting only to drag me down with him. We had to present our case, and the jury had to hear from me.

At 10:37 A.M. John called our first witness: Dr. Thomas Smith, M.D., a psychiatrist specializing in drug- and alcohol-abuse cases. John asked Smith if blaming others was a typical trait of the alcoholic personality. "Blaming is a very common trait," the doctor said. What about resentment? That, said Smith, "is one of the most common traits of alcoholics. If we list the various traits, resentment is going to be on the top."

"And what does 'resentment' mean?" John asked.

"Well, in everyday language, holding a grudge."

For alcoholics, was the resentment usually short-term or long-term?

"Well," the doctor said, "for some people it's a lifetime."

Dr. Isadore Rosen was called to the stand. Rosen was an elderly man, a retired physician who lived near New Orleans. Telephone records showed that Moises Chayo had called Dr. Rosen on the afternoon of the day Chayo was killed. Rosen didn't remember what the conversation had been about, but he did remember how he'd met Chayo. They'd played gin rummy together at the New Orleans Athletic Club. "For money?" John asked. Yes, Rosen said, for money. And where was the New Orleans Athletic Club? It was about a block from where the Ponderosa Bar used to be.

Clara Sparks, my old roommate, my old friend from the *Princess Louise*, was called to testify. John asked her to describe what happened on the day in July of 1970 when I left California for New York.

"I heard Ginny up in her room," Clara said. "I heard her choking and moaning and gasping for breath, and there were cries for help."

"Had you heard those sounds or any sounds like that before?"

"Similar sounds."

"And when you heard those sounds before, who had been involved?"

"Jack Sidote."

"When you heard those sounds, what did you do?"

"I went up the stairs to see what was wrong with Ginny."

"And when you went up the stairs, what did you see?"

"I saw Jack leaning over Ginny. He had been choking her."

"Did Jack do anything as you came up the stairs?"

"He just—he came out of the room and he—he came towards me and he was yelling at me and he was screaming at me, and he was saying, 'I'm going to kill her. I'm going to get even with her if she ever leaves me.' "

"When Jack came out in the hall, did you subsequently go in to see Ginny?"

"Yes, sir."

"Would you describe what you saw?"

"I saw Ginny lying on—partly on the floor and partly on the bed, and her face and her eye was all swollen and her lip was all puffy and blood was draining from it, and she had her hand around her neck and she was moaning and she was gasping for breath."

"Did you and she then make some decision to do something?"

"Yes."

"And what was that?"

"We decided that we'd better get Ginny out of town, get her away from Jack, get her on a plane, send her home to her mother . . . where she would be safe, where she'd be away from Jack."

Clara described some of Jack's earlier visits to me, times when she heard "gagging and vomiting sounds" coming from my bedroom. On those occasions she waited for Jack to leave and then came in to help me.

"She was throwing up. I would help her into the bathroom so she could finish being sick, and we would brush away the loose strands of hair that were falling, that were loose—loose on her head. They were just kind of coming out in gobs."

I looked at the jury. Some of the women looked as sick as I felt.

After Clara was finished, John called John Boyd, who had been Clara's boyfriend in 1970. It was John, a former Air Force medic, whom Clara called to help get me to the plane on that day in July. He was asked what condition he found me in.

"She was very badly bruised and beaten about the face," he said. "She looked like she'd been used as a punching bag in the face. One eye was already starting to almost completely close, like a fighter's eyes in a fight. Her lip was very badly cut and bleeding. It was very hard for her to talk. Her neck had bruises on it and she had a great deal of upper body discomfort from the bruises that she had received."

John was asked about my mental condition.

"She was on the verge of emotional collapse," he said. "She was hardly capable of even dressing herself. It was very difficult for her to do anything without being helped. She'd put her purse down and then forget where it was; it was very difficult for her to keep her mind on any one thing for one minute past another." He described what

I was like at the airport. "I had to put her on the plane like a small child," he said. "It was very difficult for her to decide to do anything."

On cross-examination, Konrad asked sarcastically why John hadn't insisted that I see a doctor if I was in such bad shape. On redirect John explained. "She wanted to leave and go to New York as fast as she could," he said, "because she was afraid for her life."

My sister, Emilia, testified about my homecoming. "I couldn't touch her," Emilia said, "because she was so badly bruised." And after Emilia came my mother. She had been so scared of testifying, so worried that she wouldn't know what to say in front of all those people. But she was wonderful. I hated her having to be there, but I was so proud of her. Watching her, I knew that whatever the jury thought of me, it would have a hard time convicting Virginia Galluzzo's daughter.

Mother testified about the letter she and my father got from Jack after I left California. "It was such a vile—the language in that letter was so vile, my husband and I—we tore it up. We just didn't want it in our home."

"And did that letter close with any particular remarks?" John asked.

"Yes," Mother said. "The last statement was, 'And I'll get even with your'—and he bad-named Virginia—'and if it's the last thing I do, I'm going to kill her.'"

Then Mother was leaving the stand and I knew that the defense had only one witness left to call. After thirteen years there was no place to run anymore and no place to hide. I heard John's voice: "Ginny Foat," he called.

chapter 36

I tried to remember the advice I'd been given about testifying. Anne had told me to sit all the way back in the chair and to plant both feet firmly on the floor. It would make me feel stronger, she said, more grounded. I did as she told me, but there was no sense of safety or strength. I felt utterly vulnerable, exposed, and afraid. I knew what I had to do, but even now, on the witness stand, I wasn't sure I could do it. How could I ever look anybody in the face again after they'd heard what I was going to say, after they knew . . . But I pushed that thought away. There was no time for it now. I had to concentrate. I had to take it one step at a time, one question at a time, and sooner or later it would be over. Sooner or later everything would be over.

Bob and John had told me to listen to each question carefully, think about it, take my time answering. They told me to look at the jury as often as I could, to address my answers to the jury. I tried to do all those things, and at first I did pretty well. I told a little about my arrest in January and the arrest in 1977. I talked about the threats that Jack had made against me. I spoke up. I looked at the jury. But then John's questions were taking me back to when the nightmare began, and I found myself lowering my eyes and I couldn't seem to raise them again.

"Ginny," he said, "what were the years 1965 to 1970 like, in a word?"

"Horrible. Shameful. Terrifying."

"Have you ever told anyone publicly about those years?"

"No. I have never told anyone privately about those years."

"Can you tell the jury about those years?"

"I don't know," I said. "I'm so ashamed."

Of what? John asked.

"I'm ashamed of having loved him. I'm ashamed of having stayed, ashamed of my own stupidity."

John asked me to go back to 1965, take the jury back to 1965, and I did. I tried. I began telling the story, and I could hear myself telling it, but whose voice was it? Whose was this scared, soft, halting voice? No time to think about that, either. I had to go on. I told about my family, about all the things that led up to my falling in love with Jack, about the fight with my father, about leaving for Florida. I'd promised myself that I wouldn't cry, but I was crying and I couldn't stop. I was trying to tell about the first beating, the one in Florida, but I was crying too hard and a recess was called. Then I tried again, and I got through it. I told about the beating and the story of murder that went with it, and afterward I pulled myself together a little bit and went on. But then I came to the beating in New Orleans, and by now the crying had turned into heaving, wracking sobs, and I looked up at John and whimpered, "Oh, John, I can't . . ." And he said, "You've got to tell the jury, Ginny."

So I told the jury. For more than two hours that day and then on into the next day I told what the years 1965 to 1970 had been like. All too often I heard that strange, strangled voice that was mine saying "I can't remember . . . I can't remember . . ." but I told everything I could remember. I went through beating after beating after beating, the psychological torture, the sexual torture, dredging up every detail, every degradation. John had learned a lot from those sessions with Anne and me. Every time I broke down, every time I couldn't go on, I would hear, "What is he doing now, Ginny? How is he hitting you? Where is he hitting you? What is he saying?" And I answered. I choked it out and gagged it out, but I told it. And toward the end of it I was dimly aware of hearing from somewhere in the courtroom sobs and moans and gagging sounds that did not come from me.

By the time John was finished with me on the second day I was sick to my very soul with shame and pain and disgust, and with fury, too. I felt like raising my eyes at last. I felt like screaming at those strangers staring at me: Is this what you came to see? Is this it? Well, here are the wounds, with all the scabs ripped off, and I'm raw and I'm bleeding and I may never heal again. Is it enough? Am I innocent now?

John was finished, but I was to spend almost three more hours on the stand. At 1:30 P.M. that Tuesday Konrad began his cross-examination. Oddly enough, it was by far the easier part of my testimony. Konrad didn't hurt me, he only made me angry; and the anger, though I had to suppress it, steeled me and kept me calm.

He wanted to know about the logistics of how Jack and I had left New Orleans in 1965. Did we fly or drive? I couldn't remember. I'd already testified to that in the direct questioning, and I could only repeat it to Konrad. But he kept coming back to it, over and over. It was clear that he didn't believe me, and I wondered why. If I'd wanted to lie I could simply have said, "We drove," or, "We flew, just as Jack said." I couldn't understand why the question was important, and of course I didn't ask. I just kept telling him that I didn't remember. That was the truth.

Konrad was also concerned about money. How much did Jack have and when did he have it? Did he have a lot in New Orleans? After New Orleans? Again, I couldn't say—not because I didn't remember, but because I'd never known. I'd already testified that Jack handled the money and I didn't ask how much he had or what he did with it. I was afraid to ask.

Aside from those questions, Konrad's main interest seemed to be in my love life. Did he understand correctly that I'd been married four times? How long did each marriage last? Didn't I know that I was breaking up Jack's marriage when I started dating him? Wasn't it true that when we left New Paltz, Jack was motivated by his great love for me, while I just wanted to get out of town? Wouldn't I have gone with anybody willing to take me? Didn't Jack's drinking problem begin after he met me? What about Ray Foat? I'd slept with Ray while Jack was still in jail, right? Was Ray still married at the time?

The questions confounded me. Even assuming that everything

Konrad was trying to imply was true, was I being tried for adultery? For home-wrecking? For perpetrating multiple marriage? But I was even more surprised by the questions he didn't ask. He never asked, for instance, whether I killed Moises Chayo.

John asked me a few more questions on redirect and then, at 4:05 P.M., he turned to Judge Burns. "The defense rests, Your Honor," he said.

A recess was called. For the next forty minutes I followed the minute hand around the large clock on the courtroom wall and listened to the anxious talk around me. Bob and John and Kay and Annabelle Hall were rehashing our case and speculating about the prosecution's. Should we have called our expert witness to talk about battering? No, everybody agreed. We were right to stop with my testimony. The jury had heard all it needed to hear. Would the prosecution bring Sidote back to try to rebut? Would there be some surprise witness? I listened, but I said nothing. I felt no anxiety at all about what the prosecution was going to do. For the moment I was too numb to care.

At 4:45 P.M. court reconvened. "Your Honor," Konrad said, "the state would rest also."

On Wednesday morning, the ninth day of the trial, the closing arguments were presented. John Mamoulides, who had left the rest of the trial to his subordinates, spoke to the jury for the first time. The case was basically simple, he said. All that really mattered was the murder that took place in 1965. Everything else, "the life-style, the marriages, the beatings," bore only on the question of who was telling the truth. That, the DA seemed to imply, was a fairly minor consideration.

Then Tom Porteous, presenting once more the crux of the prosecution's case, argued that the truth was on Jack Sidote's side. It wasn't logical to believe that Sidote would have confessed to murder out of any motive other than contrition. It wasn't logical to believe he would wait seven years to take revenge on me. And, Porteous said, it was obvious that I was lying. I could remember things like feelings and beatings, but I claimed not to remember important things, like how we left New Orleans.

Then Bob spoke for me, at length and very eloquently. He answered the prosecutors' major points. Why didn't I remember how we left town? Because, he said, at a distance of eighteen years the things people remember are those with emotional weight. I remembered the relationship between Jack and me. I remembered pain and fear and threats. Jack recalled how we left New Orleans because the issue was emotionally freighted: He had just killed a man and he was getting out of town; the means of transportation was important. For me, though, the way we traveled had no such significance. "She doesn't remember how they left," Bob said, "simply because it's not important."

Then he turned to the motivation for Jack's confessions. Did the motive of vengeance make sense logically, rationally? Perhaps not, Bob said, but the yardstick of rationality could be applied only to the acts of a rational man. Jack Sidote was rational only when he was sober, and for years he'd been sober only when he was in jail. The Jack Sidote who confessed in 1970 was not a rational man. He was a suicidally depressed alcoholic, suffering from hallucinations and DTs, obsessed with resentment against a woman who'd betrayed him by escaping from him, a woman who, finally, had refused to go on validating his existence by submitting to his brutality. Later, jailed and sober, a rational and con-wise Jack Sidote found ways to make the confessions he was stuck with work for him. He could use them to try to get his parole transferred, to get attention, to make some money from *Penthouse* magazine. This was the man, Bob said, whose truthfulness had to be believed beyond a reasonable doubt for the jury to find me guilty.

The case boiled down to one issue, he said. The jurors had to believe Sidote or they had to believe me. And the facts were, he concluded, "that Ginny Foat is innocent and that Jack Sidote is a crazy person and a liar."

Then John spoke, very briefly. "Don't let Jack Sidote do it anymore," he pleaded. "Tell Ginny that it is over, that she is out of the cage, that he can't come back . . . that she can be free again and that Jack Sidote isn't going to haunt her for the rest of her life and drag her down whenever his sick mind so chooses.

"I ask you as a jury to look at her and to tell Ginny that she need not be ashamed anymore," John said, "that she need not fear Jack Sidote anymore."

The last argument, the rebuttal, belonged to the prosecution, and it was Gordon Konrad who rose to make it. It was up to him to convince the jury that I was the dominant, evil influence that caused a good and decent Jack Sidote to go wrong; I was the one who led him to murder and murdered along with him. To rehabilitate his witness, Konrad had to undo the effect of my testimony to five years of brutalization. I watched the jury as he talked, and it occurred to me that he might have been wiser to have left well enough alone.

Jack Sidote, he said, "became an alcoholic because of what he did with this woman. . . . Now, I don't know whose cage who was in, but all I can tell you is that Jack had lots of things going in 1965, and when he left New York with Ginny Foat the nightmare of his life started; and from 1965 until now, that nightmare has continued."

The suggestion that I'd ruined Jack's life caused so much laughter in the courtroom that Konrad could only stand there flushing and wait for it to subside. But that suggestion wasn't the worst of his miscalculations.

The defense had painted Sidote as a monster Konrad said. At the same time, it wanted the jury to believe "that our little lady is so good, so true, so pure of heart, that she stuck with him, even though she left three other men *and even left a child without seeing the child for one hour*."

I flinched at what he said about the baby. If Konrad wanted one last gouge at the deepest wound of all, he'd gotten it. But it was clear that I wasn't the only one who thought he was being unnecessarily cruel. I heard little gasps and grunts from all over the courtroom, and when I looked at the jury again I saw that one of the jurors, a young black woman in the front row, was glaring at Konrad with what looked like pure loathing.

chapter 37

Within walking distance of the Jefferson Parish Courthouse was a little tavern that served home-cooked food that was inexpensive and very good. Most of the press corps covering my trial had taken to eating lunch there every day, and I often went there as well. The proprietor was a wonderful woman, hard-working and earthy, who always did her best to see that I had some privacy in what little time there was away from court. On the day the case went to the jury she set aside a back room just for my friends and me, a place where we could be together, have lunch, and wait undisturbed for it all to be over.

It was by far the strangest lunch of my life. There were about thirty people in the room, among them those closest to me in the world—Kay, my mother and sister, John and Bob, Jan, Annabelle, a number of women from California who'd flown in to be with me during the trial. We were gathered for a supremely important occasion, but none of us knew yet whether it was a celebration or a wake. There were times when all of us seemed to be laughing and talking at once, and times when whole minutes passed and nobody talked at all. We needed to be together, and yet I think each of us was alone, waiting to have confirmed either a best hope or a worst fear.

My own emotions were a tangle of hope, confidence, fear, sadness. I had to believe the world was sane and people knew the difference between true and false, right and wrong. If that was so, the jury could not convict me. But I'd lived through so much insanity that I feared it could. And even if the verdict was acquittal, what would it mean? It couldn't restore my reputation. There would always be people who would believe I was guilty just because I'd been accused. The months I'd spent in jail couldn't be erased, and I knew mornings would come when I'd wake up listening for the jail sounds. An acquittal wouldn't ward off the nightmares or still the fears. Jack Sidote, among others, had taught me all there was to know about vulnerability, and even an acquittal could not make me feel safe.

But there were ways it could free me. I thought about what John had said about cages—the cage Jack Sidote had built for me, the cages I'd lived in. As terrible as they were, I realized now that the cage I'd made for myself was worse. I'd carried that cage on my back for years, the way a snail carries its shell. Its bars were the old shames and guilts, the festering agonies that couldn't heal because they hadn't been faced. Well, I'd faced them now, and though there would always be scars, the healing could start.

One of the strange silences had settled over the room, and so I stood up to make a toast. I thanked John and Bob. I told them that no matter what happened, I knew I'd had the best possible defense. Everybody applauded them and settled back to order coffee or dessert. We knew there'd be plenty of time. The jury had to eat lunch, too, and then elect a foreperson, and then begin deliberations. It could take hours. It could, I thought miserably, take days. But just as the coffee was arriving, a reporter stuck his head in the door and shouted that we all had to get back to the courtroom. The jury had come in.

All at once everybody seemed to be running in different directions, but I found when I tried to get up that my knees were shaking so badly I could hardly stand. How could the jury possibly be back so soon? It hadn't even been out for two hours. What did it mean? Bob and John helped me up and we started back toward the courthouse. A crowd was moving along with me and television cameras were whirring, but I hardly noticed. I was as alone as I'd ever been in my life.

I'd heard somewhere that jurors who have voted to acquit always look at the defendant when they come back into the courtroom. They look happy. They smile. But as I stood and watched my jurors file back in, not one of them looked at me. Not one was smiling. Judge Burns addressed the foreperson of the jury:

"Have you arrived at a verdict, sir?" he asked.

"Yes, sir, we have."

"Will you hand it to the clerk, please?"

The court clerk took a slip of paper from the juror and delivered it to the judge. Burns looked down at me and then read from the paper: "We, the jury, find the defendant, Virginia Foat, not guilty."

I slumped back into my chair, hardly hearing the bedlam that had erupted all around me. Then somebody was pulling me to my feet. John was hugging me, and then Bob was, and then I was in the middle of a crush of people—my mother, friends, strangers, all laughing, crying, hugging me, hugging each other. The jurors, all smiling broadly now, were bringing over their lunch napkins, asking me to autograph them.

It seemed to take hours to get out of the courtroom and into the hallway, and there another crowd was waiting—more spectators from the trial, court workers, even a few matrons I recognized from the parish jail, all of them laughing and waving and cheering. And outside the courthouse there were still more people, more cheers. It seemed that all the women were crying as they cheered, as though some long war were over and a victory had been won, a victory that was theirs as well as mine.

And I was crying, too, with the joy of finally leaving all the cages behind me. The jury had made its judgment in one hour and fifty minutes, and I, after an agony of years, had made mine: Ginny Foat is not guilty.

exposure to racial prejudice, 9–10, 29–30
extradition to Nevada, 173–75
fails secretarial course, 20
fears insanity (1977), 167
and female sexuality, 142
and feminist books, 144
and feminist movement, 139–55, 203–5
fights extradition, 168–69, 229–30
files for divorce from Raymond Foat, 157
financial worries of, 191, 198
first political awareness, 29
freed by Nevada judge (1977), 188
freed on bail (1977), 185–86
and friendship with Morton and Becky Brown, 83–84
and friendship with other women prisoners (1977), 170–71
as full-time wife (1976), 153–54
graduates with honors from high school, 17
and guilt feelings, 39–40, 44–45, 256–57
and gypsies (Jefferson Parish jail), 235–36
held as fugitive on murder warrant (1977), 164
helps organize and joins Dr. King's March on Washington, 32
and home for unwed mothers, 37–42
imprisonment of (1977), 164–73
and indecision of Louisiana authorities (1977), 188–89
influence of black colleagues on (Wiltwyck School), 30
involvement with U.S. draft evaders in Canada (1972), 131
and jail in Nevada (1977), 175, 184–85, 188
and Jefferson Parish jail, 235–38
and job friction with Raymond Foat, 133–34
joins civil rights organization, 30
joins Dutch Reformed Church, 16
and J.P. Stevens boycott, 199
and Lake Tahoe, Nev. (1977), 185–86
and letters of support from women (1983), 228–29
and Life interviews, 224, 232
and life with parents, 7–10
and living conditions in Sybil Brand Prison, 167–68

and male chauvinism, 151–52
and march on Washington (NOW demonstration, 1978), 194
and marriage vs. romance and adventure, 17
marriages of, 25–26, 87, 126–29, 198
and mental blocks (1983), 251–55
and mental breakdown, 166–67
moves to New York City, 22
and murder accusation, 214, 229–30, 267–71, 289
and National Organization for Women (NOW), 139–55, 191–201, 204–10, 227–29
and New Paltz, N.Y., 7–10, 14–15, 44–46, 118–19
as NOW chapter finance coordinator, 148
and other unwed mothers, 40–41
and Pacific Bell job, 101, 103, 106
as party and wedding organizer, 138
and Playboy Club (N.Y.C.), 59
and police interrogation, Los Angeles (1977), 157–62
and police search, New Mexico, 78
and power as an objective, 204–5
pregnancy of, 34–41
and preliminary hearing on murder charge (1977), 186–88
as president of California NOW (1981), 200, 207, 209
and press conference, New Orleans (1983), 239–40
and Princess Louise job, 107–8, 110–14
and Princess Louise II job, 121–24
prison experiences of, 3–5, 164–73, 186, 215–24
and prison visits from NOW women, 172
rearrested on behalf of Louisiana authorities (1977), 188–89
reconciliation with parents, 119–20
refused bail (1977), 164
released on bail (1983), 239
and reporters, New Orleans Airport, 235
runs for vice president of NOW, 208–9
and San Pedro, Calif., 101, 103–4
separation from Raymond Foat, 155–56
and sexual attitudes of 1960s, 42–43
sexually abused by Jack Sidote, 67–68, 74, 83, 91–92, 100–1, 117–18

— 303 —